AND SO IT BEGINS ...

YOU HAVE MORE POWER OVER LIFE THAN YOU REALISE

STEPHANIE J. KING

(Co-written with the aid of Spirit)

DERWEN PUBLISHING

PEMBROKE · DYFED

This edition published in Great Britain by Derwen Publishing 2011.
Published by Inner Sanctum in 2004 with the title *The Winds of Change*.
Published by Hay House in 2008.
The author wishes to thank Inner Sanctum and Hay House for the
support of her work.

Derwen Publishing
3 Bengal Villas,
Pembroke, Dyfed
Wales, SA71 4BH

A CIP catalogue for this book is available
from the British Library.

ISBN 978-1-907084-12-6

Production by David Porteous Editions.
www.davidporteous.com

To my family…

Simon, Christopher and Natasha

…with love

I am.

I can.

I will.

These words come to us from spirit.

All we must do is decide how to use the time that is ours – the time that is given to us.

(I am I) I have created man so that I may experience at first hand the pleasure of life itself. It is only through this channel that I may know all aspects of life on Earth. Man is My own experience of experiencing. (I am I)

CONTENTS

ACKNOWLEDGEMENTS

A special thank you is given to my spirit helpers, Mr Mie and Mr John Benjamin, for their patience and wisdom in pulling *And So It Begins...* together. This book could not have been written without them.

Thank you, too, to all my relations, for without their love and support I would not be the person that I am and would not have been in the place of life where I found this book.

INTRODUCTION

Despite all the freedom you have in your life, how often are you actually happy? Take a look at your family and friends. How often are they?

(I am I) For many people life seems empty, repetitive and pointless. No matter how hard they work or what changes they make to their life and to the things that surround them, peace and happiness somehow elude them or seem impossible and life keeps getting harder and harder. I have to tell you, this is not the way it should be. I have to help you move on. (I am I)

This is your life. You create it, you choose it, you alone decide what you will do with it. Don't believe you're a victim, at the mercy of others. Don't wait around for them to recognize and help you. If it all ended today, if this life were over, would you be proud of your achievements, of what you've left behind, or would there still be much left undone? There is no defence in 'I couldn't because ... I just didn't know ... or understand ... or have the time...' You choose for yourself. And you alone know how life is for you...

You are unique, completely individual. Your life, your influences, all your experiences, your talents and strengths, your outlook and projection, your character, position and private thoughts have all served to make you that way. All you are now is not all you can be, though. It is just a fraction of what you can become.

And So It Begins... is a deep healing, talking, interactive tool specifically designed to highlight your potential, to help you grow and expand, to help you understand exactly where you are – and then to help you move on. When read in the usual manner, from front to back, it will take you on a personal life journey. You can know who you are, why you are and what you're part of, know your strengths and your weaknesses, where you're heading, where you're stuck and where you've been, how you personally react, relate and communicate, how you connect and create daily life, how you can plug fully into the mainframe of life and creativity, smash patterns you're locked into, whether consciously or not, and let go of old baggage and trauma, learn to send healing to loved ones, to problems, situations and friends, ask productively for help and, even better, recognize when it comes in, understand people and influences around you and recognize where things are stuck...

When dipped into daily, *And So It Begins...* is a valuable life tool that speaks directly and specifically to you. It establishes a soul-to-soul link between you and your own guardian/angel/guide, giving help and advice as you need it. You know what is happening around you, so for help and advice, why not try it now?

> Still yourself. Place the book between the palms of your hands and as you do so your guardian will step forward into your space. Feel yourself start to relax, then begin to fan through the pages. Let them flow through your fingers like water. Think of nothing, hold on to nothing, completely let go. Feel yourself relax even more deeply... You are physically

placing your energy onto the pages – and so too is your guardian. You are blending.

Don't be tempted to stop too quickly, as you'll jump in before a connection is complete. Keep on going until you feel you've done enough. *Feel* it, don't think it... This is a time for you to be quiet – and a time for your guardian to speak.

When you *feel* ready, stop. Open the book at the place you are drawn to. As if sticking a pin in at random, read from the point where your eyes first land, even if it's mid-sentence. Read a paragraph, a line, a few words or pages. You will know when to stop as the content will change and finish speaking to you...

Guidance is there for you at any time. Use the book first thing in the morning for the day ahead. If something happens personally to or around you during the day, or if questions or thoughts cross your mind, just let them go, pick up the book and repeat the whole process. Use it as much as you wish. Take it to work, share it with family and friends – but they must do the same as you did. They, too, must link up with their guardian, they must blend and connect for the process to work as it should. Don't worry about energy interference; the point at which you fan is the point of energy transference. When you get the book back, simply repeat the whole process with your guardian. Whether for work, family, love or home affairs, you'll always receive the tailored advice that you need to keep your day and life in general on course.

This will help you to make better sense of life and your own experiences, calm your mind, see more clearly, become happier and healthier, love better, concentrate more effectively and change your thinking in ways that will always support that. You will gain greater clarity, focus, confidence and understanding and become more compassionate and peaceful within. *And So It Begins...* will stop you chasing your tail and give you quality of life and peace of mind.

The journey of your life is unique to you, so the assistance you require will be also. Make your time on Earth count. Be proud of who you are. Get back to creating and know your importance to the planet – to the 'now' window of Earth life itself.

Author's Note

- This work is a three-way link between you, your guardian and God.
- Any reference to 'man' in this book is the universal word for humanity, for mankind as a whole. It is not intended to place the male gender over or above the female. They are equal.
- All writing by 'I am I' is channelled directly from God – from the Universal/Earth/Mind energy source. This is speaking directly to you.

(I am I) You are all connected to Me. Whether you know it or not, whether you accept it or not, it cannot alter.

All (I am I) references come from Me. I am the consciousness of Earth. I connect to each one of you. I am who and what you call God.

Why should this surprise you? It should not. You have a mind and a voice of your own – so do I. I have many voices in each one of you. I have many links back to My own mind – again, through each one of you.

Why should it be difficult to believe that I can talk and communicate? I will speak often throughout the course of this book.

And So It Begins… *will help you understand who you are. It will help information and energy flow. It will help you remember your heritage, your dreams and your purpose.*

I will work with you throughout this inspirational journey. I will lead you back home. (I am I)

PROLOGUE

We all come from spirit. We are matter and energy beings. All we can see and touch is matter. Matter is energy at its slowest vibrational frequency. The slower the vibration, the denser the object will be; the faster, the more translucent. Science has explained this to us admirably over past years. It also has an explanation for many other things in the universe that we see, yet much more exists that we can't. Only now is science even willing to acknowledge that there is indeed an underlying intelligence that governs and operates through the planet we live upon. Science has explained the *how* of the universe, but cannot yet explain the *why*. We are as much in the dark today as our ancestors and theirs before them, and we still don't understand our true connection to this planet that gives us life.

CHAPTER ONE

And So Was the Past

In the Beginning

Long ago, the planet we live on was born. At that time it existed only as pure transparent energy. Then the conditions that surrounded it changed. Atoms and molecules began to move and rub against each other. Cells began to grow and split, just as cells do in a mother's womb. In the universe, conditions altered and the intelligence that made all things began to know itself. Just as a drop of water will always be just that until it becomes part of a river, a lake, an ocean or a cup of steaming hot tea, so things will always remain the same until the conditions that surround them change... And so it was at the start.

The first energy was intelligent. It sensed the change coming within itself and all was good. This energy in its true form vibrated at a frequency not yet known to man. As changes began to occur, the frequency at its centre slowed further. These changes took billions of years. At the heart of the energy, matter began to grow, vibrating at a lower rate than the pure energy giving it life. Cells continued to grow and change and slow down at different rates, just as a child grows inside its mother's womb. The Earth we live upon grew – and is growing still, just as it did at the beginning of evolution and time.

Man is part of that Earth. He lives on Earth's surface. He is part of Earth's structure and form. Man could not appear until living conditions were ripe – then he, too, began to grow and take shape.

We too are still growing, still in the belly of the energy that first existed, still, as it were, in its womb. Energy is all around us, filling all space the eye can see. It exists within us, without us and in all living things. It is this – and only this – that gives us life. It *is* life…

We are botanical bodies that grow on the surface of this Earth, just as trees and flowers and animals, but the difference between man and other living species is that we have the gift of thinking mind – we have consciousness, we have intelligence, we have the power of deduction. We have the ability to know ourselves and our surroundings.

All things on Earth are interconnected and always have been. All things are made of one energy that came or grew from one source… Each living thing, large or small, has its own part to play in the existence of our planet, and this is no less true for mankind. Man has in fact the most important role of all and this is on no account being big-headed. Man has the role that was destined for him by designation of Earth planet itself, just as each limb and organ we possess plays an individual role unique unto itself and to the body that it belongs to. Man has the role of an energy converter. He is responsible for the smooth movement of energy between Earth and sky, above, around and within him. Everyone everywhere plays this part, regardless of who they are, where they live and what they know, do and possess. Everyone is the same, and this cannot be stressed strongly enough.

Energy movement is the prime function of the human body, but we often seem unable to do it. During the course of normal daily life, the energy channels we possess become blocked through stress and turmoil, just as the guttering system on the roof of a house can become blocked through dirt. When blockages arise, the energy we generate and use is unable to ebb and flow the way it should, until over time we become ill. Illness is often caused through the misalignment and malfunction of physical energy built up over time but unable to disperse, because the physical condition of the body dictates otherwise. All illness, at its most basic level, is merely a form of blockage or malfunction of our body's energy systems, regardless of the symptoms an ailment might produce.

Energy plays a vital role in everything everywhere. It existed before Earth was born and will do so long after the Earth is no more. It is eternal – and so is the energy that lies within us. It is this that is unique and can never die. That energy part of the whole that exists within us all will always be imprinted with the essence of who we are, and as we grow and change, so will the imprint we leave behind, long after our physical body has perished. We can never die, because nothing ever dies; all life merely evolves back into its original form. The energy part of us – *that part that really is us* – has never separated from the rest of the energy ball and it is this that is known as our soul. Through our soul we experience life and all that we do. It is this that is responsible for our joy, for our pain and for our intelligence.

Man has learned how to recreate matter, how to grow trees and how to reproduce animal and human bodies, but he can never reproduce the spark of life that exists within, because it is not made of man. It is eternally and essentially a part of the whole of the planet that we live upon. It is God.

'Why "God"?' many will ask. Why not? 'God' is merely the name given for identification purposes. Just as we and every other thing on Earth have a name, a label, so does this conscious, life-giving, intelligent energy. All things are part of this God, and this God has been part of all things since time began. I am a part of God. You are a part of God. We are all a little part of the whole that exists, much as a single strand of yarn will remain exactly that, but when put with others can complete a beautiful rug or anything else we weave it into. It becomes embodied to form its own part of the whole.

Combined, we form this planet that we live upon. We each have our own portion of conscious intelligence, but from space we are merely part of the Earth we inhabit.

It took millions of years for Earth to evolve. It will continue for many more, with or without our help; but here's the thing: our help is needed now, and urgently so. Our role, apart from living our own life, is to conduct energy between the sky and the dense matter of the planet. Together this forms a living, breathing, growing, intelligent cell. The ground is its nucleus and the sky its food, its vital life force. Without the energy transference being properly carried out, this Earth we love and depend upon will die, just like the Moon and other planets that surround it.

We, mankind, are keepers of the Earth in a very real sense. We are vital to its continuation because we are part of it. We are what keeps it changing, for without us it would simply be a garden, unknown and unexplored, as before. It is we who have consciousness. It is we who can grow, change and experience all there is to experience. It is we who can enjoy what has been grown and created like no other living species on the planet. It is we who can help the energy that is God to know itself. We are a vital link to the creative force.

In the beginning, the universe, the planets and the Earth were created. All grew as a consequence of energy slowing its vibrational frequency enough to form matter, at the time when the conditions were right. All things became the way they are today – the mountains, the trees, the animals and the seas. All things would have grown even if man had not grown also. But man did grow. He was meant to, because he was part of the mechanics of the world he lived upon. No part of anything on Earth should not exist, everything matters, everything fits – and so does man. But now he is not performing the function that nature gave him. We are not transferring energy we are supposed to. Too many of us are locked into our problems of daily life. We have become closed channels instead of working ones. That's why it's so important for us to get our act together to sort things out…

The Bible is a collection of books written by learned teachers who lived in early times. It was designed to help us understand ourselves and our connection to the all that is. All bibles, regardless of denomination, were designed for the same purpose, but we have become too tied up in dogma and words. We are too caught up in the view that only 'our' religion is right, that ours is the one truth that all should follow.

Admittedly, in the years that have passed, many original words of the Bible have been changed to suit the power cravings of influential people. Yet, for all that it may be full of faults and texts that appear old and outdated, the Bible is one of the earliest representations of our true selves. It clearly states that we are more than what we think. It tells of our troubled past and the pressures of today, but it also holds the key to peace tomorrow. The words (not only in the Bible, but in other religious books too) tell the story of all we were, all we are now and all that we are able to become. I, too, am the product that is described in its texts and I, too, have realized my true connection to God, to Earth and to life.

The basic message within the Bible remains the same as it ever was: we are a product of the world around us. We live in a garden that was grown for our enjoyment. This is it... *This is the Garden of Eden* – created long ago. We are here to enjoy it, to physically experience, enhance and grow through it and then to return to our own (and God's) original energy form. We can come back here as often as we wish, or as often as we need, but the point is that we do come back – we choose to – and we will experience the effect of all that we and our species have ever done. We are not part of something else and we do not leave it all behind. We come back again – to live physically on Earth again – by choice.

Now you can see the importance of *And So It Begins...* Eternal life is not a myth or a fanciful fairy tale. We really do choose to come back, for many reasons, so it is important to get life correct – right now.

CHAPTER TWO

Acknowledging Changes that Need to Occur

The Way Forward

Growth is change, and changes must occur as part of the process of life. All of life exists as it was meant to from the start. This is how things are. But now mankind has reached a life-enhancing plateau and it is time for personal growth and redevelopment. In order to proceed further along the course of life, we must know ourselves and our connection to the world.

Many of us amble along our daily paths looking neither left nor right. We allow life, circumstance and other people to propel us until all we can do is pick their pieces up along the way. Within ourselves, we come to a virtual standstill. I, too, had reached that point, but was lucky enough to wake up, to go forward – to write this book.

All of us must reach and pass a point like this in life. We must stand still and take stock, recalibrate, redraw, rechoose. We must reconsider choices available here and now, but the problem is, how do we know that we have reached a standstill in the first place? How do we know when we and life are stuck?

Life itself will always show us. Life will offer all we need – provided we can read its signs correctly.

All through life we have been following instructions. From infancy to adulthood, anything we needed to take the next step was provided. Always through our own choice and conscious thought, all was given for our next link in this life. But then we reached the point of saturation. Too much good living in any form you care to think of became the norm, it became expected. Instead of wanting less, we became stuck within the programme of obtaining and amassing more – bigger houses, more money, better jobs, expensive clothes, more food than could be eaten, more gold than could comfortably be worn, etc., etc. Even holidays that extended into usual working time were gathered freely, without thought or thanks to anyone. The more we got, the more we wanted and the more we felt we needed or were owed.

Today life has never been so good. We are living far beyond the dream we always wanted, the dream our ancestors gave their 'whole lives' to achieve, but we still don't really recognize what we have. We want more, we expect more and we want it faster, at any cost. We rarely realize the true cost of what we're living.

This roller-coaster madness has to stop. We all see it, we all recognize it, but we must do something now about it. It all must cease or world resources will burn out. A wheel will keep on turning for eternity if treated properly, but when constantly pushed too hard, too far, for too long, it will buckle, break and splinter, it will burn or wear itself completely out – and that is exactly what we're doing to our planet.

The Earth cannot cope much longer – without a slowing down of life. All we could ever need is here already – for the taking, for the asking, but right now we must go easy – not chill out for days, but with an intelligent, conscious decision to ease off, to take a softer, slower pace in our daily life, to recognize our limits and live within them, for now at least, to help the physical world around us all catch up.

Take a look at the world you live in. Not the world as a whole, but your own sector of it. Each of us lives in our own private space, our own little sector of the universe, and signs indicating its state and wellbeing are present all around. Do we see them?

Is there discomfort in your family, in the lives of work colleagues or friends? Is your own life as easy or worry-free as you would like? Are you on an ever-moving treadmill of work, bills, arguments, stress and illness? Is your life as you hoped – even with all you have amassed? Does everything you have achieved hit the spot? Are you working far too hard or do you not have a job at all? Is it a pleasure to wake up – or a chore, a burden you must face? Do you wish the day was over before it has even started? All these and many more are clear indications as to the state and wellbeing of your life. Are you happy? Do you ever think to check?

We all strive for happiness every day of our lives, but rarely find or achieve it. Happiness is the most natural state in the world, but it can appear the hardest to come by. I, too, had to learn how to achieve this state, at the cost of much pain and heartache along the way. Gurus and holy men take years to finally get there, so why should it be any different for us? Yet happiness and peace are the greatest gifts we have and if we can pass them on to others along our pathway, then our journey and our lives have been worth something. I, too, had to learn this. I, too, had to study, and no matter who you are, it is worth striving for.

We all are the same. We are made of the same substance. We feel the same emotions. We dream the same dreams. We are different – yet still the same as one another. I had to learn this after my own trials and tribulations came to a head. Again and again life appeared to let me down. I thought I had changed all I could, but still it wasn't enough to make a difference. Then I knew that it must be something I was doing. A word came to my attention – it was 'karma'. I began to search and learn. I began to look inside. I began to see myself in ways unknown to me before. I saw the world about me from a different angle.

The answers coming back were staggering. They were far, far too big for me alone. Yes, I could apply them to my own life, but my family would simply meet the same brick walls and obstacles along their own paths... I could still choose to ignore them, but that I knew would never feel quite right... It is impossible to unlearn what you have known and learned. I had to share this information and to write it in a book was the only answer. Incredible insights being given were flowing fast.

We are born into life through our parents. From them we inherit family similarities and DNA, but that is all. Each soul born into each body is completely individual. It is a single thinking part of the universal soul called God. It comes to experience physical life, to live, breathe, dance and cry. It comes to sing and laugh and eat and drink and know. It comes to feel the wind and rain and sun. It comes to be part of the planet that it will live its life upon, to make a difference, to contribute and repair – some way, somehow – somebody or something. It comes here to create, in the most basic form there is, the form of matter, it comes to love and manifest its own life story. Every soul born into this world is individual, yet it is also very much the same as every other soul that has ever lived.

Not all matter is alive or contains life: it is always energy at its slowest vibrational form. It is energy that has converted into forms we can hold and touch and see. It is solid, it is physical, but has no life. Life is a spark of conscious living energy that exists in all living things, and it permeates all forms of matter that have no life. From a flower to a tree, from an animal to man himself, it is the same form of energy, but the differential factor is that man has the capacity to know and grow beyond his physical form.

A flower can grow only to its limit – and then must die. It cannot grow beyond the point that it was destined. It cannot know anything beyond its current capability. The same ruling applies to everything else upon the planet. Nothing can grow beyond its inherent original form. An animal can learn tricks, but it can never understand its earthly placement. It cannot educate and know itself beyond its basic survival instincts… But man can. Man is the only species on the planet's surface that can do all these things and more. Man has the capability to be anything and everything he wants. He can know how it feels to fly, he can swim like a fish, hunt in the dark, sing, dance, learn, invent and investigate. None of these things is born of necessity. They are not things man does because that is the nature of his species, but he does them because he chooses to experience what those things are like. He can choose, while other forms of life never will.

Each thing on Earth has its proper place, but man can exceed all his limitations – by choice. Therefore he has no limitations. He is free.

It is this freedom that we often take for granted. In fact, very often we forget we even have it. Never before have we had so much, yet still we reach for more – and more again.

Life for our ancestors was different than it is for us. Their time was neither better nor worse, just different. Life was hard, but slower. Today everything comes quickly. This is not necessarily a bad thing, but it does mean that we have less scope for configuration or for error. It is more important now than ever that we get life right. The faster our pace, the more compact our problems when they arise. It takes more effort to put things right than it does to do things properly in the first place – and this is no less true for our own lives. We barge ahead, looking neither right nor left, to achieve what we think we desire or want, yet often when we get there expectations fall far short. We wish we had waited a little while longer, or maybe searched a little harder. This seems to be a trend of the life and times in which we live. Yet it is not all doom and gloom. It is not too late to change our patterns or the course of life we've set. The first step is being taken even now. As you read this book, you are becoming more in tune and more self-aware. You cannot argue with truths you already know and as you reach periods of change and of clearing out old habits, you let go of behaviour patterns that no longer serve you.

Change of any kind takes time to manifest. But manifest it will, with or without your help. You can swim against a current and have a long and uncomfortable time, or you can recognize the change in the tide and swim with it.

Change is inevitable. Just as the world must turn and seasons rotate, so changes must occur, and this is also true with us. From the time of our birth we are destined to change, grow and alter. We push past our limitations throughout the whole of the time we are given to walk the planet. Change is the fundamental nature of all life and all we know. To remain stagnant is to be like stone, and there is little point in that, yet even stone must change as it falls and crumbles back to sand, then dust, and then again to nothing physical at all.

CHAPTER THREE

Realization

Our First Intimation that Something Is Amiss

We are born. We grow and change. We explore, learn and understand. We store every shred of information we come across within our system. Once we have seen or experienced something, it becomes a part of who and what we are. It becomes imprinted on the blueprint of our soul.

We are the product of every experience we have had since our time began, yet when exactly did our time begin? If it began when we were born into this physical, earthly life, then how can brand-new babies that exhibit talents be explained? Or super children with exceptional gifts? How can siblings be so different within their family unit – even if they've had the very best that life could give?

Family differences run deep. Yes, similarities can be apparent between each family member, habits and opinions can rub off, but fundamental differences lie deeper than you think. Each person is an individual soul on an individual journey through Earth life. Members of a family might be born and live together, being physically and chemically interlinked, but each is a separate entity in their own right. Each will go entirely where their life and choices take them, provided other limitations don't apply, yet sadly, this has all too often been the case.

Looking Back

The life we live on Earth is short. Old people can see that as they look back through the years. Life whizzes past, but with each passing day we gain a sense of the rest still to come. We gain a purpose, a sense of direction and a goal. We move through constant change that always leads to something, somewhere. We choose and aim where we want to be and strive to get there.

But where do these urges come from? What is inside that propels and spurs us on? And why is this process so unique for everyone?

The answer is old: it is born from that part of us known as our soul. It is the soul that yearns for knowledge and experience. It is the soul that propels us forward, on a journey of progression, knowing exactly what we are and what we could be – always.

This soul we are given or inhabit or own (however you choose to address it) is an individual part of Earth's own soul. A grain of sand will never be the whole beach that it came from but will always be one part of that same beach. It could be nothing else, and that same analogy applies also to us. You, I, your parents, siblings and friends are all individual but equal parts of Earth's own soul. They are no more or less important than one another, regardless of social position or anything else. We are all individual parts of energy that's divine, with a chance to explore this planet's own life and body as we see fit. And regardless of all we may or may never do with that opportunity, when it's over we'll return again to our original state – in energy form.

We are primarily spirit/energy beings – whichever you choose to be called. We have been on Earth in a physical body many times since the journey of man began. Countless people have proven this through many years and situations, but that is another subject for another book, another time. The point being made here in this one is that we do come back. We choose to come back to experience a new life, in another form, in another way, from another angle. Each time we return we learn and grow. We learn to make a difference to ourselves and to the world that we live in. We also come to contribute, to reap and know what we and others have sown before, and this what today we call karma.

Each time we come back we choose what we need to experience to grow and perfect ourselves further. We choose parents, situations, crossroads and trigger points, and the many lessons that will take us closest to the people we are striving to become, often choosing who will cross our path at specific points or times along the way. Right now most of us can recall a handful of such people, people we will never forget, who have impacted our life at various stages to take us in a new direction or make us think. There are no wasted meetings, no such thing as coincidence, there is a reason for them or you behind everything – no matter how obscure it may appear at the time. Everything is part of cause and effect. I, too, see this at play when I look back over my own life. Not all of it was pleasant, but it took all of my experiences in all shapes and sizes to bring me to the point I'm at today. Without any one of those experiences, I would be a different person from the person I am now.

We are all the product of our complete life's teachings and experiences, and this goes back much further than we know. Past influences really do affect us in the present.

For instance a fear of water, fire, heights, dogs, horses, birds or anything else you care to name could stem from a past lifetime experience – but so could the nice things. A talent for something or an immense love of or interest in something you know you must do, could equally be brought forward by your psyche (or your soul) from a past life to affect the one you're living now.

We are influenced as much by the distant past as we are by experiences of the present or thoughts of the future. We are the life product of all the encounters throughout our lifetime. This varies greatly from person to person, brother to sister... This is actually where the saying 'They're an old soul' comes from.

When you begin to realize that a lifetime is short, that it's continuous you appreciate the one you have now even more. It hammers home how precious every day, each moment is. Instead of wishing the weeks away, you want to hold on to them as long as possible. Even the not-so-great moments can be seen as gems when you are able to look back with an open, balanced mind and the gift of hindsight. It is not that you will enjoy those bad times more than you did before, it is more that you will be able to understand what is occurring, and with greater understanding come compassion, tools and lessons that will help as you move forward towards sturdy ground.

All lessons in life are necessary as part of a regrowth cycle. Nothing is ever for nothing; all things are part and parcel of who we are. Problems make us push past our limitations; they highlight and examine parts of life that no longer work in our favour. Problems are more help than hindrance than any of us recognize, because they force issues that need attention to the fore. They make us move and change things, do what we've been putting off, whether through laziness or fear or sheer neglect.

They even put our life into better order, when we would prefer to be doing other things instead. Problems are a natural aspect of life that push us to ever-greater heights. They are our friends, not our enemies. They should mean no more to us than a flashing light when things need attention or go wrong. They are warning signs, signals that say all is not as it should be, and without them we would merely procrastinate. We would stay just as we are almost indefinitely.

Today trouble of one kind or another is everywhere. We have passed saturation in much of what we do. We are beyond the flashing-light stage; life/the world at large is telling us to now back off, to slow right down, take extra care. This is not all bad, but neither is it good. We must make urgent adjustments to bring chaos into order. The question is not 'What shall we do?' but 'Where do we begin?' and the obvious place is within ourselves.

We are each the centre pivot of our own universe, the central starting point of the life we're living. From this premier vantage point we influence, create and affect all we do. Life revolves around each one of us completely. We are responsible for much that happens day to day.

We hold the keys to the sadness and happiness we experience. Life and people have always told us that the opposite is true, so much so that we believe it now ourselves. But these facts are not the truth. Truth lies somewhere else – in the feelings, thoughts and emotions that we carry, that pump through us by the thousand each hour and day that passes, every waking moment of our lives.

It is time to take stock of the life we're living, dreams we're dreaming and thoughts we are thinking, but before we can begin we must realize the importance of such a task. Every day hundreds of thousands of thoughts flit across the horizon of our mind scope. They are like streaks of lightning, appearing and disappearing in an instant. Some are deep and meaningful, some are connected to time and the particular life frame we are presently experiencing, but most are absolute rubbish and mindless chatter. We take special care with the food we put into our mouth, but do we consider the food we unthinkingly give to our mind? Do we ever? Likely, the answer is not. We allow our mind to wander freely wherever it wants or wills, like an unruly child. We hardly notice it at all, morning, noon 'til night. We hardly care or notice anything we're thinking.

During the course of a normal day, ideas come forward that have little or no relevance to things we're saying or doing. The course of an average conversation is much the same – countless possible answers come pouring in and, given the individuality of the people we are, isn't it a wonder that we ever get it right?

Communication is an art form even unto itself and to do it well we need a mind that's free of clutter and emotion. How often are we ever like a blank page that allows the moment we experience to lead the way? Mostly we rehearse our answers, thoughts, questions and things we want to do before the situations we anticipate even come into play. We imagine all the things our opponent could possibly say in response to an imaginary conversation, and their actions too, and then, when the event comes around, when the real thing actually happens, we put our well-rehearsed rehearsals into play.

We often live a life of fantasy instead of the reality that it should be and then wonder why life rarely goes as planned or needed. We achingly wonder why we are never understood or why no one sees what we are trying our level best to achieve.

Could it be because we treat life too much like a script than the interactive program it should really be? Do we take too much for granted – or leave too much unclear and unsaid, waiting for someone else to slot it in? Does our imagination sleep too much or race too far ahead?

Life is not a game. It should be fun, but it is serious. The days we live can never be replaced. We all can be exactly what we want and what we dream of, but it will often take more work than we've allowed for.

We are spirit/energy beings that live and operate through a physical, biochemical, degradable body on an ever-changing, growing, decaying physical Earth. The body we are in is incapable of living life all on its own. It cannot do anything without our spirit being attached. A car is nothing more than components until its engine is switched on and it comes to life (so to speak). A computer is useless, too, until power surges through its motherboard or a boot-up program reminds it what to do. The human or animal body is but a lump of flesh, incapable of movement until united with its energy/spirit counterpart, or soul. The two parts must unite properly, completely, to power physical life as we now know it on Earth.

(I am I) I, too, am unable to write this book without the use of a physical body – the body and mind of this author. (I am I)

Matter is incapable of intelligence. Intelligence is the function of the soul. The soul completely enwraps all matter existent within its space. It can be seen only because of the body that gives it physical shape in a physical world. The body is necessary to anchor the soul, or energy, to the body or the ground of Earth itself.

Now you can begin to see the importance of the soul connecting properly to the matter of the Earth and the importance of man's own channel being in open, working order, for live energy the planet needs to filter through. Man's important channel must pass energy from sky to ground and vice versa. Without this fundamental task operating at its best, the Earth we live upon would slowly die. Starved of the life force that it needs, although existent all around, it would die like other planets orbiting in space – not because it needs mankind to keep it alive and kicking, but because mankind is draining too much out. If everyone died today, Earth would recover to its original form.

Earth does need man to help it, to keep it healthy now. That is a huge part of our physical function whilst we're here. And this is precisely why we must keep our species going, not in the technological, materialistic fashion we are now, but in a balanced, healthy way that sustains both us and the planet. It's time for us to move to another level of existence, to fulfil our role and purpose for the planet that sustains our soul and physical life.

There is energy in abundance in the sky and in all space surrounding physical Earth. The ozone layer is the outer skin of Earth's spirit and physical self, just like the outer membrane of any single cell. The Earth is a giant intelligent cell, living, breathing, self sustaining within its own right. Beyond that, man has no need to know – not yet and not in this book anyway. Earth's body is the matter that is growing in the heart of the ozone-protected cell in which it exists. This cell is intelligent, just like any cell in any form of living matter. It knows just what it is. It knows the shape it must become. It knows all it needs to know. Just as a sperm knows it must swim to reach an egg, so the Earth knows it must continue to reach maturity. Once maturity is reached, it can obviously grow no further. It only can sustain itself and that is that.

The Earth we live upon has reached that final point. It can grow no more. It cannot change its shape or what it has become. It now needs nothing more than sustenance from live energy that surrounds it, but man is closed and locked, blocking the way. Man is stopping vital life force from entering as it should. Man is killing Earth in ways he does not know – not by mining and over-usage, but by failing to perform his most basic function as a channel for live energy to flow through.

Man does not realize the significance of his attachment to the Earth. He is blind and impervious to it. Throughout history giant leaps have been made in the advancement of medicine, science, manufacturing and technology, but inside man still appears to be the same as he always has been. It is as though he has been asleep to his inner self, impervious to everything except the outside world. Historical events have not helped his own 'internal' development, but in this age of free thinking and speech it's time to wake up to reality.

Life on this planet revolves around balance. Nature needs balance. All balance revolves around balance. This Earth turns flowing energy into manifestations of physical matter. It relies on all of its systems and these must be working correctly. This is not happening today. Balance and harmony are falling apart – and the reason behind this is man – through his lack of understanding and respect. We have lost touch with the reasons we're here. We are out of synch with general life, with ourselves and with Earth. We are wrenching its systems apart.

We hold the key to make or break the systemic changes that are occurring. We can help put things back to how they should be or continue the way we are now. The choice rests always with us. If we stay as we are, we will wipe ourselves out and damage the life forms remaining in place. The way things now stand, we do have a chance, albeit small, to correct what is hurt and out of synch.

(I am I) This task must not wait – this window in time needs help now. (I am I)

CHAPTER FOUR

Transformation

The Way We Behave

We have the power to change anything. We have the ability to think, act and foresee. We also have the ability to access and analyze information. We know what has happened before and what might happen again in the future, but the time that matters most is the time that is now. All of life exists most strongly in this time-frame, in this window of instant reality. It is now and only now that change can commence to make a difference.

We can all see evidence of our progression as we interact with life and look around us. I, too, have helped in my own way to form the world as I see it. We have all lived as we have always seen fit, but the problem is we have never really looked deeper/further than that. This is not to say that we have stumbled aimlessly along, but we have lived to achieve our individual aims. This is not so bad as long as it makes us happy, but the news each day is proving otherwise. Too many of us are sad and extremely unhappy. We find ourselves wandering lost and alone in our thoughts, in our life... In fact, many of us are unable to glimpse even the happiness that ought to be ours, no matter how much we try. And try we do, day in and day out, to get a balance and a straight run at life, but problems and people always get in the way. We catch glimpses of what we want in other people's lives, but again, when we get there ourselves, we see that that was not what we thought it would be or wanted either.

We are lost in a sea of plenty. Times have never been so good. We can be anyone, do anything and have anything we can ever want. Our ancestors fought life and limb to get us to this point in life, yet we still don't recognize that we are living a real-life, living dream. We have got where we wanted to go, yet we still reach out for more. We are locked into a pattern of striving outwards as far as we can, but inwardly we are no more than children. All day, every day, we are little children in the games we play, things we do and things we say, but worse still is the fact that we don't even realize it. We are locked into a game of acquisition and power, and blow anyone who gets in our way.

The world is our oyster. It is a balance of charm and destruction. It is fertile and it is barren. It is kind and it is ruthless, just as we are within the make up of our own selves. When the world was young there was no hostility. Yes, there were savage animals, but they were just that – animals. They did purely what their instincts asked of their survival. Now it is different. It is man who chooses to be hostile. Yes, there is much good and kindness, but hostility and fear appear to be more widespread than understanding and love, and this is where our problems really lie.

As already mentioned, we are channels for energy to pass through. Earth needs this energy in order to survive. It needs it to keep the cycle of life in harmony, rotation and control. Nature needs this energy to function as well as it should. Life needs it to continue all cycles correctly.

We need it, too, for our own health and wellbeing. We all need it to survive and exist. Energy is supposed to flow through us, day in and day out, for the whole of the time-frame we're here. It is too late to recognize this when we cease to live physically on Earth, because our channels will be altered through physical death. Yet we do not die but become part of the whole, part of the all that is, part of the soul energy of the Earth, much the same as we are now but no longer in our present physical way.

We do not perform the same function after crossing over the bridge of death. It is when we are physically alive that we hold the key, while we are still a part of this living Earth's matter. It is here that we must love one another better – to keep our channels open and the world alive. This is not a joke or a fanciful story, it is for real. It is the truth. It is all that matters now, all that will keep the Earth healthy and turning.

The Earth is matter. Matter is energy. Energy vibrates at a high speed and matter at a slower one. The nearer we dig to the Earth's core, the denser the matter and the slower the speed of its vibration. The core of the Earth is all but dead to the eyes of man, while the surface seems more alive, because it vibrates faster and is teeming with life. The outer layer of most of the Earth is still very much alive and will sustain itself for millions of years to come, yet the Earth is dying from the core. It has slowed its vibration too much. It has been starved and depleted of energy for too long by man himself.

History clearly shows the destructive nature of man, not physically but mentally and emotionally. Throughout the ages there has never been a level period where man was happy, either within his own self or the world about him. This is even more evident in the world we see and live in today. And man can only fulfil his purpose when he is relaxed and happy. Not the 'lie down and chill forever' kind of happy (although his channels will be open because he's zonked!), but deeply, mentally, emotionally happy – every waking moment of every day. Man can only be a positive channel for Earth's life force when he is in a state of attunement with both himself and the world around him. He can only be 'open' when he is in a state of harmony, balance and love – real love from deep within the soul of his being.

Man is both the destroyer and the saviour of the world. He is capable of such love, such beautiful dreams, and also of such devastation and hate. He is a strange mixture of good and bad, happy and sad, love and hate. It is precisely this that makes him a good channel when he is operating correctly. Life itself is good and bad, new and old, birth and death, destructive and eternal. It is a place of contradiction, of opposites. It is ending yet unending. It is all or nothing. This is the way life has always been and also the way it always will be. All these things are equal parts of the 'whole' that make up the life of the world. All these things must be in existence or there can be no balance. Too much good is as tiresome as too much bad. All must be equal to keep the scale of balance at its central gyrating point.

The World Is Born

How did these opposites come about? In the beginning the 'all that was' or the 'intelligent energy' wanted to know itself, but there was nothing to compare, to know or measure itself against. In our own life, if there were only hot, not cold, how could we know it was hot? Hot needs cold so that we can know the comparison. We need the two to know and fully understand their difference.

It took millions of years for Earth to form, but the all that was did not know itself yet.

(I am I) I was not alive. I could not experience what had been created because there was no form of educated conscious thought on the planet. What there was – was good and healthy and growing, but there was no knowledge to any part of anything until – man was born to experience, to feel, to think and to live the life that was offered. I had to live – to know that all that was created – would work as it should. I made man to be My eyes, My tastebuds, My hearing, Myself. I made man to complete this work of art, to finish what I had begun.

I made man as Myself because I am the creator. I made man think for himself because then he could create too. I made man to live – as I do now, upon the planet that sustains him. I made man so that I could experience the world I had made.

I need man to help 'Me' now. I need man to help sustain all that has been made since time began. The world would still continue if man were not here, sure enough, but it is presently in a state of imbalance and I need man to set it right on My behalf.

Because man has total free choice, anything that I would do alone would countermand all that I stand for. This decision belongs to man... He must decide all by himself what he wants to do, but the key is this: he has been here before, he is here now and most likely he will be here again – not out of pressure or malice, but out of love, out of free will and choice. Man will be here again to experience all he has created with his fellow men. (I am I)

In order for 'the all that was' to know itself and the world that had been created, opposites had to exist. Good and bad are equal parts of the whole. Without one, the other could not be known, either by man or by God/ man/creation itself. (Remember that the term 'God' is only a name. It is a reference point, like the names we have ourselves.)

In order for man to experience life, he had to be a conscious, intelligent, contributing, physical being. He had to have all the attributes of God. He had to think for himself alone. He had to have freedom of individual sight, touch, smell, hearing and taste. He had to be an explorer from the moment of his birth and that is why he had to be born completely helpless, like a blank page that was waiting for input, like a virgin computer program. All his functions were there, he just needed to learn of their existence and then how to master and use them.

Man is a born explorer of life. What he makes of his life is totally his own affair, from its beginning to its end. Yes, at the start he is at the mercy of his surroundings, but thereafter, once he learns to exercise his free will, he can do as he pleases. This is the only way a true exploration can achieve results – unique, individual results. Just like a true explorer, a child must have guidelines for understanding, good conduct and safety, but thereafter he will do whatever feels good and works well for him.

Adults are little different. They also have guidelines to follow, but each has free will and the discrimination to choose whether those guidelines are correct, useful or not. They can push their boundaries at any time and redraw and refine them at others. Just as a child looks to their parents and peers for guidance, so an adult should look within at the wealth of knowledge they have collected through their years. Each person has their own individual buttons and triggers. I, too, had those that served me and led me along my own path of discovery. I, too, had freedom of choice, but unlike you, I did not realize where I was going until it was too late. Not too late to experience life, but too late to put it to good use. I had to cross the bridge to know my own self and my function.

Man is the master of his own life. He is slave to none. Our ancestors corrected this so we might enjoy the freedom we do. But as well as enjoying and exploring this life experience, man is also here as a keeper of the Earth. As we now know, it is his job to pass life force to the planet, but he can only perform this function, this task, when he is in a state of contentment, happiness and love. Only then is he truly open and unbiased.

Energy radiates everywhere – it's our life force. We are born completely blank, open, unbiased and unconditioned, but all of us get blocked during the course of our lifetime and this is the root of the problem. If we do not correct this, we become ill or depressed. The life force that we should channel becomes blocked within us. It does not move and filter through as it should.

Imagine a long row of guttering running around the top of a house. It performs its function well, day in and day out. Then one day a twig is dropped into it. Silt builds up, leaves get stuck, dust and soil congregate and the obstacle continues to grow bit by bit until the water channel is completely blocked solid. It becomes ineffective for the purpose that it was designed for. Instead of water gushing or gently flowing correctly along its surface to the downpipes, it spills over the sides or floods areas down below. At other times the guttering will remain full to the brim with stale dirty water that has washed down from the roof and roof tiles. Until it receives some attention, the system loses its purpose. Over a period of time, if still left the same, it will become obsolete or even destructive – and the same thing is happening to man.

I, too, was like this. During the course of living my life I, too, became blocked. It took much time and effort to correct this within myself, because as the years pass by it is always far easier to compound a block, a problem, than it is to acknowledge and address it. It's much easier to continue as we are than to stop and take stock of the person we have become and the life we are sharing with others. It can be difficult to analyze your life's direction and focus, even with professional help. It is difficult – but it is possible. It is also necessary at some point. We need flushing out, just like blocked drainpipes or guttering. We need to be living life as we should, not as we often do, in order to be fully functional as nature intended and, more importantly, as nature desperately needs.

CHAPTER FIVE

Energy Channels

Our True Being

The Earth needs energy to replenish itself. Energy keeps it moving in a regenerative state. It must flow freely between sky and Earth and is necessary for the correct weather conditions. The Earth needs clear blue sky and the warmth of the sun, but it also needs the clouds and the rain and the storms that they bring. A good storm is nothing more than energy movement between the Earth's elements. It needs all the power that is generated by the currents at work as much as it needs the heat from the sun and moisture from the rain. In an ideal world all these things would always be equally balanced, but they're not – yet another system that's not working properly because of mankind.

Energy must flow freely like water in a stream. Energy creates growth and harmony. It is the cause of all new life. It is the food that feeds all aspects of this world. It keeps nature on its course. It keeps the elements as they should be. It keeps the air fresh and healthy and it keeps all that we know as we know it to be. It keeps life and humanity on course.

I am a channel for life's energy to flow through. So are you. So is everyone, everywhere. I must remain open and unblocked, so must you, and so must everyone. This is our function. It is easy, yet so many of us fail. All too often we are blocked by the trials and tribulations of our individual lives. Aside from personal health, which may be damaged because our life force is not flowing as it should, many areas of our planet are barren, dry and troubled. Good examples would be the turmoil in Afghanistan, Iran, Iraq and the Middle East and the many, many more conflicts we hear about daily through the news. There is unrest all over the world and has been for years. In these areas the ground is dry and lifeless and the people are troubled and sad. Almost no growth exists either in the ground or above it. Their flowing energy is almost at a standstill. Similar examples of long-term unrest, war and disease can be seen throughout the history of man, with similar life patterns too.

Man is in a state of flux. He is mostly discontented and disgruntled with his life, despite the many opportunities that surround him. He chooses those which suit him best, yet his life is still upside down. He finds it difficult to settle into a happy style of life. I, too, was the same. I, too, became upset with the content of my life because all that I was doing had become a burden to me – or to others. Everything I had chosen with my free choice and will had become that burden. Every day was an effort. I was tired and misunderstood. I had to strive harder and harder for the recognition and love I felt I needed.

So, here is a story of life…

Once upon a time there lived a man. He was a simple man both in his needs and his desires. Then one day he found a magic lamp. He rubbed the lamp and a genie appeared.

'I can grant you your heart's desire,' he said, *'but only on the condition that it will bring you happiness.'*

The man thought for a while. He considered all the options that were available to him – riches, travel, gems, women, friends and neighbours, fast cars, corporate business, holidays, jet planes, boats, fame, etc., etc. He looked at the possibility of owning or experiencing those things. He searched his mind for the outcome and the pleasure those things would offer him. He thought of the women… He thought of the popularity… He thought and thought about all it would bring and mean. At last he had made up his mind.

'I wish for every man to be at peace with his life. I wish for heartache and sorrow, illness and fatigue to be things of the past. I wish for each person to attain their own personal goals and I wish for them to be content with their choice. I wish for world hunger, illness and deprivation to be no more. I wish for each person to get all that they need to survive. But most of all I wish for love. I wish for each and every person to have the deepest love they desire.'

The genie laughed. 'But these things are yours already. All you ask is already in place.'

'How so?' said the man. 'I look about me and see only famine and war. Some people kill and others are sad. Most never achieve their dream of success or their pot of gemstones or gold. They argue to get love and the respect they deserve, as do their children and friends. Famine is rife in half of the world, while the rest has more than its share. How can you say my wishes are already in place?'

The genie smiled. He looked the man in the eye for a while. Then he looked to the right and destruction was there, desire and heartache too. So were man's hopes and dreams, achievements and abilities. He looked to the left and it was the same. All was in place. But mankind still had a long way to go to find true happiness.

'I can do no more to fulfil your request,' the genie said. 'All is in its proper place. It is up to mankind to fill in the blanks for a wonderful love-filled future.'

The man was put out. 'But my wishes – where are they?'

The genie just shook his head sadly. 'I have given you the Earth, the sky and free love – a life that is full to the brim. I can do no more. The rest is up to you. If you cannot love one another, the rest will not matter. No riches and dreams will fulfil you. The love that you search for is with you from now till the end.'

He was gone in a flash – no more than that.

The man just stood there a while.

The genie was God, who had come to help mankind. The rest has still not been written.

We hold the key to our own future. The past has been and is gone. We live in the present. I, too, am a product of today. My future will be fine, because the present that I live in is rewritten day by day. It is a product of love, of peace, of contentment, commitment, hard work and hope – hope that the future will be fine for us all. And it will be, as long as we each play our part. And as we do come back to live here again, it matters very much what we make of the life we are in.

Over the strands of time man has done many things to make life comfortable for himself and in this respect he just keeps on going. I, too, enjoy the comfort of past inventions, but what do we do in the future? When material life is as good as it can get, what will we put our efforts into? Will we just want more of the same? I, too, fell into that trap. I worked hard and enjoyed the fruits of that labour, but in the end did I really gain all that I thought I had? I did not, and neither does anyone else. Once survival and comfort have been achieved, what more should we do, what more should we plough our time into?

We come into this world with nothing but the life we are given. When we leave we take that life force back with us to the place where we all belong and graduate to, but what of all the wealth and possessions we have accumulated during that life? What of all the good intentions we have had and the things we intended to do with them? In most cases we leave our worldly goods to our relatives and friends, but does that serve a purpose other than for remembrance's sake? The things that we hold near and dear do not have the same meaning to those we love and bequeath them to.

Possessions can never be any more than that. I, too, have experienced this a few times in my life. I, too, now wish I had done things a little differently. It is easy with hindsight, but what matters more than any possession we have ever had is the way we have lived our life – the happiness and the love we have shared, the good things that have resulted from the fact that we have been here, the legacy of knowledge that we have left behind – even the smallest seed. That is what we take forward with us…

Only knowledge and truth and love have any clout in the place where we will all end up. In that place we will be seen as the sum total of our accumulation and activation of these things. These will be our true colours. The rest will drop away as meaningless.

CHAPTER SIX

Capability and Growth

The Way Forward

The life we are given is a gift, a precious gift, and it is the nature of that life that dictates that we should change and grow. Only man is capable of growth. All other species of life remain within set limitations. A dog will always be a dog. His options will be limited to what dogs always do. A bird will always be a bird for the same reasons, and so it goes on with whatever life form we care to examine, but man is different. At birth he is actually far more helpless than other living species, but a natural feeling flows through him. It keeps him going forward – he needs more… It is this that makes him different. It is this that makes him grow, and as he does he stores the data of his experiences, just like a computer stores information on a memory chip. Only man has this ability, because only man will use the information he's accumulated at a later date.

We are like probes on an expedition of knowledge and experience. We are the sum total of all our experiences – not just those we choose to remember, but all we have ever said and done and had cause to interact with. We cannot lay a single thing aside, either good or bad, because then we are not who we have actually grown 'til this moment to become. There abides in reality neither good nor bad;

all things simply exist as they are at any given time in our lives. Every choice we have ever made was right – or seemed right at the time, or we would not have made it – but then comes the consequence of those choices, and it is those that must influence the next ones we make. I, too, am a product of consequence. I, too, am responsible for all of my past, whether I like it or not, but I have learned to step off that spinning roundabout of chaos.

How we change our life is up to us, but do it we shall, each one of us, at some point. How and when depends on how happy we are with the content and direction of our life right now. Remember we have total free will from the time of our birth. Yes, we must operate within existing family boundaries and restrictions, but even from an early age our likes, dislikes and preferences are our own. Very quickly we develop a character and that uniqueness grows and develops as the days, months and years travel by. At some stage, at some time, something will activate triggers, something inside will push us forward or pull us back. We will make the choices that will keep us where we are or help us reinvent ourselves or change direction. This is all part and parcel of life. I, too, made many choices that had great impact on the direction of my pathway, but more than once I came to realize that those choices were not all that I had anticipated them to be.

We are all the same. We are made of the same chemical components. We all feel happy, sad, lonely, angry and desirous. We all grow in an upward and outward direction that will conquer the obstacles placed in and along our pathway. Normal family restrictions are the first and keep us safe from harm, but later we push past those boundaries and explore.

All of our life is lived in this fashion. All of our life we aim and fire to attain whatever our heart desires or tells us at that time. We analyze and assess all we encounter to measure and validate it for ourselves. We choose whether to remain on the level we are on or to try a new one.

A life without opportunity would be no life. We need to go forward to keep ourselves happy. Growth is one of the most important of human characteristics. It keeps the world turning and Earth's energy flowing as it should. Without the opportunity for growth, man would become stagnant, stale and fed up. He would appreciate little and individual choice would be a thing of the past. He would never reach up or out of his existing state and would never know the wonders that exist all around him – for his enlightenment, entertainment, choice and delight.

(I am I) Only man has the ability to create and to know for himself on the journey of his making forever more. He is the eyes, ears and understanding of Myself. Only he has this inherent capability – through the will of Me, his creator, his consciousness and his soul. (I am I)

We do all we can to be happy, to make others happy and to make something of ourselves, but too often we are unhappy, dissatisfied and stuck in the life we are living. It seems that no matter what we do and how hard we try, we still end up being misunderstood and unfulfilled. We search far and wide for the love we deserve, but again people and life let us down. I, too, have been there, but the amazing thing is that so has everyone else. No matter what we are experiencing, even right now, so is everyone else. Everyone is the same. We are all searching, looking for that niche where we can completely fit in and belong. Everyone is feeling the same thing – on one level or another in their life. Their packages might change, but underneath, everything everywhere is the same.

The new millennium was a prime example. Every new year – and the new millennium more than most – we look forward to the changes we hope that year will bring, but as the time comes and goes we see that everything remains very much the same. In reality, how can one more day produce all we expect it to? The changes we desire are far more deeply rooted and must come from within our own lives. The changes we require are on a more individual and personal level that when activated would alter not only ourselves but also others and how they relate to us. To understand the changes on this personal level is like a breath of fresh air – or a wind that gains strength as it blows across the desert. It may be all-consuming, but it blows with strength and conviction – and the promise of a brighter tomorrow.

Man cannot change the world alone, but he can change his little part of it. He can make a conscious decision to alter the way he behaves and the way he reacts to others around him. Each man is the king of his own empire. That is the way of the world. It does not matter if he is rich or poor, what matters is the kindness he gives to those who need his help. This is not to say that he should become a doormat. Some self-restraint will go a long way to earn both the respect of others and of himself. A man who does not respect his own self is often full of sadness and despair. He has learned to let others use him in any way they like, just so he can feel that he is needed, and that is not a good thing.

Each man is totally responsible for his own life and all that it means and entails. Each man must gather his own strength, his own juicy bounty and his own rewards. There will be times in every life where a helping hand is needed, but when that hand is openly extended – too often providing a lifeline – then balance will quickly shift to burden, and no man should be a burden on another. The problem needs to be adjusted to give the first man back his independence. That is the will of the creator. Man must keep his own life in order, once the tools have been granted or found – and that is itself another story.

Each person holds the key to their own failure or success, but this key is often hidden by fear or self-doubt. So many give up when the going gets a little tough while others soldier on for their whole life without seeming to get where they once aimed to be. This is life that has missed a beat. Somewhere along its pathway important decisions, connections or roads have been missed or misinterpreted. This, when apparent, will often place a person on a side road, completely cut off from those who could help them to establish the connection they need. Anything will be hard going at that point, but the worst thing would be to give up or to throw in the towel. I, too, have been at exactly this point in many different ways on my journey, but I, just like many before me, managed to clamber back into the mainstream of society and flow of life.

Only man has the ability to backtrack and alter direction. Only man has the chance to change anything and everything that he may choose. Only man can 'change his spots', so to speak. An animal of any description will always be exactly the same as it has always been (unless it evolves) and exactly the same as all the others of its kind, but man changes at leisure into exactly what he desires to be.

In years gone by, a life was a whole, complete lifelong experience, but today we have the ability to taste many different lives during the course of one lifetime. Because of the freedom of the world about us we can change direction as many times as we wish, and each time we do, we embark on another angle, another facet of that life. These little snippets of evolution all sow the seed of the next experience we will encounter along the course of our chosen individual life pattern. Man can grow in any direction at any time in his life-frame, but first must come the desire to do so. First must come the realization that something more exists – that he can reach out, experience, grow and go forward.

Only we can find the key that fits our own destiny and that is why it is up to us alone to take the next step along the path of our journey. When we rely too heavily on our friends and family to help us out, we can miss something vitally important for our next step, something that only we could ever have seen. If, instead of dancing to our own tune, we look to others for the answers, we may end up dancing to theirs. Very often that is what puts us out of synch both with our own life and with reality.

Our experiences are always completely individual affairs. No two instances will be the same for any two people. Each situation that we encounter will lead us to the next piece in the puzzle of our life picture and only we can know what is right for us at any one time, provided we can be honest with ourselves (and that is a whole other story). Only we know who and what we are. We know where we have come from, on an emotional level as well as on a physical one, and we know exactly where we are going, or where we intend to go. Only we can know the experiences we have encountered along the way, so it makes sense that only we can know the next step to take. Very often we do know, but choose to dither and dally instead, because we are fearful or unsure, then because of this we look to others for confirmation and approval of what we are thinking. We believe that others know better than we do and if they voice an opinion about our next step, everything will turn out much better. And it might prove to be that way for a while, but if something was missed along the pathway, or if that solution was too quick or not correct for us right now, then we will have to repeat the experience from scratch all over again, perhaps in a different form, but the same experience nonetheless.

Life is a strange thing. We all begin at the same point and end at the same point, but what goes on in the middle is a miracle of innovation and intricacy. I, too, am a constant jumble of works in progress that cannot be completed until the whole of my life has been lived, just as a priceless piece of art or an intricate Chinese rug cannot be what it was intended to be until the last detail has been put into place.

Only man can do that for himself. Only man has the knowledge that is personally structured to fit his needs. He alone must learn what makes him tick, what makes him happy, what makes him sad. Is he happy with his life and if not, what areas need adjusting and why? Is there any more he would like to accomplish in the time he has left? Are his friends and loved ones happy or are there family feuds around him? Is his life full of stress and worry, pain and struggle, or is he carefree?

I, too, had to delve down deep to find the answers. I had to find the reason why I was not as happy as I thought I should have been. I had to find out what was bringing me down, what was going wrong, because, like many others, I was not a bad person and I thought I was doing the best that I could with all that I had and was available.

I began to learn differently. I began to learn that we are all the same and in the same boat. We are all looking for happiness and a place to fit snugly in life. We are all constant works in progress that alter daily as time goes by. In my own life, things were occurring that appeared out of my control, yet I somehow knew that I was contributing to them. We add more to where we are in life than most of us realize. It is easy to blame others for our predicaments – indeed, we are taught to do just that from a very early age – yet really it is down to us, but in subtler ways than you can imagine at this time.

All of life is based on the laws of cause and effect. Nothing is exempt from this ruling. All of nature is based on the same thing – and we are part of nature itself. The world was born because of cause and effect, when conditions that surrounded the first energy changed.

We may think that this current span of life is all that we have, but it is not. We must work to grow and change our opinion of ourselves, of who and what we are. Only we can change the paths of distress, disease and destruction we find ourselves on and only we can come back to do better than before. That is our given right, but we have a chance to do better, to be more than we are and to claim our birthright here and now – in this lifetime.

We are under the influence of our emotional self much more than we should be. Only we can make the necessary adjustments that are needed to correct this imbalance, but first we have to realize that an imbalance or problem exists. From a very early age we learned to relate to the world about us by the way it felt. When something felt good we did it again and when something did not we shied away. Even our parents led us on by our emotions, and by theirs too. We quickly learned to read the emotional cross-currents of all those who surrounded us. As we grew up, this experience extended to school and playmates and to anyone we encountered along the way, but what we did not know was that energy currents also flowed from us to them. It was these currents that tripped our emotional switches just as much as the emotions and mood swings of other people, and they still do. When we walk into a room that we have never been in before, we feel at ease or not, but we don't know why. What we are relating to is the energy that already exists in that space, the energy of what has gone on in there before.

We are both physical and etheric beings. This means that we are equal parts of matter and energy. We are familiar with the 'matter' or 'body' side of ourselves, but often unfamiliar with the energy side. All energy flows around us, about us and through us, but just as dust particles settle down in a room, so does the residue of energy particles left there by other people and other conditions. All the objects there will also contain residue – the chairs, the table, furnishings, etc., everything will affect the feel of any room...

Man is structured in a way that allows the free flow of energy to pass through him at all times. He is made to be happy and contented with his life, so when the opposite occurs he clams shut, just like a limpet on a rock face. Only peace and harmony allow him to perform the function he was made for, and that is why it is written in the Bible that 'God does not recognize sorrow or fear, anger or war'. When man operates from within those behaviour traits, the energy that is his life force and also the planet's does not pass through. It cannot, because he has blocked its pathway or channel, and this is how, as we said earlier, man is slowly killing the planet he loves. Its life force is not flowing as it should and therefore cannot reach as deeply into its core as is needed. Man is not doing this deliberately. He is not acting out of vindictiveness or vengeance. It is the cause-and-effect law in operation again. Man is unhappy, so both the planet and man himself are starved of vital energy that they need. This is not God's will. It is not man's wish either. It is simply the by-product of the life he is living at this time, and has lived in past times, as history clearly shows.

Man lives to be happy. It was the way he was designed to be. He has around him all he could possibly want, need or desire. The possibilities for contentment have never been so great, so easy, yet it seems almost impossible for many. Somewhere deep down inside, love, laughter, happiness and contentment are being lost or misplaced. Each and every day we tread the dreary, hard path of life and each and every day we fail to reach our goals. Something is wrong somewhere and that something lies embedded in each one of us. Only we can sort ourselves out, because only we can find our own true happiness and peace.

That does not mean we should stamp on each other, point the finger of blame at those in range or take drastic action to compensate for our unhappiness. It is easy to blame others around for their failings and for our own shortfalls, but these things are as much a product of their life as of ours. Nobody deliberately sets forth to make those that we love or know unhappy, but mis-communication and misunderstanding play vital roles in this, not to mention our own overactive emotional behaviour traits, and we are all victims of them. Only time can put things right once more, but we first need to understand there is a problem and why. We need to take stock, to understand that we ourselves play a greater part in our own unhappiness than we realize.

The time we spend here on Earth is but a drop in an ocean of time and space, only a moment, yet many of us don't accept this is true. That is the reason why those we have loved and lost through seeming death are coming back to be with us once more. *They are letting us know with every ounce of their being that death is not the end, only a transition.* Those who take their life as a way out of sadness and turmoil simply continue where they left off as they cross over that bridge. Life does go on – and so do the consequences. So do Earth's laws of cause and effect. The 'heaven' we are all waiting for is the continuation of the here and now. Here is the only place where we can make a difference, an instantaneous physical difference. Here – on the face of the planet, on the physical body of the all that is, on the body of God itself.

Many will throw up their hands in uproar at that statement, but only because they are still asleep. That is not a problem. Many different tracks and pathways lead up the mountain, but they all reach right to the top. There is nowhere else to go – unless you are on a round-and-round route. Each person will find their own truth. They will wake up at some time, a time that is right for them, but that does not mean we should drag our feet and wait in the meantime. We are on our own journey and if we speak words of truth and love, others will see the light and follow. Truth needs no long lullaby to back it up. It stands straight and tall on its own merit, in its own strength, and once it is spoken something deep inside all of us makes the connection with it. We don't even have to realize it. It will just happen, because truth is like that. It is what man has been unconsciously searching – for through the aeons of time he has been here.

Truth is an unchangeable force. Truth stands up in its own glory – regardless of what is thrown at it. Truth can be examined from any angle, and indeed it is, but each time the same conclusion is reached. Truth needs no coloration to make it palatable. It withstands time and space – eternally. Truth waits quietly by the side of man until he is ready to accept it, whether he believes in it or not. In fact, believing or not believing does not alter a thing. Truth is truth and that is all there is to it.

'I am truth. I am the light. I will lead you through the valley of death.' These are words that hold great weight and meaning. These are words that are timeless. Yet these are words that are simple and true. Only now can we realize their full potential. Only now we can take them on board in our own life's situations. Knowledge of any kind is only useful if you put it to work, otherwise it is taken back and rendered useless by the mind. It is here and now that matters most and we have all that we need to help us make things work.

Life is not a gamble. It is not a game. Only a life that is lived moment by moment can be bought to successful fruition. Only this will make the difference that we all wait anxiously for. '*I am the light*' means that we have the light of truth and knowledge always, at all times, within us. '*I am the truth*' means that we all, each and every moment, know exactly what is best for us and what is the better option to take, but to recognize it fully we must still our emotions, because it is those that lead us astray. '*I will lead you through the valley of death*' means exactly that too. It is not concerned with physical death, because that transition is automatic – we automatically return whence we came – but with the seeming death and fear of the spirit in life itself. It means that in our darkest, saddest, most fearful hours we will be taken by the hand and led back to peace and light. It means that we can always find that glimmer of hope that takes us forward to another day, a new day – and each new day is exactly that. It is a blank page that we can write upon exactly as we would wish. This means that we do hold the key to our life firmly in our hand at all times and that we are not the victims of circumstance we like to think we are. There is always a better option available to everyone and we are led by the hand until we find it.

We are boss of our own life and only we can make the moves and the decision to change it. I, too, have had to pass this point and I still do on an ongoing basis. That is the nature of free will and individuality. We are not the product of haphazard circumstances, but of the choices that have taken us to this point in time. Each and every day we have the option to change at least one little thing we don't like or something that no longer serves our purpose. That is all it will take to get the ball rolling – one little thing, one issue at a time. Life does not call on us to make catastrophic alterations that will change its course overnight; indeed, these are often the changes we should not make. But again these are more obvious with hindsight. I, too, have had my share of catastrophes, and have taken decisions that could have been better, and once again it is life itself that has shown me these things as I have pondered and looked back upon it.

We all have a wealth of information and experience at our fingertips that we don't often access. We are too busy looking forward to a point of reality or illusion that we would rather be to notice exactly where we are here and now. This seems to be the norm for today's fast lifestyle. We forget to stand and take stock of what is right under our nose.

Life comes at us one step at a time. One day, one hour, one second. Every moment of every day we have the opportunity to 'gently' say our truths, but do we? How often do we say exactly what we need to say to sort a problem out? If you are like I was, then the answer is not very often at all. It is easier to smile and keep the peace than to voice a truth that might bring conflict once it is aired. But that is not always the answer because terrible storms build up deep inside.

Sometimes the signals we send out are not as clear or as obvious as we would like to think, and then we wonder why others don't seem to take any notice. But how can they when they are stuck in their own train of thought and behaviour and our signals are not clear enough? It is truth and kind words that are needed to put our point across. This is more necessary than we realize. Only we can help ourselves. There is no knight in shining armour coming to whip our troubles into shape, no magician and no genie. All of our future stems from us alone – and that will happen one step at a time.

Chapter Seven

And So We Begin to Wake Up

We are all the same. We share the same hopes, the same dreams. We all look for love, acknowledgement, comfort and hope. We would all like world peace and world health. Each and every one of us is entitled to the most basic of human necessities as our birthright. We look to our parents to love and to guide us, to know us at least as well as we know ourselves and to be proud of who we are trying to be. We look to our friends for upliftment and to share our good times. We look to our siblings and children for a sense of belonging and understanding. We look to many people for many different reasons, but do we ever really look at ourselves? Do we know ourselves as well as we think we do? My guess is that we don't, not often anyway, yet we expect, completely expect, others to know what we want, what we are about and what we are thinking all the time. We look to others to mend the broken parts of ourselves that even we can't fix, and then we wonder why life continually falls short of our expectations. But is it really any wonder in reality?

We are our own worst enemy, travelling through life dashing here, there and everywhere, without often achieving or aiming at anything. We proceed miles along pathways that need never be travelled at all. So much time is wasted in being busy that need not be spent if we would only realize the many patterns we repeat. I, too, travel along this road. It's as if we need to be busy in order to prove our own worth, to prove we can cope and keep up, when in reality we don't – there's no need. We could achieve much more by consolidating our activities and focusing our attention on the task in hand. How often do we mindlessly perform menial tasks as our attention haphazardly wanders all over the place? It takes us two or three times as long to perform something we could do in minutes if we put our mind to it and focused properly.

We rarely consider the connection between the tasks we are doing and thoughts we are thinking whilst doing them. Energy flows where attention goes, and given that our attention wanders freely at will, no wonder we are tired and lethargic at the most inopportune times. I am also guilty of this. I waste my energy like water down a drain, and it's only with practice that we can stop. But how can we stop until someone tells us or highlights just what we are doing in the first place? We are not taught things such as this ordinarily, and then we wonder why time flies by so drastically fast, why we rarely achieve what we set out to do in a day. With our head in the future, the present that we experience sprints by. It's easily done. We hold imaginary conversations with those we are intending to speak to. We pre-enact dramas as if to practise what needs to be said and imagine what will happen in response, then when the event comes to be, we wonder why those concerned do not react as we thought or imagined they would. Instead of relying completely on the moment we are in, we reach into the future and rehearse it, either in our own mind or in conversational form with colleagues or friends. And the same can be said of the past. Not the distant past but this morning, yesterday, last week. We replay scenarios as we would have liked them to be so often that we recompute and add to the memory over and over again.

How can we ever know the truth or let life take its course when we are not even present in its now? We must experience every moment exactly the way it occurs – innocently, spontaneously, without preconception or rehearsal. How can we know how others will respond when life has not even got to that point yet? The answer is that we cannot possibly know. We think we do, based on past performance and experience, but really we don't know at all. Each and every day, every event, every moment is individual. No two experiences are totally alike, so how can we anticipate them correctly?

Helping Ourselves

We can help ourselves, but only in the moment we are in, in the time-frame of 'now'. Yesterday has been and gone. Tomorrow is not yet here and 100 things could happen in the meantime, so it stands to reason that only 'now' can matter. It is here that life is actually taking place. It is here that we can make a difference to our future, to life's outcome – one step, one second, one minute at a time. It is here that all change is possible, where what we do and what we think count for something. 'Now' is important – too important to be left unattached to conscious thought. All the decisions that need to be made are only of value in the now. All of life occurs at its highest state, its highest energy potential and frequency, in the now. Now is all that matters. Now is the only real time window that exists, where life's potency, fine-tuning, precision and conception take place.

This is not to say we should throw caution to the wind and totally ignore tomorrow. On the contrary. Our thoughts of the future show us the direction we want to travel in, the goals we need to head towards, but it is only in the now that those changes can begin to take shape – one step, one decision at a time.

Many hours are spent in longing. We long for different physical looks, lifestyles, bigger and better jobs, houses, cars and attachments. Few are content with what they themselves have accomplished, and this is sad. We have more available to us in every way than we care to imagine, yet deep inside many of us are disappointed, discontented and even angry.

I, too, have experienced my fair share of this kind of life. I, too, had to go within to understand what was going on. Each goal that we reach should make us happy, but instead of enjoying the experience, we look past it, ahead to the next. How can we ever be pleased with our lot when we keep changing our mind and direction? There lies the paradox. We don't know our own mind. We don't even know what we want. Yes, we have an idea, we really believe that we do know, yet when we finally get there, reality falls short of high expectations and we feel that in many ways nothing has changed at all. We have all experienced this countless times in many forms and this is also why we go through so many major life changes today. It used to take a whole complete lifetime to build up a home, a career and raise a family, but today we can experience as many different lifestyles as we see fit...

We are complex machines, capable of so much, but too often achieving so little. Many of us never reach our goals or fulfil our dreams or our desires, and the saddest thing of all is that often we don't even realize that we can.

Only we can make the life we lead a happy one. We have travelled far to experience all that we have, to live, love, be happy and content, to make a difference and contribute in some way. We think that at death all is over, that it's too late, that our time is up forever and that we must face our maker – as well as review our flaws, but what we don't realize is the truth – that life carries on from the point where we seemingly leave off, just on another level, that's all. Life continues. We are eternal. We do not die, because we cannot die. There is no death for humanity, only change. We relinquish our physical bodies, they return to physical dust, but we ourselves continue and live on in a more transparent, pure energy form.

What we do with our life, what we make of our choices and chances, does matter. It matters very much, because when we get home, when all is said and done, it's too late to activate or physically accomplish any more. At that point we will be the sum total of the person we were before our life's journey, plus all we have gained whilst on Earth. So it is here on Earth that we matter the most. It is only here, in the now, that we can make any difference – either to the planet or to ourselves.

As we have seen, man is the keeper of his own life. He is master of his own destiny and no one upon the planet can tell him otherwise. Yes, he has responsibilities, but even those are the outcome of past events or present necessity. Other than that he is free to come and go as he pleases. He alone makes up the rules he must live by. He is responsible for the day-to-day running of his life. At some point in the past he himself made every decision for which he now faces the consequences. Regardless of whether these were made in haste or not, or whether the outcome seems good or bad, he is responsible for exactly what he faces today.

Again I hear people say, 'But what about this, what about that? If only other people had done this or that… If only so-and-so had not placed me in that situation or that predicament…' There will always be 1,000 if onlys, buts and maybes, but the truth will always remain the same: each decision that was taken along the pathway has played a contributory role in the current situation, and as every day passes, we make the best decisions we can at any given moment that occurs.

How many of us can relate to this? How many of us have done and said things that in hindsight we should or should not have done? But at the end of the day we are only human and unless someone stands there and cries, 'Hey, this is a better way,' we carry on regardless. Our own worst enemies, we are all guilty of this trait – but then isn't that what being human is all about?

We all like a quick fix, too, and if we see a short cut it would be unnatural for us not to take it – only sometimes it may not be the best option in the long run. Only things won through effort, over time, can be sturdy and long-lasting; the rest will fall by the wayside as quickly and as easily as it appeared. When we search deeply within, when we see any situation from the correct viewpoint or bottom line, any options available become clear and so does the best route to take.

We have already examined how when we are young we look to our elders for direction and leadership, but what we don't realize is that those elders themselves are still searching for their own direction and answers in life. We come along, as innocent as the day is long, and take on board every word that is said – until we learn otherwise. We are like sponges that soak up all we find. We always think that others know better than us – but do they?

In many cases adults only know what they themselves have been taught, and again, this may not always have come from the truest source. Yet all that we see, hear and experience throughout our lifetime gets ingested into our mind. We take on board everything that interests us or that we relate to, and the rest gets filed away or discarded. That is our personal choice. But all that we do keep is stored. It becomes a part of our belief system, and once we form a belief it remains with us through time unless it comes to light to be challenged or we have cause to refine it. Most of the beliefs that we hold near and dear have been unaltered through time. Buried deep within our foundations, they have been a part of us since childhood and we have very few reasons to check their validity or their content. But what if those beliefs are incorrect? We only know what we have been told by people older than us, and they too only know what they have been taught, and so it goes back for generations.

Our thoughts and convictions are as varied as stars in the universe. We look to our own belief systems to lead us through life, but what happens when they are wrong or incomplete? Who knows? Who can tell? We are all we are because of everything we have experienced along the way. We are guided by our parents until we grow up – but when do we actually grow up? At what point in time do we know that we have and who can tell us? It is assumed that once we leave school we can handle ourselves and our life, but can we? All at once, what has changed? We think we can stop learning and get on with life, whether we are equipped to do it properly or not, but the truth is different. The truth is that many adults are more like children than children are themselves. They are so busy surviving, building and accumulating that everything else falls by the wayside. When do we grow up? Who on Earth can honestly say we ever do?

What Do We Really Know?

Life is full of ups and downs. Often we learn hard lessons along the way that appear cruel but are necessary. The problems that we encounter are not meant to make us buckle and break; they are valuable lessons that we must learn, tests we must pass, stepping stones that lead us to the next stage, the next phase in life… The more quickly we can recognize this, the more quickly and easily we can overcome them. Yes, sometimes those stones feel more like boulders, but their very size indicates that we must have missed a few red flags along the way. It is generally the case that we have buried our heads in the sand and ignored the signals, hoping they will go away, but if a problem gets bigger or keeps reoccurring it means that it needs our attention. Something needs addressing somewhere to instigate a change, and that is usually for the better in the long run – even if it hurts like mad at the time!

We are working too hard. Every day we get up and spend hours at our places of work. Work is a natural part of life, but we have become 'stuck' in work mode. Only man spends his life cooped up in a room while the days of warmth and sunshine pass by. Days roll into one another and suddenly a month has passed without his conscious mind even realizing.

The time we have is precious. It is too important to waste. We have become trapped by the rules and regulations of society, yet it is not society's fault. It is ours, because we use and expect too much. We work hard to earn more money, to pay the bills and to buy more stuff. We are not content with waiting and saving, so we borrow money we don't yet have and this becomes a millstone around our neck. We work hard to pay it off, but in the meantime we need or just buy more stuff. Debts rise. We work harder to pay them off, but still keep living and buying and working and borrowing. We are stuck in a loop, in catch-22. The only way out is to stop, to get off that merry-go-round and stand still.

Take a look at yourself. Do you really need all that you have around you? Is it worth working your life away for? We all need a roof over our head because of the climate we live in. It's too cold to sleep outside forever! And we all need the basics, but we have enough clothes alone to cover a football pitch. We have enough stuff to keep a small village happy. Where does it all end? And who cares? Do we? We worked hard for it, and we can do whatever we like, but are we happy?

Because we buy and want so much, society must create more and more to replenish its stocks and keep up. If we stopped for a while and took stock, we might feel better – lighter even – for it. Just look about you. Look in the shops. Look at all the stock that is sitting there waiting to be bought. Imagine double, treble that amount in the pipeline at all times, waiting to come from manufacturers, in transit or on the drawing board as new lines for each new season. Do we need it? Should we really want it or should we take a look at ourselves and wake up? There is more to life than work and perhaps we should look to easing our load, to enjoying what is outside our door every day.

Alone we are small. We think we can't make a difference, but we are wrong. We absolutely can make that difference. I, too, am one small person, but I am trying and that effort counts for more than I realize. *(I am I)* I can, I am and I will. *(I am I)*

Much of what is done today is totally unnecessary within the scale of life itself. If we pulled ourselves together and sorted our own lives out we would be amazed – not pleasantly surprised, but *amazed* – at how much we could accomplish.

At this moment in time we are teaching our children to be exactly like us – to work and want and eat and sleep and work and spend and work and eat and sleep… Is this what we actually want life to be like, or do we want more time to visit, to enjoy, to chill, to have fun, to savour the moment or day? Only we can answer these questions. Only we can make that choice and instigate the changes that will make it happen – not overnight, not through rebellion or skiving off work and neglecting commitments, but one step at a time, with acknowledgement, understanding and the right choices.

We all need to reach a certain standard in life to feel a sense of self-worth and stability. It is good to reach goals we set for ourselves, but other than that this world is our oyster. We must work to survive and play, but in reality that is all. However, today this is often not the case. We are so used to working to achieve that now that is all we do. We work hard, too hard, in a time-frame in history when the general standard of life has never been so good. There are more gadgets and gizmos than ever before – and still we look to produce bigger, smaller, faster, better ones that will cut our use of time even more. But what do we do with that time? Extra time is only of use if you appreciate having it, yet this is also not apparent today. We use that time instead to cook, eat, sleep and work some more. We have ground to an emotional halt, having lost our sense of enjoyment and zest for life.

I, too, have been in that place where every day is like the one before. I, too, have had to leave the treadmill. It is easy to be bogged down by routine, and indeed we do need organization, but when all is said and done, by the time we do get to sit down or relax, we are too tired for anything else. The hours slip by and off we go again. Is this the way of so-called civilization? 'It is a sign of the times,' we say, but fail to recognize that we ourselves add to all that keeps us as we are every single day. If we ate only when we were hungry and bought and wasted less, we would see that we needed less. Because we needed less we would buy less, therefore we would be able to work less to produce less, and because we worked less, we would have more free time to enjoy. But now we are doing the opposite. It is another catch-22 that we have got ourselves caught up in and again we have no one to blame but ourselves...

I was the same and still often am, but the more you can pull yourself back, the more you will start to break through old habits. Notice the times you automatically do things you need not do and begin to curb your actions. It need not be drastic, just one little thing at a time. It is not comfortable to change overnight, because then you feel deprived. When you feel deprived, you want to spoil yourself to make yourself feel better and so you begin the cycle again – until the next time... But one step at a time is enough to dent the habit and with practice it will slowly become a complete reversal. I should know, because I am still going through the motions myself. It's not easy and it sure takes time and patience, but keep on going and eventually you will get there!

Life is a joy to be lived. It's not always a bed of roses, but then it's not supposed to be. If we never had anything bitter, how could we enjoy the sweet taste of honey? Life is equally good and bad, and that is exactly the way that it should be.

Life is a gift to wake up to each day. Each new day is ours to live as we would like to live, to do whatever we desire to do. Work plays a vital role, but so do happiness, contentment and satisfaction. Yet, given the fact it is necessary to work, how many of us completely enjoy what we do? Too many hours are spent doing jobs that we really don't like. This is not to say we shouldn't take a job that seems menial or below us, because in reality joy can be found in any vocation if you put your whole self into it, but why don't we find jobs that we would really enjoy instead of just working for a pay packet? The answer is that we sometimes forget what we really wanted to be in the first place, and then become so bogged down with necessity and the life we have formed for ourselves that we have no possible means of backtracking.

Life is too short to gamble and play at it. Before you know it, time has run out. It is never too late to change your goals, but do it with love. Do it with consideration to yourself and to others, but do it. Look for that job that will fulfil you each day. Recognize your strengths and talents that you own and work with them. It's too late when you go back across the bridge of death. What will you say? 'Yes, thank you for my life, but I didn't enjoy it because...' or 'Yes, I had the opportunity, but I couldn't because...' There will always be obstacles in your path, but if you are sincere and move those boulders one stone at a time, you will gradually win through.

Life is not a game. It is serious, and we seriously need to get happy in all that we do. Make it count for you. Make it work the way you would want it to and get happy in the process – not chilled-out drug-type happy, but happily content with your lot. No one else can do it for you, so do it for yourself and for all those who love you.

It is easy to put a smile on your face, but even easier for someone else to remove it. Each and every day someone somewhere can place a spoke in our works. Only we can stop them from doing this by making a choice: we can choose not to let them. Nine times out of ten those who spike us are only venting their own bad mood or anger anyway, so push it subconsciously back to them, like a snowplough clearing snow, until you can learn how to recycle it. Make a decision that today no one can get to you and it's likely that they won't be able to. Stand firm but happy on your own ground and any storm that occurs will pass you by. If you are worried, in your mind make yourself small, like a grain of sand, and remain so until you know what to do. We are great at making our presence felt, but if we did the opposite more often it would be better. Make yourself small every day and life will flow around you much more easily.

If someone is causing a rumpus and you are quaking inside, send your thoughts up and ask silently for help. Ask for the person/people concerned to be made small as well. You can do this once or 100 times in a day and it will always work. There is more that goes on in life than you realize, so have a little faith.

Life responds to us – we don't respond to it. This statement alone runs counter to much that many believe and say today. I, too, had to learn this in not-so-easy lessons. But life flows according to its own rules and regulations. Man is given this life to live but he does not – or should not – control it. He owns it, but he cannot control it completely. He is just a part of it, like a player in a team or an actor in a film. Man is the keeper of his own life, but life also flows about him. I, too, learned this when I was young. Life was not always kind then – but neither is it today. Much has changed for the better, yet we often barely notice as new trends and problems break through.

Only we can make our life work for us. Only we can help it flow in the direction of our choice – but we must *help* it, that is the key.

> One day a man sat on a stone with his head in his hands. All day he had laboured to clear the leaves from a garden, but each time he did, the wind blew them back. All day this went on till in the end he gave up.
>
> The problem was not what he was trying to do but the way he was doing it. He was sweeping them into a pile to be picked up together at the end. If he had moved the pile out of the wind's reach or put the leaves in a bag along the way, he would have been finished hours earlier.

The moral is to work with what is available to you in the most efficient and effective way you can. Nature will lend a hand – but only if you stop working against it. Two streams that flow against each other will simply stand still, whereas two streams that meet as they follow the same direction will flow softly, softly until they reach the sea. Work with the currents that flow in your life, not always subconsciously against them.

Signposts

Only we can determine the direction of our life, but if something is wrong we will always find out. Problems are the markers that keep us moving on. If we are on the wrong path, it will come to a dead end at some point and we will be forced to reconsider or reroute entirely. This is one simple example of how life gently guides us to where we ought to be, to a smoother existence or plateau. Only we can make the alterations that will get us there, but life will give a signal first.

It is we who decide the direction we wish to follow, because we have personal choice, but once we have chosen, it is life that carries us there, that places the opportunity in our grasp. Babies offered a rattle at first do not know it is there. Then they are shown it, but still they must reach out for it themselves, and that is what happens to us in life. One door closes and another takes its place. This is nature working with us. This is the creative process of life at its best.

But who and what places these things in our pathway at exactly the right time? Someone does. How many times has a leaflet dropped onto your mat at just the right moment? How often do we overhear a conversation and think, 'That's funny – I need that too'? How often do we see something on the television, hear something on the radio or read a newspaper or magazine article that gives us the right information at exactly the time that we need it? I, too, have experienced this. It is called coincidence, but there is no such thing as coincidence. Each time something of this nature occurs, it was meant to. You are being given a helping hand, a nudge, or are being shown an alternative direction that will help you out, or a place where you need to be to receive another direction.

All this happens so ordinarily that the average person thinks little of it, but begin to take notice of it from this time on. The more you notice and silently acknowledge that you have noticed, the more it will happen – with things that are more important to you.

Sometimes this happens but the timing is not quite right. Sometimes we say, 'If only I'd seen that last week' or 'I could have done with this yesterday.' If that is the case, it is a sure sign that you are changing your mind too often, that you've fallen out of synch. It can even signal that you are living more in the future than the present.

You are wishing your life away. But if you operate fully in the moment, you will be pleasantly surprised at how often 'coincidences' occur and will continue to do so if you let them.

Many of us believe that we must hurtle through life to get what we can when we want it, but often this is wrong. How many times have you moved hell and high water to obtain something you thought you wanted, only to wish you'd waited a little longer to get it? The answer is 'very often', if you are like the rest of society. We charge through life at a great rate of knots and often miss much more than we see. It is time that we slowed our pace to allow the universe to catch up, to help us once more. We do not need to hurry through life quite as much as we presently do. Time passes the same whether we enjoy ourselves or not, so we may as well use it to our advantage – but that's not to say we should take too much on board, because that in itself is another problem.

The majority of us are good and kind. We look to make this life work as smoothly as possible. Life is hard sometimes for everyone, but usually at different times and for different reasons. As we pass through those difficulties, we become wiser and stronger and happier. Life holds lessons for us all and we try to help those around us overcome their difficulties. We do this because we want to. We enjoy the end result when all goes well, and often it does, but more often the difficulties only appear to be solved and if this is the case the problems will simply return and the person concerned will be back where they started once more.

Every problem has a different lesson behind it, even if it appears to be the same on the surface. If a problem seems hard, it is because it is meant to. Its lessons lie deeper than is apparent. Usually a lot of things will need to be addressed and altered to make it disappear and never return. The only way to prevent a problem cascading is to address the little things at the time that they arise. One step at a time and the life we are living will be different.

Life goes by in seconds, minutes, hours and days, but we often don't notice that time passage at all. We are so wrapped up in the things we are doing that we hardly notice hours passing. We are forever on catch-up, rushing here and running there, without living or perceiving the day at all. We are the only ones who can slow our time down, only we can make it work for us and all we need do when we want help is ask. When time goes too slowly and the day appears to drag, send a signal up to your guides. Ask them to speed it up a little. When time seems to fly faster than you can work, ask again. Ask for it to be slowed right down so you can achieve all that you want in the time that you have available for the project in hand. This can be done as often as you wish, but remember to put it back to normal when you are finished, or you may be on the opposite side of the problem. You have total charge over your perception of time. It can work for you, but you must remember to ask for what you need. No one else can, because no one else knows. Only you do.

Only we can help ourselves, but first we must realize that we can, and this is just one little trick of many that will work in our favour. We should be glad that we are not just skin and bones, that we are more, and are capable of more than we understand right now, because all these things will work in our favour forever, once they are mastered.

Life works for us depending on the rules by which we play. We set the scene and also the pace. We are able to choose pretty much everything. Yes, it often appears that we are at the mercy of outside events and people, but in truth they are just living to their own beat, to their own rules and desires. If we are influenced by them, it is because something somewhere has been overlooked.

Wherever we are in life, we are exactly where we are meant to be. When something needs to change we will know by the signals at work or by our innermost feelings. When we are bored, or have had enough of the life about us, it is a sure sign that we need to reach out and explore once again; we need new knowledge, new circles, new experiences and new energies to explore and digest. Sometimes this may be a small step, such as joining a new club or doing a new activity, but at other times this may not be enough. At these times, send out the thought that you need some help and watch closely to see what arises in response. Remain in a state of truth and love and openness and you will be surprised; drop into depression, stress or fear and you will only succeed in shutting out all that might be. You will clam up once more and feel the weight of the world upon your shoulders. But if you ask for help in an open, true and sincere way, it really will come to you.

Be watchful and remain open for new thoughts and experiences to filter through. Sometimes we are so bent on what we imagine the solution to be that we miss the subtle things that offer a change of direction. Don't be too rigid in your thinking – remain flexible. A solution may not appear in quite the form you anticipate.

When something does appear, don't rush headlong into counter-activity and drastic measures. Be gentle with yourself. Imagine you can be as small as a grain of sand and sit tight for a while as things readjust or realign themselves to and around you. I, too, have travelled this none-too-smooth road and there are plenty of adjustments that need to be made. Be patient, watch for the signals and above all be kind – not indulgent, but gentle on yourself. Remember, you are where you are now because that is where you are supposed to be at this time.

If you observe the people around you, you will see they are often just as stuck or unhappy as you are. But the wind that will blow your cobwebs away will also send gusts out to those who interact with you in your circles of movement. If you make the changes that you need, no matter how small, you will also unblock the flow of life of those around you.

Sometimes these changes might feel a little painful, but that is only because we are creatures of habit. We would rather remain in an uncomfortable situation just because it is familiar to us. We can be too frightened to change because of the unknown factors it may bring. Life can be like a pair of old slippers that we don't want to bin because of their comfort. They may be threadbare and inefficient, but we hold on to them just the same. Often we would rather remain unhappy and moan about it than alter the smallest thing. But really, that is not the answer. Instead we should enjoy a happy and content frame of mind (for many reasons).

We are each assigned at birth a guardian/angel. It does not matter whether you believe this or not, because belief is not the key. The angel is there and will remain so until you die, or cross back over to home. The important part is that in your darkest moments, when you feel totally lost, you know you are not alone. You are being helped, supported and guided.

Just as only we can see the spokes in our works and the areas that cause us pain and discomfort, so only we can focus our attention on the alterations that need to occur. Sometimes these changes will involve other people, but sometimes they might simply be down to a change in our own attitude. Don't do anything at all until you know exactly, without doubt, what to do.

Only you can know how you feel, and if you are unhappy or stressed, you need to understand the cause of it. There are many books on the market that will open new windows of understanding for you. Go to a bookshop and browse in the self-help section. Remember to remain open and flexible. Notice the kind of book you are attracted to and read it. This will be the first of many stepping stones that will lead you to a new understanding of yourself and of others around you. *Families and How to Survive Them* by John Cleese and Robin Skinner is a good starting point. If you are in relationship difficulties, try *Men Are from Mars, Women Are from Venus* by John Gray or *The Relate Guide to Starting Again* by Sarah Litvinoff. These excellent books will give you food for thought and will also lead you to others.

A book is like a breath of fresh air. It is like discussing your problems with a friend or counsellor and you will take on board only what you need. Your subconscious will do much of the work for you, as it disregards, reseats and catalogues all thoughts and rubbish.

Change will come slowly, one step at a time, but, just like a child at school, if you hold up your hand, someone somewhere will answer your call. They were meant to. Many of us are like children who need redirection and input from another source. When we are small we look to our parents and our teachers, but in adulthood we go forward as best as we can – often alone or following the guidance of others who are as stuck as we are. This is nobody's fault but everyone's problem. At this point in time you are luckier than most simply because you are reading this book. You have already begun to wake up and look around you. You are sending out the ripples of change simply by looking at yourself in another way. The wheels of life are already beginning to move. Be pleased and be happy.

CHAPTER EIGHT

The Winds of Youth

The Child and the Parent

We are born and we grow. We naturally adapt to our surroundings and to those around us by simply blending with all influences along our path, but what proof do we have that those who surround us know as much as they think they do? We live by their rules, regulations and standards, but what if they themselves are out of synch with life as it really is or should be? Should we not look to find out?

It takes all sorts of people to make a world and those 'all sorts of people' operate on many different levels, with different thoughts and behaviour patterns. Anyone can be a parent. There are no restrictions of any kind. Many adults struggle daily to make their own lives work, then all of a sudden they become parents and it is assumed that they know what they are doing. But do they?

Being a parent is the most important task in the world, yet most of the time we do it alone – surely the stakes are too high to take risks with this? We only know what to do from the examples we ourselves were given, but often those were way off the mark and we can never know how well we are doing because there are no objective standards to measure against. Out of love we make many mistakes, but how can we know? Who can tell us? There is no operator's manual. Perhaps we don't know as much as we think we do. Being a good parent is not easy. Being an adult or a child is not easy either.

Each child is completely different and being a parent is a unique experience for us all, but should we go through it as blindly as we do? From birth to school age our children are almost completely alone with us. They are at our mercy, but should we carry this burden and should they? Is it right to leave such an important task to chance? And what about adults with learning or behaviour difficulties? They too are completely on their own in adult life. It is assumed that they can cope, that they know what they're doing, but do they? Can they?

We are trained for every job we ever undertake – except parenthood. Teachers are trained for years to handle children, but as parents we are expected to do it automatically, without help or guidance of any kind. It is assumed that parenting comes naturally, that we know what to do. And of course we love our children and would lay down our life in an instant on their behalf, yet we unknowingly hurt them with over-indulgent loving intentions all the time.

Children go through definite stages and behaviour patterns, but how often do we fully understand what they are and how best to help and guide them through those experiences? Many parents are too locked into their own trials and tribulations to notice. Small signals that would highlight a problem get taken on board as a child being naughty or needy, and then, when a full-blown problem comes to light, we wonder how it got there and where it came from.

Children need our examples and guidance as well as our food and board. They tell us what they need at the time they need it, but then it's up to us to keep things in balance. Life is full of opportunity for a healthy happy child, but a child who is different in any way can come up against barriers that are very difficult to break down.

Each child is unique. Each family unit is too. Each has its own set of problems, talents and needs. Each is on a journey unique in its own right. How can we expect to automatically get parenting right?

We have much to put right, but first we need to know ourselves and our patterns better than we do at this moment. What makes us tick? What pushes our buttons? Why do we laugh or cry? What makes us angry? Where are our boundaries? What are our beliefs? All these things and many more play a vital role in the person, in the character we see ourselves to be.

Only we can know the answers to these questions and more, but it is not as simple as glancing in a mirror. Knowledge of this nature will only come to light as we pay attention to the things we do daily, many of which are so engrained and automatic that we don't even realize we are doing them at all. To know ourselves properly – from inside out – we must piece together all our patterns and recognize our triggers and the things that we do without thinking. We must rebuild ourselves correctly, in a much kinder and more mature way.

When we were small we learned about the world from those around us and by the time we reached school age we had a pretty big picture built up in our head. We knew how to behave, to respond and to interact with others. We knew our likes and our dislikes and how to play up to get our own way. Our basic character was already well on the way to being formed. We had learned about family, about our neighbours and peers. We had learned about love, interaction and sharing, and had already decided whether the world was a good, kind place that made us feel safe and happy or whether it was not. Many impressions such as these have stayed silently within us into adulthood, but they form just the tip of a tree of understanding that is still growing inside us even now.

We are who we are because we learned to be that way from our earliest understanding. We learned how best to get along in life, how to make others notice us, how to get attention, how best to get what we wanted or needed, what to do or say to make others laugh and like us, and how to behave when there were bad times or bad vibrations around. Perhaps we saw our parents work hard and perhaps we saw them argue or fight. Perhaps we learned how to make ourselves scarce or how to stand up for ourselves against siblings. We learned what we liked and what we didn't from the experiences of others, from their likes and dislikes as well as our own.

No one but us experienced all that we did in the exact way that we did and everything intermingled to form the basis of who we are now. These were character-forming years that we rarely have cause to re-examine, times that had the greatest and deepest impact because we were like blank, open pages that needed to be written upon or a blank new computer that needed software to know what it was. We were open for input in every way, shape or form that we could get it, and that is how we became the character we are today.

Only we know whether we are comfortable inside with being that person and with how we feel the world interplays with and relates to us today. Try as we might, it can be hard to be accepted and acknowledged for who and what we are. But if we feel unrecognized or misunderstood, we are the ones who carry the weight of those thoughts on our shoulders and we are the only ones who can lighten that load – not by bullying and badgering our way through life, or by being a doormat, but through a deeper understanding of why we think and feel the things we do.

There is so much more to who we are than we realize, not just in the way we look, act and talk, but in the thoughts we produce in our head all day and every day. We are careful, sometimes almost to the extreme, about the food we put in our body, but do we ever consider what we feed and allow into our mind? We are susceptible to mental bombardment all day every day from every direction. Our own thoughts wander freely, unchecked, in any direction they want; in fact, we grow up believing that we can think what we want to about anyone or anything, but this book will aim to teach you that is wrong…

We have already spoken about energy and the fact that it plays a larger part in our existence than we understand. Energy must flow freely both through us and around us at all times. Thought is pure energy itself, so wherever thoughts go, energy flows – always. When we are happy and relaxed, we are at one with the world and at peace with our surroundings. Even troubles seem to come and go without disturbing our equilibrium quite as much, but when we are stressed or sad, we send out different thoughts. These are the difference between black and white. Kind thoughts are white, while others range from shades of grey to black, depending on our attitude at the time. When we are happy, pleased and balanced, we send waves of love and contentment to all that we think of. These waves emanate from our bodies in a constant flow and are felt by everyone and everything around us. A calm person will automatically calm all those they come into contact with just by being themselves. Their presence will be felt the moment they walk into a room, while the opposite effect will be generated by stressed-out, anxious or angry individuals. When we are uptight in any way, the vibes we expel fly out in all directions. They, too, affect all they come into contact with, acting like sparks to dry kindling. All this comes to pass from the thoughts that we think and what we are in our innermost selves. Our private thoughts do matter very, very much, whether we believe we control them or not.

Only we can control the thoughts we think because they emanate from us. We may blame people all day long for putting us into a bad mood, but the truth, as we have seen, is that we *allow* them to do so. So we let others control our every thought – without any recognition of that fact at all. We were taught to do just that by parents who were taught likewise by their parents, and so on, for generations. But it is time to make a change. We have allowed too much of ourselves to run on automatic pilot every second of every day, and this needs addressing most urgently.

Automatic pilot is a good thing when used properly, because it stops our systems from overloading. It takes the pressure out of the moment. It helps us because it temporarily removes our conscious attention from the repetitive and mundane tasks we are doing. Often these tasks are as natural to us as breathing or blinking, so the automatic brain action can take over, but the downside is that it leaves our mind and our chaotic thoughts free to wander at will. When we have mastered our thought patterns better, automatic pilot will be an unequivocally good thing, but at the moment, depending on our mood, our thoughts fire all over the place at random.

Mood swings hinder our lives and our productiveness, yet can be deeply engrained. It was in childhood that we learned how to react to them, taking our cues from the standards and behaviour patterns of our elders. Adults who let their own emotions charge freely at one another give false information and signals to their young. So we are told not to fight, not to get cross, not to be nasty, etc., but is that enough to help us understand and harness these emotions? Mostly it is not, so we grow up feeling bad and frustrated when they surface, being told one thing, witnessing another and doing what we feel like in the process.

Anger in its most basic form is as natural as laughter, and as necessary. It clears the air and puts your cards on the table, just as a good thunderstorm is sometimes necessary to clear hot and sticky conditions. When we are not taught to handle our anger in a productive manner, though, it gets bottled up and festers. Eventually, we explode like a pressure cooker and all sorts of things come tumbling out. But anger, properly vented, should address only the moment you are experiencing, nothing more. What happened last week, last month or last year is irrelevant. That time has passed and nothing can alter it now. Anger is a release of irritation and should be no more than that. When we feel a flash of anger it should be recognized as a signal that all is not as it should be. It's an indication of imbalance.

Anger is very recognizable. It always starts in the same way, as a feeling of being uptight in the stomach, or chest, or neck. This will differ, depending on where you personally carry your stress, and it would be useful to help our children find and recognize theirs. An unusual, uncomfortable feeling inside is a good indication of what is building up. Once we recognize it, we can address its source straightaway rather than waiting for it to control us.

An angry child can become destructive, because they have no means of addressing and venting the strength of the emotions they are experiencing. They have not learned how to handle their feelings, so the feelings gather intensity within them, just as a trickle of water can become a raging torrent. They might live with parents who do not recognize their own emotions, who push emotions down or who themselves let their anger run wild, or they may live in such a restrictive family that showing emotion at all is out of the question. But being angry in its proper form (one that corresponds to the moment only) is as healthy and as natural as a smile.

Energy flows naturally through, to and from us with every thought we think, through the words we speak and the looks we take. It flows from anger and flows with love. Because it is the natural thing for our body to do – it's unavoidable. However, man does not yet realize the immensity of everything he does during the course of a lifetime. Every minute of every day he is responsible for the vibrations that operate within his own self and those that he sends out to others. If he could see this energy transference, he would be totally amazed. He would begin to understand not only what happened to his thoughts but also where he fitted into the scale of life. He would begin to see life and his own connection to it in a completely new, enhanced way. He would be awe-struck.

The fact that he is unable to see all this with his eyes does not make it less real or important. It is part of the movement of nature. Just as the sea ebbs and flows with the tide and the moon, so man moves with the flow of the symphony of life. He is part of all things and all things are part of him. He is a vital instrument in the whole of the Earth's life as he knows it.

Each long and lonely day we spend with ourselves, hooked into the thoughts we are thinking, we are emitting energy waves to all that we are thinking about. When we ponder past events, even events of just that morning, we send energy to those occasions and keep them alive and burning in the present. I, too, play my part in this. We all do, as we reminisce. Sometimes we look back and wish things were still the same. At other times we replay conversations and interactions as if on a movie screen, inventing all kinds of outcomes and things we could have said and done differently at the time, but what is the use? That moment has been and gone. We can never get it back. Revisiting it only brings forward the emotions we felt then – to the detriment of the present and future.

Only we can put the past to bed properly:

Imagine for a moment that you can wrap up all the events that have caused you pain. Close your eyes for a moment and bring one instance to the fore of your mind. Take the whole thing, the whole memory, out of your mind and put it into a blue bin-liner. Because you are doing this in your head, the bin-liner can be as big as you need it to be. Tie it up tightly. Let a huge hook come down from up high, lift it up and take it away, like on a dry cleaner's garment machine. As you watch it go, see it getting smaller and smaller until it disappears into the distance and vanishes out of sight. It is gone – but don't check, because that way you will be inviting it back to your consciousness and mind. Just know and trust that it's over. Know it is being recycled for you and that the pain and the hold that it had on your life have gone with it.

You now are standing, relaxed, near the hole that it came from. Imagine that hole being filled with warmth and light and love. The golden light touches you and you feel good. Open your eyes and continue with your day.

This can be done as often as you wish – once a day or 20 times in succession – but each time you do it, it will work. Some things might take far more working on than others, but eventually you will look back and the pain and emotional turmoil will be gone. They will not hurt you any more. The truth of the event, whatever it may be, will still remain the same, but you will not bring the emotional energy of it forward to the present day to hurt you and keep yourself locked there. You will be relaxed, detached and in a more logical frame of mind. You will be able to meet those concerned in a balanced manner, devoid of old anger, pain or regret. You will be able to operate completely in the moment you are in, without the invisible ties and strings that before would have been pulling you down.

The past is past and how we choose to look at it is our own affair. It can have no strength or hold in the now. This is where you are and this is where life operates. This is where all things matter and all things are possible.

The future is no different from the past. It will be just the same unless we make the changes that matter – in the now. How often do we wish our lives away in a trance-like state as we imagine how we want the future to be? And how often are we disappointed when the future arrives? We build it up to be any number of things, but when reality comes along we feel let down. The truth is that we build things up too high. We send all our energy, all our hopes and all our dreams forward to the day we hope they'll finally come true, to events we think will finally make *that* difference, but when that day comes around, we deflate. How can things ever measure up to our high expectations when most of what could have happened to enhance it has fallen by the wayside through our lack of understanding or attention to the present? We have let time rush past us without changing anything at all. Only we can know the reality of this statement, the times we said, 'If only... If only I had done this, if only I had done that...' We bounce back to the past from the future and from the future to the past over and over again, but life is *here*. It is now. It is present in the here and now and nowhere else.

Only we can make life work. Only we can make it count. Only we can improve upon what we already have by relearning and readjusting ourselves to fit better into the world we live in. We hold the keys to all possibilities in life, we make the choices that take us forward or hold us back. There are no limits, no boundaries that we can't overcome, and it all starts from deep within us. I, too, had to learn these lessons and this book is the result of that journey.

We can each work wonders in the world in which we live, or at least in our own little section of it. We can each make the difference between light and darkness to somebody somewhere, even just by being a better person or a better parent. We presently do that job blindly and alone, but it need not and should not be that way. Parenting is the most important job in the world and our children, the children we love, deserve better. Something needs altering somewhere, so let it begin right here – in our now.

CHAPTER NINE

Actually, What Is Love?

Love – the most sought-after thing in the universe. Everyone wants it, everyone needs it, everyone searches for it, but few truly find it. Only a few even know what it really means.

Only man can understand the immensity of this emotion. Wars have been fought in its name; deaths have been arranged in its honour. Love. Only we can know what it really means – but that is the twist. What *does* it mean? It means something different to us all. Who can explain it? Who can put it accurately into words? Ballads have tried since the dawn of time. Love – it makes the world go round. We love it and hate it just as quickly. Only we can make it work for us, but first we need to understand what it does *mean*.

Yet, how do we know? How can we? At no point in our life has anyone explained its meaning to us. We just know – or we think we do – from somewhere deep inside. We grow up with an expectation of love that reaches the moon. We expect it to warm us, to uplift us, to make us happy and to complete us. We love to love at all times, at all costs, all our lives.

We grew up feeling loved – or not, as the case may be. Our impression of love and what we expected it to be grew with us. We unconsciously learned to feel it from the first time we lay in our mother's arms – or not, again as the case might be. Only those who have experienced it fully, innocently, can know and recognize it, while the rest can search all their lives but never really find it. They look past it without even knowing.

Love is delicate. It is strong. It slams itself into your face, yet it creeps quietly along. Love has no definition; it just is what it is. We love with our heart, our soul and our mind. We love with every breath we take and every thought we think. We live for love for the whole of our life's journey…

We learn about love from our parents, from our brothers and sisters, from our friends and neighbours and grandparents. We unconsciously build up its picture all through our learning years. We recognize it by the way it makes us feel, depending on what we are doing and what we are thinking at the time. Slowly we build up a comprehensive picture that will lead us through life, and it is this that shapes all we do and become.

Everyone everywhere just wants to be accepted for the person that they are. They just want to belong. Yet it is this sense of belonging that is so hard to come by, even when we are small, within our own family unit. From a very early age we start ducking and diving our way through the attentions and affections that are put upon us – or not. We learn how to play each other to achieve favourable results and to score points. We learn that we like to be in our parents' good graces and also in those of our peers. We gradually learn the difference between like and dislike, happiness and sadness, love and distress. These early influences form the basis of how we love and how we see love. They also teach us what we expect to feel when experiencing love – of any kind.

So, only we can know what loving and being loved means to us, and 100 different explanations will be given by 100 different people. Love is an individual experience, but one that we all hunger after and expect. Love is the most important thing in our lives because without it we feel like nothing. It is what gives us a sense of self-respect and self-esteem. It is what keeps us going through thick and thin. In many cases it can seem like the be-all and end-all of life, but this in itself is another problem.

Love is important to us. It can fill our every waking thought, our whole being. It can lift us up as high as a cloud, until we feel just as light, or it can dash us deep down to the ground. Love is the centre of all we feel. It can rule our lives. It can be so strong that all other aspects of life seem to fade into nothingness. Only love can do so much with very little effort. Only love. Only, only, only – but the cost of that 'only' can sometimes 'be' our life!

Man is not the only species to be driven blindly by this force, but only he can move mountains to get it. Love is behind all he has ever done, all he will ever do and all he will ever aspire to be. Love is the key to his life and also his kingdom of heaven and hell.

Only we can know what love means to us, individually. Answer just with your heart as you read the next questions. What do *you* need in order to feel loved? What is it you expect to receive?

Only we can harness the power of love and loving. We can help it work within us, for us, or we can let it rule our world, but whatever we choose it will always be the key to the type of person we are.

I, too, have had my share of this emotion. I lived every day under its control until I knew nothing else. I, too, had to harness it and help it become a kinder, gentler but stronger, more adult, realistic love. I, too, have had my heart broken and have unwittingly broken others – all in the name of love.

Only we can help ourselves. Only we can help each other and only we can turn this 'loving' thing around so it can again become all that it was made to be – the life-giving force within us all.

Early Lessons

From the time we are born we are subjected to the force of love. It fills our whole being at a time when we have nothing more in our head. It gushes from our parents and all who come to see and welcome us. We don't know what it is, but we feel it. It feels good and it makes us feel good. Happy and secure in our new earthly form, we reach out for the security of it every time we cry, and when we're babies, unless we physically require something else, we get it. As we grow we learn many things, but in the end the majority of what we receive is encased in love once more, gently flowing forth from parents, siblings, friends and others that we know. We reach school and have to learn new rules that are sometimes less than kind, and when things go well we feel a different feeling – but it's a kind of love just the same.

All love comes from the same source and hits the same response points or emotional triggers in us. Regardless of how old we are, we need this interaction. It is how we measure ourselves in the world. It is how we know if we are up to scratch or if we are way off the mark. It is how we fit into the life we carve out for ourselves and that of our family too. Families that are too way out will not fit into society at large. They will feel out of place and uncomfortable and surmise that the world and all its people are against them. When we fit, we have friends and happy neighbours. Life feels good. ('Fitting' in this instance is not the same as 'conforming to the same standard as everyone else' – it just means that you are balanced and totally at peace with your life, yourself and your surroundings. To fit is to be content with your lot, and when you are content you automatically operate within the love mode and the currents of life flowing happily and easily along.)

As we grow from childhood to adolescence we learn to express the feelings we have. We slowly learn to manipulate them, to let them work to our advantage. We learn to read others. We learn what helps us to feel good about ourselves and also what feels uncomfortable. Feeling either comfortable or uncomfortable about the choices we make and the actions we take is an important part of growing up. Feelings such as these keep us on track with our life and become signposts and guidelines to help us both now and in the years to come. We learn once more how to stay in the love mode – the happy, comfortable and good side of life. We inch forward bit by bit into the person we will become. We grow into our character and love is the force that leads us on.

Again, this is where good parenting skills play their part. Within a well-adjusted family unit, all aspects of life are equally balanced. No person has too much power over another. People are not pushing and pulling and shoving each other on a never-ending roller-coaster ride of emotions and conditions. They are generally happy and able to speak their mind, to live and to interact successfully together. It will not be this way the whole time, but then neither is it supposed to be. We have already discussed that anger is as healthy as laughter, but in a balanced way and in the correct proportion to each event. All members of the family will see and respect each other as individual beings who have a life and mind of their own. They live together, love each other and help each other along the course of their time and journey together, but they do not own each other or try to over-control or over-protect. They just fit and interact, as good friends do. Being a blood relative is a privilege, not a hindrance, and in a happy family this is how it is seen.

Not all of us will have grown up in such a family. We must relate to the experiences that were individual to us on our journey so far. Only we can know if they were adequate or lacking in any way and whether we were happy and content for the most part or not. Only we know if those about us understood and knew us or if they did not, but whatever we experienced, it was what it was at the time and now it's gone. All that remains is the product left behind and this is the total sum of what we are. We are what we have known and have experienced up to date and that's all there is to it. If we are lucky we will have had all that we needed when we needed it, in an emotionally secure sense rather than just a material one, but if not, then the base bricks of our life will be scattered all over the place, like foundation stones that were not correctly set under a house. We will be fine of course, because we learned how to be, and through it we will have gained strengths, but it is also likely that we will have gaps in our subconscious instruction manual of life, and every now and again little blips will arise, the most obvious ones being in love, finance and parenthood. So we too will repeat inherent mistakes – probably the same ones our parents made and theirs before them. Life is like that. It takes us all along the same old chiselled route, until we stop, until we choose to make it different. Yet that's just it – we *can* choose.

(I am I) I gave man the free choice to choose his own life. He can be happy or sad, poor or rich, upbeat or downtrodden,

worried or content, mean or kind... All these things he has the power to create and control – for himself. This is the freedom of life. (I am I)

Only we can make the choices that will ever make a difference, but first we must remember that we can. It won't be as simple as changing our look, our partner and our job. These things may appear to assist in the short term, but really never help at all, because fundamentally we ourselves have remained the same. We are still the same person that we were last week, last month, last year, with the same basic personality and life structure. We respond, attract and interact to everything in exactly the same way we always did.

We might not like many things but we cannot run away from ourselves, no matter how much we might like to try, so the only thing left is to look inside at the connections and workings of our own inner self. If you do this with patience, time and effort, you will discover that even though you thought you had changed the rules by which you played, fundamentally you remained the same, easily finding yourself in exactly the same situations you were in before. I, too, have been in this place and it hurt. It hurt like mad, but things did get better. I, too, had to learn what put me there and what was needed to break the pattern and get me out, but I did it, one step at a time, as you will, as everyone does. Remember that...

All that you have experienced so far, all that has bought you to this point, in some crazy way was meant to be. It has brought you to this point in your life, to who and where you are now, and without any single one of those experiences you would not be you. You would not be where you are now but in some other place, probably facing a different set of problems and setbacks – but problems and setbacks just the same... Yet you are exactly where you are, and only being there, in the now, can take you forward to the next step, to the next stepping stone, the place where you need to be to go forward, for whatever reason... Life will get better and so will love.

Do we know what the word 'love' means individually for us – and in all the contexts that it comes to affect us? We are driven by love. It is the force that lies behind everything we do. It is what helps us feel at home in our family surroundings. It is what attracts and attaches us to friends, new and old. It is what directs us to be the person we are in all that we do and say. We do our job because we love it (or should). We visit new places because we think we will love them too. The hobbies we pursue, the clothes we wear, the food we eat, the music we enjoy, the colours we have around us, the perfume we wear, the car we drive, the name we call our child, the people we mix with, the person we date and perhaps eventually marry – are all chosen because of love. It hides behind every decision we ever make in our lives. We are love ourselves, in its purest physical form, yet do we understand the part that we ourselves play in our search for love? We automatically look to others to give us what we need, but do we ever consider what we give to ourselves? We play the greatest part in our own executions and it's all in our search for love.

Only we can sort this out and it won't be easy, but putting one foot in front of another is a good beginning, and it all starts here, with us.

We have already discussed the fact that the majority of us know little about the way we formed our opinions and expectations of love. At some point in our life our expectation of this emotion became automatic, an expected achievable level, a part of ourselves we thought little about – but expected others to recognize and know exactly. But only we ourselves can know the answer to this riddle, only can know the love that we crave for. We must search within to fill the missing gaps in our lives, in our relationships and in our soul.

During adolescence we play and explore the realms in which we find ourselves. We explore at leisure all avenues of adult life. We form opinions that will help us during that adult life and these stay with us until we either outgrow their need or something gives us cause to update their content. We often carry so much outdated clutter in our head that we can feel overrun or suffocated by our own private thoughts. Just as a home needs periodical attention, so does our mind, our thoughts and our beliefs. By always remaining the same, we stagnate – we become bored, boring and stale. A clean sweep will go a long way towards attaining inner peace, harmony and balance.

Adolescence plays a large part in clearing the mind of childish thoughts and notions that would otherwise lead us astray or cloud our judgement in later years. It helps us grow out of childhood gently, but distinctly, and into adult thought patterns and beliefs. After early toddler years, adolescence is the next vital step to becoming the individual character we will be. It is the blueprint of the adult now emerging from innocence. It is the formation of the being we will become.

We all need to pass through this stage under the safety of a secure family umbrella. All manner of things might happen, and indeed should happen, during this period, but what remains the most important aspect is the amount of emotional security present to enable this metamorphosis to take place. Any child that needs to hide aspects of themselves is not being true to the character that is forming, and this is itself a problem in the making.

We are all the same, with the same hopes, dreams and desires, so in the end it's only natural that we explore the same avenues and make the same mistakes – until we know not to. We are the sum total of all facets of ourselves, comprising the good and the bad, so having the freedom to make mistakes while still in the safety of our own family unit is priceless. We learn by things we do in much greater depths than from words that are spoken or aimed in our general direction, and these lessons will remain with us for life. That is why it's so important to live a life functioning totally in the now, without colour or illusion from past or future. Only in the 'now' can we find the balance and truth to live life as it should be.

During adolescence there is the opportunity to play out the beliefs and opinions we have formed, and if we are lucky most of them will serve us well. We are also extremely sensitive to the opinion of those around us at this time, and not just in a negative way. We are liable to pick up and keep all manner of things, both good and bad, from every direction. This is the time when we need the most help, but ironically it is also the time when we are most likely to spurn that guidance. We are learning to stand on our own two feet, not only in all that we do but in our emotions, thoughts and belief systems as well. We are cutting the apron strings that until now have been our lifeline and security.

We go to school, we grow up, we leave home, we go to work, we stand alone, we fall in love, and so the story unfolds... But how do we know that we are right? We only know what we know because somewhere along the line we were told or we saw and did what we did at any time, but what happens when any of that information is flawed? Who will ever know? How will we know? And what will happen to the next steps that we take? A building is only as strong and as straight as its foundations allow it to be and if in our earlier years the influences we had were incomplete or offset, our next steps will be too, unless we have cause to update them. But again, who knows, who can help or even notice and then tell us? And who would dare? No one. No one can unless we veer off the beaten track we are treading...

All of us are in the same boat. We can't help it because humanity has been the way it has for generations. Not only have we passed advice, information and knowledge to one another, but we have passed on any flaws we have as well. I, too, had to understand what I was doing wrong. I was doing the best that I could. I was being the best person and making the best effort, giving and receiving that best I could in every way. My life led me all over the place, yet fundamentally it was all the same. Nothing ever changed and I found myself repeating what I would rather not. I had to step back and take stock, to readdress the situation and understand what repeated and was going wrong.

Only we can know the thoughts that we carry and all the things that we do and have done. We know what we have seen, the people we have met and the many experiences and influences we have had along the way. We know the hopes and the dreams we have adhered to and won – and those that fizzled out or were dashed. We know everything that we have done to feel accepted, happy, loved, secure, and exactly how that has brought us to where we are. We know all the changes we have made – and at other times where we've fallen, only we can know or say when things have worked – or not, whatever be the case until today.

Some people appear to be lucky. They seem to have all they need to live life to the full. Everything they touch comes together as it should, but things are not always so easy for the rest of us. We try, we work, we try some more, but then it appears that with each step we take, we only slip back even further. Sometimes years can go past and life seems relatively fine. We turn a corner and wham, everything stops. Not necessarily due to our own actions, but maybe more to life and other people letting us down. So we try to get up, to get going once again, and so this trend continues on and on.

Work, life, friendship, love – all these change, grow, fizzle out and grow stale, but why? What determines what will work and what will not? We do all that we do with the best of intentions and effort, so what makes us fall down as fast as we try to get up? The answer, you will not believe: we cause our own destruction and our own heartache – without ever being aware of it at the time. We do it all by ourselves, automatically, because we don't realize it or know any better.

We follow the path that many others have trodden because it appears to work at the time. We do all that we do to the best of our knowledge because again it's right at the time. We do everything to the best of our ability, yet we are where we find ourselves today – even though it might not feel comfortable or right, or be the obvious place of our choosing, it is the place we should be 'here and now' to grow forward, it is the place we will find the next step.

Only we can move ourselves through this process. To understand it, take stock, take a rest, take time out. Even if your world seems to be tumbling down, don't fret or worry, don't add to it or do anything more – until suddenly you know for sure what to do – and you will.

Man only loves with half of his heart; the rest of the time he waits for love to come to him. He waits in vain for the love of this life to appear to him. I, too, was guilty of this. For the whole of my life I felt alone, unloved and unlovable, yet I was not.

Where do we derive our opinions and ideas of love from? Who told us what it should be like? And how many of us even know what it is that we are looking for? How long must we wait before we feel the love that has been sitting on our laps all along? So often we wait for others to return love in the same fashion and format that we gave it, but life is not like that. Love is an individual thing and no two people are ever the same (or at least hardly ever). Yet we wait and hope that the people we care about will hit upon the buttons in our heart – but how can they do so when they don't know what they are and, even worse, neither do we?

Definitions of Love

Love is a feeling. It is within each and every one of us as part of who we are. It is that part of us that determines how we feel about life, about others and about ourselves. It is the look of the world about us; it is the wellbeing in our heart. It is the peace in our mind and the way we seem to swell when we are happy. It is the way we interact with other people and why we place their needs above our own. It is every ounce of our being that reaches out to touch the world we live in. Love is the way we care, the way we hope and the way we dream. It is the way we pick ourselves up, and others too, when we or they have fallen. It is the first cry we make and the last breath we take. It emanates from our very beings every day of our lives. It is the essence of all we are and all we can strive to be. Love is our life force. It is the energy that flows through the Earth and it is this that the greater world is short of. It is more of this – and only this – that can save our bacon.

Love is the key to the rest of our life. It is the key to our own happiness and to the gates of paradise, whether you believe in its existence or not.

Love will never fade away. It can never disappear. Love waits quietly in the wings of our life, waiting for us to notice that it is there. *It is always there.* Only we are stuck. We think we are alone when we are not. We close the doors to our own hearts and wait for others to turn the key that fits the lock, but how can they when we hold that key ourselves? The doors are locked from within, not without. We have barred our own way to happiness through the fear, pain and unhappiness we have felt.

Every time we are alone and sad, we place another obstacle in our way, another chink in our armour, without realizing. We trap our feelings and emotions deep inside and wait subconsciously for another to reach in – to unlock the door, but they can't... Only we can set our hearts free, for ourselves, by ourselves, because it was we who locked them tightly in the first place. No one can rescue us. No one will manage to even get close until the time we comprehend what we are doing and let them in.

When the doors are first flung open, we may feel vulnerable, even naked. Of course life will hurt at times – that's why we clammed so tightly shut in the first place, but just as a breath of fresh cold air produces a sharp intake of breath, we can learn to take it. Life is full of ups and downs, and if we don't allow them in, how will we ever learn to weather what will come about? If we lock out all the pain, we also lock out all the love – we remove ourselves from the flow of living life force that we need.

Only we can help ourselves – and when we can, when we finally learn to do this, the rest will follow quite automatically, straight from God. Love will flow from God and the many angels/teachers/spirits/guides who live to serve, whether you believe in their existence or not. A parent loves their child no less for following their own path, their dreams and their own opinions, right or wrong. A good parent simply loves – no frills, no flounces, no conditions, they just love and try to guide as best they can – and that is exactly how it is for each of us. We are just loved, every day of our lives, by the force that made life possible in the first place. We ourselves are living aspects of physical love, so how could we ever be without it? Love flows through us, is within and without us, all our lives. Let it out – it will attach to more love that's been with you all along, waiting quietly in life's wings for you to notice it.

First we must love ourselves, because without that we can never properly love each other. Self-love is the most misunderstood form of love that exists in man. It is responsible for much of the heartache we experience, both by our own hand and by those of other people. We give ourselves to everyone and every event that ever asks us, but to be kind and loving to our own selves seems impossible. How can we love ourselves when we know all that we've been up to and are responsible for? How can we love ourselves when the largest part of who we are lies buried deep where even we don't care to look?

We learn to disown parts of ourselves at a very early age and do it so very well and automatically that we don't even know when we're doing it. But as soon as someone comes close to us we clam shut even more tightly than before, just in case they catch a glimpse of some dark secret or scary sight. We have become our own worst enemies, treating ourselves much worse, in fact, than we would ever allow another person to do. And we do all this as naturally as breathing.

Only we can lighten up on ourselves and on our outlook but before that we must realize we have a problem. How can we fix what we don't even know is broken? How can we, until the time arrives that we're meant to? Only we can mend our broken spirit – and that is exactly where the problem lies. We have allowed the world to bring us down until we are battered, bruised and bleeding emotionally from within. No one person is more responsible than another, no one person has done these things deliberately, it has just happened along the course of our life, slowly and surely, and the worse thing is that we have helped it, because somewhere deep inside we have accepted it. We may have even subconsciously thought that we deserved it. We expected to be hurt – we expected it from life and situations.

I, too, have lived this saga and in many ways still do, only now I am more aware of the process when it occurs, so I can make the choice to let it be that way or not. Life will not stop being the way it always has been, because that is the nature of free choice and life itself, but now I can choose how I will react and interact. I can choose – just as we all can.

Only we can feel the emotions that are ours. For the most part we've carried them through our lives, every day. Because only we can feel them, only we can fix them. Only we know ourselves well enough to make that difference – in the thoughts we have, the words we speak and the things we unthinkingly do.

We can change all the rules that we live by – not with force and battle, but with love, understanding and kindness. We decide what we accept and are feeling at any moment, whether it be love, balance and truth or illusion. We alone make the rules and regulations we choose to follow. We alone can make our life work – no one else – and life will always support and help us if we let it. We should approach this task not in the lazy 'I'll let life take care of me' fashion, but with strength, courage and the conviction of a clear and 'open-minded' head. If we stay out of illusion and deep in the truth, we will see more clearly the best route and direction to follow. Markers and signposts are all over the place, but first we must learn to read them. We must learn to see differently what is being placed before us to gently nudge us onto a clearer path.

Life is like a symphony in motion. Each decision leads to the next. Cause and effect have more power over us than many of us care to know. We blame the predicaments we are in on any number of things, but very rarely look truthfully at our own input, and then when we do, we do it with anger and regret, very rarely with gentleness or love. It is the way we have learned to be, and we have learned very well indeed, but the time has now come to make a change.

CHAPTER TEN

We Can Mend

Only man can mend his own broken heart. Time will help as well, but man must do the physical work himself. All through life he gets battered and bruised until at some stage he can barely take any more. From a very early age he learns to blame himself for the misfortunes that befall him, and when this becomes too painful he makes the switch to blaming others. He blames all and sundry for the predicaments he is in, but most of all he blames them for the fact that he doesn't feel loved – or at least not in the way that he thinks he should.

Man has mislaid the key to his own heart. He waits for life and for other people to complete him, to recognize and make him whole, while all the time all the answers lie with him.

For the most part he feels unsettled. He looks outwardly for love, for self-worth, to complete his sense of wholeness and contentment, when really all he needs is to take stock, to stand still for a moment and look within… The majority of people follow others who seem to know what they are doing. It is easy to look at someone else and see them as they are right now, as having all life's answers – the answers that we ourselves need. It is easy to mimic their lifestyle, their possessions and their manner, but are they really any happier than us? We see the person as they are today, but do we consider what they themselves might have been through to get them to this point in the first place? And do we know where it is that they think they are going? Very few are content with life – very few indeed. Only some are happy and in love with their lot, yet this state is available to all; it is here for the taking.

If everything we need is all about us, what is the problem? Each dawning day is a brand-new page, a brand-new chance for another go at living and enjoying life. Let's use it to our highest advantage – not with force, but with a commitment to love, to self-love, to love life. Let's get on with making things better – here and now.

We have already discussed that when we were small we followed the route of our parents. We followed their example and lived by the rules that they set. This was good, because it gave us a basic structure, a base grid to follow and to keep us safe in early life.

As children, we know the life that our parents have had. We witness first-hand their dreams, trials and tribulations. We see their kind hearts and their good intentions. We live with their anger and emotional turmoil. We see the lovelessness that exists almost everywhere. We see the mistakes and the heartache that is all around. At different times we learn about the world, about love, about friendship, about sunshine and music and art. We are told that the world is our oyster and that love is all around, but the majority of us live through the opposite.

As the years go by we allow others to add to that parental grid of information in the form of influence, experience and teaching, but what if those things are incomplete or rocky? How will we know? Who can tell us? Who will see or hear the thoughts that we're thinking? No one. So we trundle along every day thinking the thoughts that we always think, just as others have done before, allowing anything and everything to pass through our mind – unfiltered, unprotected, uncensored and unchecked.

That is the general pattern of life today. We take on board and digest anything and everything we allow ourselves to, and most of that depends entirely on the opinions and boundaries set up and put in place in early childhood. Yet how can we determine at such an early age what is good, correct or right for us? We rely heavily on our peers, but they too are in the same boat, rowing along their own path of life in the same fashion, looking to fit in comfortably and be happy.

We are all blindly following a path that seems to be leading nowhere. So who can help us? Who can tell us where to go and what we've been doing wrong?

I am. I can. I will. These words have been given to us by spirit. Put simply, they mean that we are what we are, that we can change whatever and whenever we choose, and that we will do so. They are simple words that can alter the way we see our life and also the place we are heading.

So often we change our jobs, our style, our partner, our outlook, each time in the hope that that will do the trick, but all too often once again we find ourselves back almost exactly in the place where we started. Years go past in this fashion, repeating and repeating, yet we are the only ones who can choose to break the mould, to stop these things from happening anymore. We must make changes from within ourselves, not without. We can change all we wish *without* over and over again, but if we don't change within, even just a little bit, we will always end up in exactly the same spot.

A good example is love. How do we decide what love is? Do we ever stop to consider what it is that we think we are looking for or what we need to feel or to know that we are loved? Hardly ever! We just go right on looking for that something that will make us sparkle and feel complete – but even in that statement there is a problem. We are waiting for others to make us whole when we should be complete already. We should not look to others to do this for us, yet we do. We use each other's strengths all the time, then wonder why the load they carry gets burdensome and heavy.

Only we can be complete within ourselves. We should be able to support ourselves in life in every possible way and situation. That is our own responsibility. Then and only then can we find an equal partner to share our life with. Then we can choose to be together because we want to be, not because we have to be to hold each other up. Two people who come together and use each other's strengths might fit closely for a while because they complement each other, and for the most part they will feel better, lighter, happier than they have ever felt before, but then small niggles and other problems will come creeping in.

These two people have become one, but they still have two heads, two sets of opinions, two sets of needs and wants and desires, so which head will be the controlling head? Which will be the winner and which the loser? It is an impossible situation from the start. Each likes the other for their differences as well as similarities, but once in a relationship both try to mould and change the other to fit their own way of thinking, behaving and believing. They forget they are independent and suddenly switched to owning and controlling each other. Why should that be when it's precisely this behaviour that is the cause of many relationship problems?

When we are incomplete inside before we meet, two people cannot form a compatible, balanced relationship, even though we love each other and think we can. When we first meet someone we feel compatible with, we fill in any gaps in each other's life. So a shy person, for example, will be attracted to a more outgoing one, because they can be themselves but enjoy the opposite of their character in the other. The outgoing partner will provide all the stimulation and enjoyment needed in the relationship, whilst the shy one will provide the audience and the stillness. At first this can work well, but eventually the more outgoing person will burn out, as they will feel it always falls to them to provide the stimulation. They will need a rest, while their partner will feel unnoticed and even misunderstood because they feel safer and more used to just following. They are uncomfortable and unaccustomed to taking the leading role.

This is a simple example of how easily whatever feels good at first can later become a burden. I, too, have experienced this and I, too, have had to grow and change my outlook.

We must experience both the same and the opposite to know ourselves in life. If we get stuck, we often think the only answer is to break away from the relationship. We are more used to breaking up and walking away than we are to staying put, recognizing and fixing the problem. I should know, because that is how it was for me too! Life is the same for us all, only we don't often realize at the time. We look at others and at how happy they appear, wishing we too were just like that. But we've forgotten how to do it and that we can be too.

Whether we are part of a partnership or not, we will always be individual people with our own hopes, dreams and desires. When we were small we built up a picture of life, of our future, of the way we thought it would be and of love itself. We built up a fairy tale in our own way, in our mind, and because no one knew, no one could tell us otherwise. But then how could they? Who can see inside another person? Everyone does the same at one time or another, so everyone is looking for that same happy-ever-after fairy tale ending. Everyone is waiting to be rescued, to be saved, waiting for the pieces of the puzzle of their life to fit together. So who can rescue whom – and how can we know how to do it? The answer, of course, is that we don't. We blindly try all the combinations we can, but how often do we hit gold and for how long before we feel the strain? Only we can make the pieces fit within our lives. Only we can truly know how we perceive love. That is always completely individual and frankly it often bears little resemblance to reality at all. It can be so out of date that is it hardly any wonder that those who come into our lives can't match up. We look to others to fit a specific role or model that in reality does not exist, and even when we are lucky enough to find someone who does seem to make us feel complete, we forget that they are individual and human too, that they are susceptible to the same doubts and flaws that we have.

Of course, when we first get together all is wonderful. It is supposed to be. We are in love. Whether it is happening for the first or last or hundred-and-fiftieth time, love is still love. It is still wonderful, as it resonates with our soul. For a while it is all-consuming. We can't think, can't eat and can't function. We live to be together each time we are apart and so it goes on and on and on, but then reality sets in regardless. It has to. Life has to go on. We are still in love, but the feeling drops to a more realistic level. It does not matter how long after we meet that this occurs, the point is that it does. We come back down to a quieter level, to a more everyday, usual kind of love, to the love that has always been there throughout our life, but because of the ecstasy of the high we've been on, we don't recognize it any more.

Love is quiet, love is strong; it is sure and always present. Only we can make the adjustments necessary to recognise that it exists all around us always. We are used to looking for love, finding it and drawing it from one another, but in reality it is with us all the time, every day. It is often just much gentler than we expect. The complete devouring, raging love we feel when we are in love is like a torrent that engulfs us. We have searched our whole life for this moment, this time, this person, and we have found them. We feel – perhaps for the first time ever – totally at one with the world, complete in every way. The quieter love from our family and friends dulls into the background as we enjoy the experience, the ride, the high. We have arrived where we have always wanted to be, and it's wonderful. This is the most wonderful feeling there could ever be, but it is just that, a feeling, and because it is a feeling, we often distort and misinterpret its presence and its hold upon us.

Only we can know how true these words are, for we know the times we have lived through relationships such as this and know the outcome of those periods of ecstasy and all-consuming love. We are the only ones who can interpret what love means to us, how it feels, how we feel and what we expect. We are not at the mercy of it; we are not at the mercy of life. We are our own masters and we choose to love. We choose to feel what we do. The coming together of two people who care for or are attracted to each other is a gift within its own right. The feeling of euphoria cannot last indefinitely. It may come and go very frequently, but it will come and it will go, and that is the point. It will find a natural balanced level all of its own, because it has to, because that is the nature of life.

Many of us today are broken-hearted, dismayed and confused. We find it hard to understand why the love we thought would last has fizzled out. Here again we work hard, we play hard and we try to do our best, but often it seems that our best is never good enough. But there lies another key. Once more we are doing all that we can because we want to. We are trying to make all the pieces fit together tightly, correctly, because we want to, but at some stage our wanting to do these things becomes a chore. The whole thing shifts and changes and becomes a burden that we carry, and by that time it has become hard work. We can sustain the pace for a while, but unless we feel that our efforts are appreciated we break down. We change from complementing each other to relying on each other to needing each other to fix us and this happens in such a subtle way that no one even realizes it. I, too, had to learn this, but not before I had hurt myself and others in the process, and it all happens under the same umbrella of love.

Love is good. It is kind and gentle, but it is also the thorn that pushes deep into our hearts when we don't do it properly. It is the birth of a baby, but it is the cause of a war. Love is as controversial as the day is long and we live our own example each and every day.

Our lives are full. We work hard to maintain the style to which we are accustomed. We get up and the day is busy, but when we are hurt in any way by love, the world in which we function falls to pieces. In reality it does not, but we feel and think that it does. Love usually does not play the greatest part in our daily activities, yet it means the most. When our hearts feel broken, we fall by the wayside and fall apart. All other aspects of life seem dim by comparison and we almost waste away in sadness. What we do then is personal to us, but you can be sure that it hurts all the same. We march over events time and time again in our minds and feel we are bleeding to death – and in a sense we are. We are bleeding emotionally. Remember earlier we spoke of two people who joined together too strongly in completing each others' lives? That is the reason. When those people pull apart, neither is complete anymore. It is like being ripped open – jagged edges and broken bits lie everywhere. We feel incomplete. To others we look the same as we did before and they expect us to function the same too, because in reality life does still go on regardless, but we are not the same. We are broken, torn and bleeding on the inside. We scream out in pain – but it is a pain that only we can feel and know. It is individual to our life and to our being.

The only way to ever stop this happening again is to become a complete and whole individual in our own right. It is lovely to rely on someone, to allow them to perform the tasks we don't like, but when we lean too heavily on that person, it becomes their burden. So we take love and turn it into pain. Only we can do this; it does not happen by itself. I, too, should know, because I, too, have done this. I have been responsible for my own pain and that of others without even knowing it at the time. I, too, looked everywhere to find the love I needed, when in reality it was with me all the time. I just didn't notice. All over the world people are doing the same thing. We all look to others to fill the void and fulfil the expectations of our heart and we fail to recognize that those we find are also searching. They are looking to us to complete them. They, too, need love to fill that void in their being.

Only we can put things right, but it will happen one small step at a time. If you are feeling disenchanted with someone you are with, remember that they are still the same person they were when you met them. The only thing that's altered is time. Life has got in between and daily problems have muddled things and are blocking the way. If you are hurting, your partner will be hurting too. They, too, will be wondering what has happened and what has changed. They, too, will be thinking nearly every thought that you have, and if they aren't, then that proves the problem lies within you. All the unrest we ever experience must first begin in us: in our own heart, in our own mind. Even when we displace it and think it does not, it can be traced back to a change of opinion or change of mind somewhere and the trick is to find and understand it.

Only we can know when we start to feel the pangs of unrest. It stems from someplace inside that gets bolder and bigger as time passes by. We cannot put our finger on the problem and we automatically assume it is the other person's fault. These feelings are compounded when we subconsciously need our partner to prove their commitment and love. We are insecure and we lay the fault at their door when it is very probably ours. This feeling stems from our own mind, yet we imagine signals and signs in the things they do, say or don't say that prove it. When we look for reasons we can make any number of things fit the bill, but only a truth that is directed at ourselves will reveal the root of any problems as they really are. Yet love will wait quietly by until we sort ourselves out. That is the nature of its strength.

Only we can look within to find the cause of the pain. Only we can know the thoughts we think and the opinions we have. Did we have a true picture of this person from the start – or did we see only what we wanted to see? Did they hide bits of themselves that they didn't like – and did we? Did we change or exaggerate a little of our own character to impress our partner – or vice versa? Did we see something other than what was there, and did they do the same?

When we first meet someone new we often believe we have found our fairy tale, the person who can fulfil our dreams and the missing gaps in our life. But often we see an illusion, because the love we are looking to find is itself an illusion. The feelings we have are real enough, but the things we think we see in a person – we see mainly because we want to. We don't always see the reality and by changing our life patterns to fit that relationship we move even more into creating and maintaining that illusion. There is no problem with this, because it is all a part of love, but the problems arise when we rely too deeply on our partners to fill our own gaps and insecurities. Often when two people put each other on a pedestal, their expectations are too high or too unreal, and this is hard to live up to.

I, too, have been guilty of this. Most of my life I waited for my knight in shining armour to rescue and love me forever, as depicted in books, songs and films throughout eons, but of course this just could not be. A bill such as this is too hard to maintain. It is too much pressure to expect any one person to carry, especially if they are anticipating the same thing from you yourself. If you both rescue each other and both aim to be what each other needs and wants (even subconsciously), it will lead to trouble, disillusion and heartache later in the developing relationship. Filling in the missing pieces of anyone's life is a tall order.

At the end of the day we are all the same, with the same hopes, dreams, doubts and needs. We are all in the same boat, floating along in the same water. We all need to be loved, trusted and respected, but when we *need* to feel *needed*, problems arise and eventually the pleasure we gain in fulfilling that role will turn into resentment and maybe anger at the burden it causes, especially if we do not feel appreciated the way we need to be. Appreciation is the reward we expect to receive. It is how we feel important in someone's life. We will move mountains and run to the ends of the Earth for anyone, just as long as we feel they appreciate the effort, but when our efforts become expected, considered the norm, a gnawing rot sets in and we only have our own selves to blame. We opted to do those things once upon a time and how are our partners supposed to know we feel differently now? It is we who have changed the rules, not them, so it is up to us to set the balance straight – not all at once in anger, but gently, by giving them time to adjust and to readjust. We need to redraw our boundaries again, that's all.

At the beginning of a relationship we are in a more flexible frame of mind. We enjoy taking the strain off our new partner, even if it means that we overstretch ourselves. We are keen to over-accommodate each other's needs, because it is a way of proving or demonstrating our love. We show each other that nothing is too much trouble. We cancel and rearrange appointments and commitments to show that this love is important. We have the love that others speak of. We have found our ticket to heaven. For a time, even years, everything in the garden is rosy. Life has a purpose, a feel-good factor all of its own, only it cannot sustain this level forever. Once this starts to drop off, we come down, either quickly or slowly, maybe over a number of years. Sometimes this happens so gradually that neither partner notices; they just grumble a little more often at each other and anyone else who might be around. Life is returning to normal and their relationship is feeling the strain. It can show itself in disputes over silly things or there could be huge issues, but whatever the symptom, the cause needs addressing, not ignoring. All problems grow a little at a time. When niggles are dealt with honestly and kindly, then nothing more will really happen. Life will be fine. But when we bury our heads in the sand and go deeper into turmoil inside, those simple niggly things will start to fester and grow. They will become distorted, be fed by and attract larger problems.

There is no point in pretending we are something we are not, because eventually the strain will be felt by all parties concerned. So be yourself. Be truthful about the things you feel at the time you feel them, especially to yourself, because the face we portray to the outside world is what the outside world will believe. At the beginning of a relationship, when everything is new and love chemicals are running high, truths can be taken much better than at any other time. Only we know who we are and what we see in the other person. So be truthful about it.

Also, don't imagine you can change this or that about them. Love them for all of themselves, as they should love you too. Characters will naturally blend and complement one another, but if you find you must hide this and that because your partner might not like it or agree, already you are on the road of illusion and sooner or later that bubble will burst or become a problem.

It is exactly for these reasons that we should be whole and complete individuals within our own right before we take on a new partner. Only we can stop the pain in our future by knowing ourselves better first, and this comes from within, not without. Like attracts like, but so do opposites. It is an invisible process that begins on an energetic level, often before we even speak. We are like two magnets that have no hope of doing anything but drawing together, because they are propelled to do so. The way we look is barely important. It is the energy that's inside that calls all the shots, and it's this that we cannot control once the magnetic pull is in action.

We owe it to ourselves to put matters right and we have already begun by acknowledging a few things in this book. Love is what makes the world go round and it is also the essence of man, but to do its stuff it needs our help – in more ways than we can ever know.

Only we can know what we expect from love and only we can know when and if we find it. Love is an individual thing that means something different to each and every one of us. We recognize its pull within ourselves, but forget that we don't travel a one-way street. Our partner is looking to fulfil their version of love as well. They, too, have their own needs and visions. Only we can rectify the balance between love and life, and it really is a question of balance. Too much love can separate us from the world about us, just as too little can harden us unnecessarily. Life is a mixture of love and survival and it is up to us to find the right level.

Love is a two-way thing that should complement the life we are already living. It is not the be-all and end-all of who we are, but a part, a continuation, a facet. It is just a slice, an expression of our personality, our character. It is not the whole of the world, but a taste of it. Love propels us forward. It should never hold us back. Love is just what it is – in all ways and in everything that exists.

CHAPTER ELEVEN

Controlling Influences

Influences and the Effects They Have

Only we can live our life, but many influences control the things that we do from the time we are born. First there are our parents and their parents, our society and culture and any religious beliefs that are apparent in our immediate environment. Next we move to school and peers and then to the influences of the greater world. We move to college and work and social events, and through all this we are subject to music, television, newspapers, magazines, books and films. We are bombarded from the start and this torrent never lets up. We are pressured in every direction to comply with life, yet we must also retain our independence and sense of fun.

Life is hard for us all and it is different for us all. Even members of the same family will give a completely different account of what life means to them. That is how it is supposed to be and how it has always been, yet every now and again we throw a wobbly. We stamp our feet and glare at the world. We wonder why things turn out as they do and why we appear to have so little control over a life we supposedly own. We are responsible for it – or so we are taught – yet often our hands seem tied at precisely the times we ought to be free. Only we can change this, but before we do we must understand precisely what makes us tick and what influences the decisions we make.

Only we should call the shots, but to do so correctly we need a realistic view of life. Only we can say what we feel comfortable with at any time, but again that might also be a trap. From the time we are small we are led by the hand to do all that's required of us. We learn what is and is not acceptable by the response of the elders around us. We learn to make judgements and to explore, again within the boundaries that are set, but when those boundaries are spongy, absent or too severe, it can hamper the love and life experiences we find. When we feel secure and safe, we are free to explore as we wish, as we should, but when we are too bold or too timid, we overstretch or hinder our lessons accordingly, together with our experiments.

Only we can know in later life if our childhood was all that it should have been and this will depend on the support, opportunities and physical structuring we had. Yet no matter what our childhood experiences, we have the ability to turn ourselves around. All other living species remain exactly as they were created. Yes, they evolve over time, but basically they remain as they were. But man has the ability to change everything about his looks, his personality and his views. He can be whatever he desires. He can do whatever he wants and believe and think whatever takes his fancy. I, too, have become a new person since I began to delve more deeply into myself. I am all that I was before plus a whole lot more besides. I have grown into the person I was destined to be by filling in blanks that were really a sleeping part of myself all along. We all have the same ability. We are all so much more than we imagine and as a species we are capable of anything.

Life is what you make it. Even in our saddest times we are not bound and gagged by circumstance; we are free to choose differently, to pull ourselves up and out of the holes that have been placed beneath our feet. We believe that others are in charge of our destiny, but that is only because over time we have allowed ourselves to believe it. We are master of our own life. Yes, we might have commitments and obligations, but even those are things we chose at one point or another.

If the load you carry is too heavy, put it down for a while. Imagine a large brown sack full of boulders on your back. Swing it to the ground and sit down. Send your thoughts upward and outward to God. Whether you believe or not, the result will be the same. Ask for help. Ask that your load may be lightened and your spirit uplifted. Ask that you might be shown a new way forward.

Stand by all that you are committed to do, but begin to redraw your boundaries and obligations. If you make yourself too available to others and their problems are becoming your own, learn to say no sometimes. This is not an act of selfishness but of love. You are a person too. By taking charge of others as well, often you actually do more harm than good. You rob them of the chance to stand firmly on their own two feet. Perhaps they are missing something that they need to experience to take the next step of their journey. Sometimes the pain and trauma that we must pass through are a necessary process of growth. I, too, have experienced this first-hand. I, too, have had to alter much that I held dear, because in hindsight it was in my destiny to do so.

When we are going through pain and trauma we can look back and say a million if onlys, but they are only ever illusion. The truth is where you are right now, and wherever that might be, you will pull through. You will be all right, but for goodness' sake, ask for help – not always outwardly, but inwardly. Send your pleas up high. You only get what you ask for and if you don't ask you won't get. Talking to God and talking to your own guides, guardians and angels is like using a helpline. If you don't pick up the receiver, you will never know when you're through.

We often feel we have to struggle through our problems under our own steam, but this is far from what we really want. We want and we need help, and that help is there for the asking. Don't feel shy, don't feel you shouldn't ask or that you don't deserve it. You are the central spoke in the wheel of your life, the main pillar that holds a roof up. If you break, everything will tumble and fall. You are important – and so is the connection between you and your maker. The thoughts you think and the pleas you make are there for you to pass on. Remember how silly you felt when you first spoke into a telephone answering machine and now you can do it automatically without even thinking of what you are doing? The same will happen when you send up your thoughts. At first you might stumble and stutter, but soon it will be second nature.

You can do this process once a day or 100 times a day, the choice is yours. Ask and you will be given, but you must ask in order to be given – that is the key.

There is much more to life than meets the eye. We amble along on a sure course of action, unaware of the forces that are working tirelessly, silently, invisibly with us or alongside us. I, too, have had to rediscover the art of paying attention to life. I, too, have had to adjust to not always being in the driving seat. I, too, have felt the need to harbour fear and self-pity, but I have learned to let go, to view my life and the world about me through different eyes.

Nine times out of ten the situations we are in are down to our own doing, because we have allowed things to slip. We have become complacent and happy to let life trundle along when we should be paying better attention to the little things that crop up every day. I, too, was often guilty of this because most of my attention was focused too far into the future or way back in the past. I, too, let 'now' run automatically of its own accord because I did not realize what I was doing. Life goes past in seconds, minutes and hours, but my own days just appeared to fly, without my being able to stop them. Now things are different. A day is as short or as long as I want it to be and all I have to do is ask that it be that way. When time flies past more quickly than you can handle, ask that it be slowed down to enable you to use it as well as you would like. If time drags along too slowly, ask for your perception of it to be sped up – but remember to put it back to normal later or you will be at the other end of the problem scale chasing your tail once again.

Only you can know what you need to do and when you need to do it. Only you carry the burden of the thoughts that you think. You carry the guilt, fear and apprehension of things not yet done, so it stands to reason that only you can help yourself by letting these things go. Recycle them whenever you feel the weight of their presence in your chest or stomach, your neck or your head. The place where you carry stress is individual to you, but the cure is the same. Recycle these feelings time and time again and concentrate on the job in hand. Only you will feel the benefit of such an exercise, but others will notice your stress-free zone. I, too, had to learn this for myself and it wasn't always easy or automatic, but the more you catch yourself thinking or doing things you should not, the more you will slowly let them go.

It takes practice to stay focused on one thing at a time, but it is a job worth pursuing. Energy flows wherever thought goes, because thought is energy in motion. It becomes obvious that if your thoughts are all over the place all the time and not on the task you are doing, it will take twice as long and you will be drained in the process. How often do we feel totally washed out halfway through the day without ever knowing why? It is probably down to wasted energy in the form of stress and worry. These two things are like water down a plughole. Your energy will ebb away completely unless you learn to stop it happening. We can control these things, but again we must ask for help. Ask that your energy be replaced and that all unnecessary drains be severed. Ask for help to remain focused in the now until your task is complete. Ask for life to help you to help yourself and ask for peace of mind, for quiet thoughts and a peace-filled day. When life about you seems to be crazy, ask that the hype be recycled and its energy put to better use. Ask for whatever you need at the moment that you need it, then forget about it and carry on as normal. When you have finished what you are doing, look back and notice the difference, and nine times out of ten it will be clearly visible. You yourself will even feel calmer and more in control, without having done anything really different at all. You have only asked for help and allowed it to channel through to the place and the time where it was needed.

We are all part of the bigger picture of life. Like pieces of a jigsaw puzzle or threads in an ornamental rug, we each have a place and a function. It stands to reason that if we are all part of the whole, then we each have a part to play, and if we each have a part to play, then we need help to do it well and understand. This life is not supposed to be struggle and stress, but love and enjoyment, exploration and fun. We are supposed to love the life we are living, not dread it. We are not supposed to have burdens and cares and woes, but dreams and fulfilment and happiness. Problems and chores are supposed to help us grow and change, not buckle, fall and fade away. Life is a gift, a gift that we chose to receive long before we came to live it. We each have a purpose and a destiny and until we realize this we will only enjoy a part of what we can be and came to do.

Only we can make our life work. Only we can make the necessary adjustments within ourselves. Time is irrelevant; it can be now or next month, but the point is that it will happen. We can make the necessary decisions now or we can wait for life and the universe to do it for us, and if we do that we can be sure it will be drastic and painful. The universe always works in our best interest, even though we don't see it that way at the time. There is always an element of choice present during times of change and upheaval in our life, but the messages we get will be loud and clear. And only we can know what they are – even if we don't yet know why.

The world as a whole is changing, sometimes slowly, sometimes drastically, but the changes are inevitable nonetheless. The world cannot wait for any individual, so we must keep up with it if we are not to be left stumbling behind.

Only we can enjoy the life we have, so let's get on with it.

The Place We Are In Now

Only we know the experiences we have had and the opportunities we have taken up or passed over. We may have regrets about what we did or did not do, but the truth is that the place we are in now is exactly the place we should be in at this moment in time. It does not matter where we 'could' have been and what we 'could' have done – we are where we are because along the way we made the choices that got us there, and these would have been right for us at the time or we would not have made them. In any decision there are always at least two options to choose between. Sometimes we go for the easy route, the easy option or the quick fix. If that works, then all well and good, but if it does not, we are forced to retrace our steps and choose again. The end result is often the same, but it takes longer to get there, so the path we tread is surer, more secure and definite. Sometimes we are led on a detour, but that is only because there is something else we should do or pay attention to along the way. Life is like that.

The universe will take care of us if we can learn to let it, but often we are too impatient. We barge through life this way and that, to get what it is we think we want, but when we get there it is not what we thought it would be at all, so we charge quickly on to the next thing on our list. If we slowed down just a tad, we would obtain a much clearer picture of where we were heading. We would also allow the universe to play its part. How often does something land on our doormat at exactly the time we need it? Or are you one of those who gets that information after the event? How often do we think, 'If only I'd received this last week' or 'If only I'd known that then'? Life will support us if we open ourselves up to its influence, but the trouble is that usually we can't wait. We are impulsive and impatient and we want what we want when we want it. To a certain extent that is human nature too, but it is a part of us that does not always work in our favour. This is exactly a thing that we can choose to change about ourselves, and if we did we would notice the difference – in life and probably in our purses as well.

Only man has the chance every day to do something different or to get a job finished and out of the way. How many of us are self-disciplined enough to do what needs to be done at exactly the moment it needs doing? If you are this way inclined then you are lucky. You probably have little or nothing around to slow or weigh you down, but I, like many others, have always 1,000 things to catch up on. I am always chasing my tail. It seems that no matter how hard I work, there is always more to do and more I haven't done. We need to learn to prioritize. Only we can judge what is most important on any one day. Life will always produce more than we can cope with easily, but that is the nature of life. There is a fine balance between too much and too little. Life goes on just the same for everyone.

Only man can make the necessary alterations to get his life back on track in a way that will work better for him. He alone knows his obligations and his challenges. He alone knows his commitments and the time he wastes chasing illusions. No one demands anything extraordinary from him; he does it all by himself. He alone sets his pace and the distance he feels he must travel. Only he can set himself free of the chains that bind him and hold him back, even though he might not agree at this moment. Only life that's rippled with pleasure and love will make him content and happy in his daily grind. Man has built his life to fit his image of contentment and tranquillity instead of looking inside himself to reconnect the missing pieces of his greater self, but love combined with understanding and knowledge will lead him back to where he wants to be.

Our whole life is lived in an effort to strive forward, to better ourselves and to fit snugly into a niche that fits, yet often when we get there we only find disillusion and more hard work. But life is what we make it, not what we force it to be. Fortunately, when we feel at our lowest there is always a ray of hope to pick us up. We are never alone, but have merely grown accustomed to the belief that we are. We have every tool we could ever need within our grasp, and everything our ancestors strived to achieve, often at the cost of their own lives. Nothing is out of reach, so why do we think we are lost and alone? Why do we want to be like others instead of ourselves? Why are peace and contentment so hard to obtain? Only we can know the answer to this and it will come from somewhere buried deep down inside.

We are who we are, which is not always who we think we are, and that is the key. Many people rarely look at themselves through the eyes or viewpoint of another. They look at themselves through condescending little eyes of anger. They judge themselves by what they have not done instead of what they have. They are much more tolerant of others than they would ever be of themselves and then they wonder why no one seems to recognize them as the person they are. They see themselves in an entirely different light. Love must come in to soften that light now, or many of us will go pop with the effort it takes to sustain the role we are playing. Only we can help ourselves – not with force or the downing of tools, but with a little more self-restraint, understanding and love.

People can never know the effort it takes us to do the things we do, because they are not looking. They, too, are in the same boat. They, too, are pulling, pushing and stretching with all their might, in all directions, to make their life work and amount to something, but the measures they use – that we all use – are often way off the mark. We live by an illusion of what we think we should be, because we have learned to be like this through the course that our life has led. Often we live by standards that are completely irrelevant to the reality of life and the place that we want to be in. I, too, can relate to this first-hand and I, too, have come down with a bump more than once. In hindsight I can see more clearly the reasons behind the events, but at the time it is rarely easy and often frightening. It is scary to lose all that you hold dear and all that you have worked hard to achieve, but often what we cling to most is purely of cosmetic value.

We regularly undersell ourselves without even knowing. We bind ourselves tightly to things that we have been taught matter, when in truth they don't. We tread the same path and try to achieve the same things as other people. We measure ourselves against their opinions and belittle ourselves with our own. How can we expect to feel happy, safe and secure when our biggest obstacle to overcome is ourselves? We love the world and blank our own efforts while we wait for someone to notice the love we're pouring out. We wait for someone somewhere to appreciate the toil we put into our activities, thoughts and words and for someone to love us back in the same way that we love them, but they never can. They love in a different way. They see life in a different way. Life and love are different for us all, even though we think they are the same. That's why only we can know when we get to where we are going and why only we can draw the line, both with ourselves and with others. Only we can decide when enough is enough – not in a bad way, but in a realistic, truthful, self-healing way. Only we can appreciate the life we are given and the distance we have travelled in the process. So we must be the judge and jury of our own efforts.

Most of us are stuck in a mode of behaviour that once served us well but does so no longer. We are almost overloading ourselves, and the planet, with the effort it takes to sustain the life we are living. 'Extreme' is the word of the moment and we push all existing boundaries to meet it. Is this the way we want to move forward? Is this the legacy we want to leave to our children? Is this what our ancestors fought through the ages to give us? We think not! Basic human rights are the same for us all and should be available for all, but after that comes personal choice. It is time for us to make that choice, to come back to reality, to take stock, to make our adjustments and to move forward in a different manner, before all that we know today comes tumbling down. We have a choice and all we need do is use it. The rest will follow naturally in its wake, courtesy of our God and creator.

CHAPTER TWELVE

The Sowing of Seeds

We can be who we aspire to be. There is no one like us in the whole of the physical world. We are unique, because of the person we are, the character we have and the experiences we have obtained. Two people may appear to be alike, but they are not the same. Distinct differences set them apart and you don't have to look too deeply to notice them. The part that you play and the places you fill are also unique, and without your being here the world would be different. Only you can fill that void. Only you can fit within the life space that you occupy, so you must learn to do it well. Nothing left undone will ever be complete, so the role that is yours is more important than you know. The human body is itself a great example. Thousands of veins, capillaries and arteries course their way through your form, yet if only one were not connected as it should be you would bleed to death or suffer some other form of illness. Life is little different, because we are each a separate working part of the whole – when we break down or can't fulfil the function we are charged with we leave a space, a void that no one else can replace. Only we can fill that place, no matter how we opt to do it. We alone can be the person we are supposed to be and that is our purpose, our role, our function.

We are all vital components of the planet we live upon. Many might say that this is rubbish. How can we – so small, so insignificant on the scale of this Earth – possibly be that important? But we are. Because we are conductors of the planet's life force, each outlet, each person, is extremely unique, complex and important. Only we conduct the necessary energy between Earth and sky correctly, and we train our 'whole life' to do it. When we fall apart, or fail to positively open up as a channel, it is a wasted opportunity, another incomplete life cycle that we regret when we return home.

We were chosen to fulfil our role in the Earth's evolution. We elected not only to be here but to achieve other things during the course of our life-frame, and now the time has come to understand and explore what that role may be. Take me, for example. I am living proof of what you've just read. Years ago I would no more have written a book than have flown to the moon. I had nothing to write about, yet here it is. You are reading it. Somewhere inside every one of us is a purpose, a reason for being alive, whether it's to add something extra to the greater whole or 'just' to enjoy life – to really enjoy it and be happy. If you cheat in any way and are not true to your purpose, it's only yourself you are deceiving. You short-change your life's purpose by your own thoughts and actions. No one here might ever know, but you do. You know very well and you will kick yourself for it one day, if you don't already.

The past is past. Today is a new day, a new opportunity to be the best of who you are. Yes, there may be consequences, but stand up and take them. Put your life back in order, no matter how impossible that task might seem, and remember you are not as alone as you think. Ask for the help you need. Just ask.

Only you can love yourself and your family enough to turn your life around. All through your time here you have been trying to be loved, liked and recognized for the person that you have become, and only you know the price you have paid for that honour. Now it's your turn to be happy. You have earned it. We all have.

The world about us is getting faster and crazier as time rolls by. People want and expect more than they have ever done before. This is just the way the world has evolved, but that does not mean it's right or the way it should be. When someone jumps off a cliff should we automatically follow or should we form our own opinion, make our own stand? Only we know how happy or unhappy we are. Only we know if our life is as rich and fulfilling as it ought to be. We alone know the answer to these questions.

A Perfect World

Once upon a time a dream was born. It was the dream of a perfect world. That dream can still be a reality if we want it to be – if we really want it to. Many people believe this world is on a course of destruction, and in a way it is, but just as equally it is not. Since time began there has never been such a cry for help as there is now. Life has never been so good, yet for many it has never been so bad. Only we can put a stop to where we are all heading and the changes must start with each of us – inside. Only we can do what is necessary to bring balance back into this world and into our own lives too.

We can look around at the world and recognize that all souls mirror our own, that they are all fundamentally just the same. They, too, are searching for input, understanding, truth and love. The turmoil around every one of us is a physical symptom of the larger unrest that exists on the planet's surface. All illness and strife are its proof. More and more people are becoming sick with serious conditions than they are with general bugs and colds. We have mastered infection and sanitation, but critical conditions are spreading faster than ever. This is another symptom of the overload we are facing, both in terms of the planet and of ourselves. Only we can decide when enough is enough and *now, in this present time-frame,* it really is.

Yet we are fortunate that we still have a chance to redraw the rules by which we operate. We can curb our spending and reduce the intake of food and the resources we require such as clothes, cars, house sizes, jewellery, etc. These are but a few chips off the boulder that is blocking our life, our energy and our welfare. The point is that we work too hard because we spend too much. We spend too much because we want too much and we want too much because we have learned to be this way. Something inside us is lacking. We are stuck in a loop that only we can break. We can change the mould by which we live, but to do so we must wake up to the part that we ourselves play in a world we have all helped to make.

Fifty years ago we had war and export famine. We had almost nothing that would serve to fulfil our basic needs, yet look at us today. Our shops, our homes, our cupboards and our stomachs are overflowing with wealth and sustenance, with goods we don't possibly need, or even use any more than a few times. When something new comes to light we rush off to buy it, whether we can afford it or not, whether we really need it or not, because we feel we must have it, or want it anyway, or because we simply like the idea. This is how we have trained ourselves to be and we get better and sharper in the process. But is this why we work, why we love, why we are here? Somewhere inside we know it's not. When we stand on a beach with nothing around us, when we walk through the woods with our hands in our pockets, kicking the leaves on the ground, we know we have never felt happier. Do we really need to do all the things we do or are those things merely the weights that tie us down? Are we living life to the full or are we our own jailers? Who can answer the question except us – in our own mind? And who can choose to stop except us?

Many people say, 'Why should I be the odd one out? Why should I do what others do not?' Yes, why indeed? Why should you work as hard as you do? Why should you carry the burden of debt and dis-ease on your shoulders, simply to keep going as you do? And ask yourself again, do you get the use out of the things that surround you that you thought you would? Like me, you probably don't. We buy and buy with good intentions, but in the end is the price we pay worth the stress, the hassle and the worry? Once again, only you can answer this for yourself, and probably that answer will be 'no' as well.

Man has more than he needs at his feet. I, too, have all I ever wanted and more than I have ever dreamed of. I, too, am doing things that I never thought possible. Because we have no limitations of any kind, all we ever have wanted is at our disposal. We look outwardly to others and marvel at their talents. We explore avenues already taken by brave men and women. We marvel at history and imagine ourselves in our ancestors' shoes, but how often do we really attempt to follow the dreams that we carry? We live the life we live, continue to build it as we do and inside we think that's our lot. If we are content, then that is fine, but often we feel life has become flat or dull. In many ways it seems not to hold a lot for us.

So we turn to our family and friends and live their lives with them. Again, this is good for a while, providing it fulfils its purpose, but often familiarity sets in and we find aspects of them that we don't like so very much either. Because we've become too intimate with those around us, the breath of fresh air they used to bring into our life becomes stale. We have joined too closely and intermingled as one instead of remaining parallel and free. We have grown into their lives and they into ours, until we focus on their lives just as much as we should focus on our own. Again, this is not a problem providing it keeps you happy, but when friendships fizzle and arguments and niggles prevail, then that is very possibly the reason why.

The life we are given is for us to live. We need interests and stimulation to keep it fresh, to keep it moving and to keep it sustained. When friends live in our pockets and we in theirs, what was stimulating in that relationship dries up. So step back a little and do something different – either alone or together. Create a new avenue to explore, something new to talk about, to discuss, to investigate and get excited about. Discover new parts of yourselves. Push your boundaries a little and allow some change into your life. Don't throw away all you hold dear, but open a window and allow the fresh air to waft through as before. Any change is as good as a rest, because it takes you out of the norm, away from all you would normally do. You can step back into the pattern of your own life whenever you wish, and you will see it with fresh eyes. You will enjoy it as you used to before.

We used to take a lifetime to build up our life, to get a home, a career and a family, but now we are able to have everything in a relatively short period. We can chop, change and explore avenues whenever we wish. All we ever dreamed is available right under our nose, and not just materialistically. Anything and everything is possible for us and all we need do is look beyond our normal conditioning, beyond the things we would usually do – and to act properly, with care, with consideration and with love.

Only we can move forward. Only we can shake ourselves out of childish habits and opinions. I, too, must do this regularly and it is not as easy as you might think, because stress and the heavy pressures of life have a knack of pulling us back. Every day we get locked into moods and power struggles just because another person does or says something that we don't like. This is really little different from children fighting for the same toy or for a particular role in a make-believe game. Our arguments and tantrums are just the same. In reality few of us have ever grown up. We remain children until we die, just older. People we live or work with eventually learn which buttons not to press or steer clear of, but in general life we allow 100 things to annoy us every day. We mumble and groan and stomp about in our own private thoughts and this in turn affects the words we speak, the avenue of thoughts we think about and the way we behave and interact. In fact, our true feelings can be sensed for miles, even when we think they cannot. Only we can stop this behaviour by learning to recognize when we are caught in it. The more we stop ourselves in full swing, the more our tantrums will die down and we will settle back into normality.

We are well aware of our thoughts and our tempers, because first of all they knot us up inside. The most trivial things then taint the whole of the day. I, too, have had to learn to recognize this and to let go. In the midst of my anger I have had to recycle my emotion. Sometimes it has been hard, sometimes it has felt wrong because I haven't been used to doing it and at other times it has been surprisingly easy. Sometimes I have got cross with myself for backing down, but the truth is that you will be empowered, not weakened, by this action. You are more of a person for standing down, even when you know you are right, than you could ever be by adding fuel to the fire. By keeping tempers aflame you feed the issue with negative energy. Like attracts like and there will be no winners.

Stress stems from negative energy and if you do not recycle it, it will stay with you all day. Then you will get more and more irritated until your temper explodes at the slightest provocation. But we can choose whether we want to keep the worry and trouble that cross our path or whether we will let them go. We can choose to recycle anything and everything that does not fit within the parameters of the time-frame we are in.

Only we can ease the burden we carry with us each and every day, yet nothing can be removed from our being unless we make a conscious effort to help it. Nothing will change until we silently send our thoughts upstairs to ask for the assistance we need at the time when we recognize we need it. Send out a thought of love and light to anyone who makes you cross. Ask that whatever aroused your negative feelings in the first place be recycled and replaced with light and love. Ask that light and love be given to all parties concerned, then quietly go about your business.

You may seem to have done nothing more than send out a few thought signals, but in actual fact you have instigated much more. You have refused to take on the negative mood as your own and have asked for illusion to disappear, to let truth and peace prevail. You have punched through the negative and replaced it with the positive. You have asked for peace to surround you and you will have recycled the temper and some of the stress load from the other person. Not bad for a few seconds' work, is it? And we can do this anytime we choose – 25 times in a row if we wish. It really does not matter how often we do it, just that we do. So we can ease the life that surrounds and interacts with us with the simple decision to take it or not take it on board. We can make ourselves a stress-free zone. It will take practice, but we can do it. The thoughts we think do matter. They matter very deeply indeed.

Energy in Motion

Thoughts are matter. They are energy in motion. Thoughts erupt from us like water spurts from a fountain. Our thoughts are a constant stream as they chatter around in our mind, day in and day out. From the second we open our eyes in the morning to the moment we go to bed at night we think the thoughts that we think. For the most part they continue as they do without our even noticing, let alone caring. We are brought up to believe that as long as we behave ourselves and live a good life, within our own four walls we can say whatever we like about whomever we like and can allow our minds free rein (and often our tongues too). We believe our thoughts are our own and that they really do not matter – but how wrong that is. Our thoughts are as loud as a Tannoy announcement in the world of spirit. Every word we *never* voice goes forth to land somewhere, with someone. It always attaches to something. How could we be so childish as not to realize it? The laws of cause and effect rule the world. They also rule our life and all that we are, so how could we ever think we could get away with anything?

Bad thoughts are like magnetized lead balloons. They stick to the person who thought them up and weigh them down in the process. This in turn keeps our tempers smouldering and our spirits heavy, so we stay in catch-22. Because we are heavy and cross, we think more heavy thoughts and continue that way all day. It's easy to see now how recycling can help. It uplifts our spirit and stops this chain of events from taking hold. Because it changes negative to positive it enables us to remain clear-headed and unattached, so we can do all that needs to be done and then move on. Recycling helps more than you think.

The load we constantly carry within our minds is an added pressure on our psychological and physical well-being. It keeps us out of synch with reality. The moment you are experiencing now is the one you should be fully operational in, so any other thoughts simply get in the way.

Thoughts alter your mood. They will cloud your judgement and take you to places that in reality you have no need to be in. Sometimes we can be locked for hours in a deep train of thought that is painful and makes us sad. We go over and over past memories that we bring forward as easily as clicking onto a document file on a computer. We think and re-think all the things we did and all that was said when the truth is that 'now' it's all probably irrelevant.

Try to recognize when you become locked in this loop. Bring yourself back to the time-frame you are in and take some deep breaths. Ask that the thoughts you were expressing be released from your mind. Ask that their hold be removed from your system and that they be recycled. Ask that you be surrounded with love and light and ask for help to remain focused on the job in hand. Don't check that this has been done or you will be asking for it back. Just forget about it now and get on with the day.

By doing this you are retraining your mind to stop unnecessary wandering and chatter. If you wish to go back to those thoughts later, that is your choice, but you probably won't want to.

I, too, practise this regularly, but even after a couple of years I can still get caught out. It's surprising how strong the pull of the past can be and if the past is where you spend most of your thinking time, then it can be hard to bring your thoughts under control. The same can be said for thinking too far ahead. Your mind is like a young unruly child. It is used to doing whatever it wants whenever it wants and now you are changing its rules. You control it; it does not control you. What you want to achieve is peace and quiet within your mind space – peace and quiet within your own head...

Peace is a hard thing to come by, yet in reality it exists all around us. It can be difficult to retain when there is a list of jobs that continually shout out to be done. Life stands still for no one and really it shouldn't. Life is continuous – that is its nature. But when the world – our own personal world – is busy, so are we. We flit from here to there, doing the things we must all day long, and our mind has little chance to take time out. Even in our quieter moments our mind is not quiet at all. It has almost forgotten how to be, so we must help it remember.

All the thoughts we think take energy from our personal store, but we need that energy ourselves for tasks at hand. It should see us comfortably to the end of the day, or until we are able to replenish its supply. Yet so often it does not. Even though I know better, I, too, still have energy problems. It saps away without my even noticing until I feel drained and tired and wonder why. I just drip it away without even thinking and I know I must keep it under stricter control, but it takes practice, time and patience to master such a task. Yet we have our whole life to apply the many new things we are learning, and as soon as we start, we will see visible improvements in all directions.

We think that the world begins and ends with us, yet the real world is far greater than we could ever imagine, and it's all waiting there for us to discover. Even if we never do more than acknowledge its existence, we will be richer than if we possessed all that money could buy. Peace and contentment will be second nature and stress a thing of the past. Only we can discover the route that will lead us there, to a place that's available to all. Yet we are not alone on that path. Someone is taking care of us at all times, even now, and we need only stretch out a hand, or a thought, to make their connection join with ours. We are deeply programmed to believe that we must carry alone all burdens that life throws our way. But the force that enwraps us will help us through in ways far more delicate, loving and gentle than we can know.

If we could only see beyond our present scope of material vision we would be astounded. A whole world exists and integrates with ours and waits for us to notice that it's there. I only glimpse it from time to time, but I feel its presence daily. I reach out to God, to my angels, my guides and my relations, and they never fail to help. Day or night, it is never a problem.

CHAPTER THIRTEEN

Moving Forward Yet Falling Back

One Step Forward, Three Back

It seems to be a common problem that for every forward step we take, we seem to move three back. No matter how well we research a project, something always gets in the way and nothing is ever as easy as it seems.

Just as the world is driven by cause and effect, so it also needs the balance of time. Things must come to pass in the time-frame they belong in. The world itself was made by these laws and nature can conform to nothing less. Just as the tides ebb and flow, so does general life. There is a time to go forward and a time to take stock, a time to sow seeds and a time to stand still. There is a time for harvest and a time to learn, a time to go slow and a time for hard work. The whole of life operates within these laws, yet to the majority they are as invisible as air we breathe. So man must learn to read the signals and signs that are there for him to help him.

Man lives his life in the fast lane. He rushes here, there and everywhere all day long. I do the same, because that is how life has become. Everyone is in the same predicament.

We are all caught in a loop of having to achieve all that we can all of the time. Days pass outside as we sit inside and work. Too soon a week has gone, a month, a year, and we are still treading the same road to do the same jobs. At this moment there seems little we can do about life except keep up. Yet how many of us know that we make our own chains? We are the only ones who can change the pace we live by. We must learn to slow down and to utilize the time we have more effectively.

Remember that by learning to focus 100 per cent on the task in hand we can get through it more quickly and easily, and by keeping this up like a constant stream, we can gradually clear the backlog that has built up. And don't forget that we can also ask for assistance. Ask that the time in your day be slowed down so you may achieve all that you wish in the time-frame you have available. When we do this we can very quickly see the results that such a simple act can bring, and the more we can do it the more we shall see how it works. The reason we get fed up is that we attempt to squeeze too much in any one slot and when we do not achieve all we intend, we think we have failed. On the contrary, we do very well, and when the interruptions we endure along the way are taken into account, we do very well indeed. So ease up on yourself. Instead of moaning or stressing about all you have to do, take a look at all you have achieved. If the opposite is apparent and you have managed little, then make the necessary adjustments to restore a satisfactory balance. The ball is in our court and how we choose to play it is up to us.

Only during the past century has life evolved to this speed and level because of the technology that has been developed. Life has changed more for man in the last 100 years than ever before. Since time began each thing has had its own evolutionary speed, its own pace and its own time-frame. Man has broken all records and is set to go further, faster still. Yet the problem is not the speed he is travelling, but the pressure and stress he has placed upon his being. He is set to burn himself out in a short space of time and this is not the way all was planned. He has the whole of life, the whole of existence, at his disposal. He is capable of more now than ever before and he has a long, long way yet to go. So pace yourself. Enjoy the ride. Enjoy each and every day you are given and make it count – make it count for you. The things you do and the steps you take need not be monumental, but take them each and every day. Just one small change at a time can move mountains over a lifetime.

Only we can wake up and now is the time to do it. We are at the beginning of a wonderful adventure, not the end of the world. We are about to enter an age that our ancestors would not believe, so let's get this world of ours in order and go forward to embrace it.

Many of us work all day and all night too. We seem to need to do this just to make ends meet. Life – a decent standard of life – has become expensive. And what makes it worse is the constant stream of consumer goods and valuables that are paraded before us, as though they will go out of fashion. We look at the things we have and we feel shabby even when we clearly are not. We look at how hard we work and we feel we deserve better. We feel wronged by the life we have chosen, but that's the point: we chose it. And just as we chose to be where we are, so we can choose a new way of life with new rules to live, to work and survive by.

Only we can pull ourselves out of the place that we are presently in, not by more stress and struggle, but by making and sticking to some new resolutions. Make some alterations in how you approach the day ahead of you. Stop and think how much you need to do and make adjustments accordingly. Remove what you don't need. I, too, am in this place and I seem to have been here a while. The necessary alterations will not happen overnight, but if we keep up our resolve and work steadily in this direction with every day we have, then slowly, slowly, we will witness the changes occurring.

Only you can be honest with yourself. Only you know if your life is working for you in the way that it should – or if it's not and see the times that you could have done things better or differently than the way you did, but one day you will get up and the sun will be shining, the birds will be singing and you will feel glad to be alive, glad to be part of the lovely world that you see. You will realize that each new day is a gift and you will be sad that you have only a number of years left ahead of you. When you can get to this stage, you know that you will be all right, that your life will be fine – always. Yes, there will be worry and sadness and pain at times, but these too have their place on this Earth and you will probably get through them more quickly than you would have done in the past.

I have also been there and in some ways still am. Life ebbs and flows like the tide. Nothing can remain as it is. Growth and change can be hard, just as winter seems hard after the summer blossoms, but it is all necessary to planetary evolution. It is the nature of the life we are part of.

Life is a constant work in progress. It is necessary for us to go through turmoil in order to come out of the other side wiser than before. Only we can do this for ourselves, and indeed we all already are doing it. So don't think that you are the only one in trouble, that you are the only one who struggles simply to get out of bed and get through to the end of the day. Don't believe that others don't have just as many worries and fears and doubts, because they do. They have just as many and maybe more. We are all facing the same problems, the same obstacles. Problems are merely symptoms of the planetary adjustments that are occurring all around us. We are being forced to rethink our lives, our beliefs and our thought patterns. We have taken the stage we are in as far as we can go, so we are being drawn to the next phase of existence, and because of this we must all reshape our lives. That is really all there is to it. The world is in a mess, but it is a mess that's born out of necessity. Just as a room becomes untidy before it gets better as you clear it out, so our lives are getting messy because we are at a clearing-out, renewing and redrawing stage. That's all. And we're all in it together. Every person everywhere is in the same state. Their problems might be different, but in the scale of life – problems are still problems and we all have them. We are all in the same boat, rowing for the dim but distant shore.

We need to step back and take stock before we can travel forward comfortably once more. Too much of the control of our life has slipped through our fingers. We are at the mercy of our creditors and our worries. We are chasing our tails and getting nowhere fast any more, and this is what we need to rethink. We cannot continue further down this road of destruction – because that is what it is. It is a box of trouble that's waiting to pop, and when it does, God help us all.

This state of affairs is the outcome of years of striving to succeed, of trying to make something of our lives, our society and ourselves. The problem arises not because of what we are trying to do – or aiming to be, but because through all this time we have mistakenly thought we've been on our own, alone with our worries and our problems. We have thought for far too long that we alone have been responsible for making this world tick, when the opposite is true. We are players in a larger game of life. Yes, we do have personal responsibility for all that we do and undertake, but in the larger scale of things there is much more occurring than we can understand at this time. Nothing happens by chance. There is a reason behind every little thing that happens, whether we know it or not. Sometimes we never know, we never find out, but a reason exists all the same. We each have a part to play, a role to fulfil, and that interacts with others as they, too, play their part to the best of their ability. All goes well when we each do what we should, but when we don't or perhaps can't, the system breaks down. We are like the cogs in a machine. When well oiled and properly maintained, that machine works perfectly, but when one part suffers more use or more stress than another, it wears out or fails to perform at its best. That in turn stresses other parts and they seize or break up also. Eventually the whole machine grinds to a halt and is of use to no one until it's mended. And it is the same with the health of the Earth that we live on.

It is time to reassess the Earth's physical situation and to make some necessary repairs. There is no need to do it alone. All we could ever want is there to help us. All we need is to learn to trust once more, both in ourselves and in those who stand beside us in our hour of need. We only have to offer up our thoughts, and solutions will come gladly back – not always what we might imagine, but solutions just the same. Remember, life ticks past in seconds, so the help that comes forth will also flow one step at a time. Follow those steps – like instructions – as they appear and slowly, slowly, you will get to the end of the tunnel you are in.

Remember, we are often our own worst enemy. When problems loom, we take the first solution that comes to light, but often this is not the real answer. If we take the trouble or the courage to take one step back, we can quiet our mind and think for a moment. It is always better to look at the bigger picture, slightly to the side of where you are now. If you take that quick fix it may solve your problems instantly, but ultimately is it not another problem in itself? Probably. The better solution might not be immediately apparent and it may take longer and be harder to achieve, but will more than likely be better for you. Life will always deliver all that you need whenever you need it, but it's up to you to be choosy and alert. Find as many options as you can, take a little time to explore them all and choose the one that's the most comfortable rather than the quickest fix.

We are totally responsible for the choices we finally make, but making the choice that's right for us will ultimately bring us peace of mind. Peace of mind can be hard to find, especially when we have taken on too much. I, too, am learning not to take on board more than I can cope with comfortably – although sometimes work just seems to appear. If you are usually the helping hand to all who ask, it will take time and practice to retrain yourself. It can also be difficult to see those you love and care for tied up emotionally in worry and turmoil, but once you have done all you can do to help or to listen or guide, you must hand their worries back to them. We can do no greater favour to those we love than that. Whatever their experience, it is exactly what they must get through to arrive at the other side. Within the turmoil is something that needs addressing, something that needs attention before they can move on to the next stage of their life. It may be small, it may be large, but whatever it is, try not to rob them of the experience. Ask for help from the powers that be, both to give you the strength to step back and to help them clear their path. Ask that all unnecessary rubbish be removed and that only the truth remain. Ask for help for your loved ones. That help might come quickly or it might take a while, but it will come. They are no more alone in life than we are. They, too, have all they could ever require at their disposal. They, too, must learn to read the signs that will take them forward.

Life is a journey that we chose to undertake. There are problems and pitfalls along the way that seem to harm but really can only help. They are opportunities to reassess, restructure and take stock. Once we have passed them, we usually can see a clear path ahead. We may not get there yet, but each time we pass those pitfalls, life will be easier than it was before. We are led and helped over every hurdle and by learning to recognize life's signals along the way we can make it simpler than it would otherwise be.

We have come a long way in this life and if we take a backward glance, then we will see just how far that is. We should be proud of ourselves. There is no shame in making mistakes, in getting things wrong. The point is that we are all human and human nature itself is fallible. We are not perfect and could never pretend to be. Nor should we. We each do the best that we can in any given moment. Remember that the decisions we made in the past were thought to be best at the time or we would not have made them. In reality there are no bad decisions. All things have their place in the scale of life. A not-so-good move will merely lead to more problems and reassessments. We will be forced to rethink and rechoose, that's all. Nothing is ever for nothing. Yes, we could have chosen better perhaps, but next time we will do.

We must stop kicking ourselves for our downfalls, because if we don't, who will? No one would dare treat us the way we treat ourselves. We would not let them. Yet we do all that we can in terms of punishing and putting ourselves down. We let others walk all over us because deep down we think that we deserve it, but we don't. We are all (or nearly all) good-hearted kind individuals who just want a peaceful and hassle-free life. We do all that we can do to the best of our ability and when life backfires once more it feels like a kick in the face. I, too, can relate to this. We all can, if we are truthful. Only a few can ever escape the knocks that life has to offer. Fewer still are completely happy and at one.

You alone know the thoughts you think and the feelings you feel. You know the things you do each day and the direction in which you are travelling. You know if you are getting close to your goals or are moving further away from them, and only you can alter your life and its direction accordingly. When we are young, we all have hopes and dreams, but along the course of life they often fade and die as the reality of day-to-day living sets in. Yet this need not always be so. We can take the reins of life back into our own hands and we don't need brute force to do it, just truth, love and the resolve to get there – wherever 'there' may be.

(I am I) Only you can make your life count. So make it count for every day of your life. (I am I)

CHAPTER FOURTEEN

What Makes Us Tick

(I am I) Only people with love in their hearts can make their lives count for something. It is not a choice; it is necessity. All of life revolves around love, and love revolves around life. (I am I)

High Hopes

Only we can live the life that we have, but to do so we must wake up to the life that 'is us'. We alone can please ourselves and bring the happiness that we desire into being. If we are sad or down, it is up to us to find out why. Does it stem from the people around or does it come from inside ourselves? There is a difference. It is subtle, but it is there nonetheless.

Happiness starts from within. When we wait for others to make us happy, we are turning our attention away from the problem – we are deflecting it. We are putting our hopes and dreams into the hands of others and are expecting them to return the compliment. We forget that they, too, are probably waiting for the same thing, so in reality we are all in stalemate. None of the parties is giving the others what they need, because none is fulfilled within themselves. All will go through their day – maybe through life – with something missing, because they are looking outside themselves, towards others, for what they need.

If unhappiness stems from inside you, it is slightly different. It means that you are dissatisfied with your life, yourself or others around you. It means that in some way you are unhappy with your lot, the life you have chosen. Take a closer look within to see where the unrest really lies.

We live our life according to our beliefs, our hopes, our dreams and our perceptions. A perception is the way we interpret the things we see, do, hear and feel. Sometimes we see reality; sometimes we have a delusional perception of life or people or situations. We don't see the truth as it really is, but the version of reality that we choose to see. I, too, used to be this way, and indeed many people are. I, too, have lived my fantasies, but at the end of them, life was still empty. I had been living a fantasy alongside my normal life.

Remaining in the now, in the absolute truth of life, is an art. It takes practice and time to become good at it. Real life is the truth. It is the bottom line of anything and everything that is occurring. It is that which is, that which cannot be altered by any amount of explanation or coloration. Real life is the facts of life exactly as they are. Illusion is anything that lifts us out of this state of reality. It is seeing the world about us and people in it differently from how they really are. It is reading into situations things that are not really there, however much we might wish or will them to exist.

The sooner we come to terms with the reality of life, the better our life will be – instantly. And that reality is that we have no need to rely on others to give us the pleasure and happiness we desire. Only we can learn what makes us tick, what makes us think and act the way we do, and only we can make ourselves truly happy. We have the power to place the ball of control back into our own court and to play life exactly as we would have it. By 'control', I don't mean badgering, bloody-mindedness, stressing and pushing to achieve what you need to achieve by force, but by moving ahead with quiet resolution, awareness, confidence and tenacity.

Each day gather a little more back of what you have given to others to do on your behalf. When you take a look at exactly how much you require other people to do 'for you', you will probably be surprised. Life so often becomes the way it is without us even being aware of it changing. It has a habit of slipping through our fingers. It moves out of our control by stages. First others offer to take on board something small, then they take on more and more until we rely on them for huge parts of what we need to be doing ourselves. This is fine as long as all things work well and remain as they should be, but when they don't, we can spend far too much time at the mercy and energy of other people, and this is stressful in itself. Who likes to wait for others to do what they are supposed to have done ages ago? It is far easier to take these things back and do them yourself. And you will probably find it more rewarding in the process. A person who sits around with little to do is far more dissatisfied and disgruntled than a person who is busy with their own labours.

It is only by stopping and taking stock of where we are that we can get some order and meaning back into our life. Are we relying on others too much or are we in turn doing more than we should? None of us should do more than is right and fair, but we often push ourselves beyond that limit and expect others to do the same. Only by reassessing the situations we are in can we see the areas that are causing the most distress or imbalance in our lives, and these are the issues we need to tackle to get ourselves back on track. Be careful that you don't pinpoint something that is merely a smokescreen for something else that you don't want to face. We hide all sorts of things so as not to look at them and we argue over the weakest, most insignificant details while ignoring the big picture. So if you don't know for sure where your discomfort is coming from, do nothing. Sit tight, but be vigilant until you *do* know. Life will always open up your problems and display their contents to you if you let it. So simply do what you normally would do and send your thoughts up and out, asking for guidance, understanding, illumination. These things will not always come overnight, but in small steps and stages, so just deal with whatever arises at the time that it does. Use only the emotional content that befits the occasion and remain calm and collected in the process. Always ask for love and guidance to surround you at this time and do what must be done kindly and wisely.

I, too, go through this process. I, too, must remain on my guard to not take on more than I should. It is easy to overburden yourself. It is easy to help others when you feel the need, and indeed it is natural to do that, but it is equally easy to get tied up in their turmoil. When you offer yourself as a guiding light, try if possible to keep the controlling light in the other person's court, because that way it leaves you free to come and go as you must.

Life is an art of love and balance. Love is our essence and it is this that gives us the need to reach out to those in turmoil or pain, but balance is also necessary to keep all things in their rightful place as they should be. Balance is what keeps the world ticking over and it is also the law behind cause and effect. Balance is a necessary part of our everyday life. It is what keeps the world spinning on its axis. The laws of balance are universal that nature itself keeps almost perfectly tuned. I say 'almost' because of the influence man has on this subject. At this time man is unbalanced and he in turn affects many things of which he is unaware, not only in his own life, but in his mind and actions as well.

Balance must come from within. It must start and end with us all day and every day. It should be as natural to us as blinking our eyes. Only we can find it. Only we can reconstruct the fibres of our life's journey to incorporate the balance that is needed – yet only balance can return the order that it needs. Balance will render us healthy, worry-free and stress-free. Balance in love is a must and so is balance in finance. I, too, am working hard to keep myself and my life in perfect balanced order. It is not easy, because everyone and everything are clamouring to be acknowledged at once. Life has a way of throwing itself at you when you really don't need it to be that way, but a forceful resolution will help to see you through. Be gentle with yourself but firm – not too rigid, but firm all the same – and slowly you will begin to make progress. Remember that the place you are in now has taken you a lifetime to get to. It is only natural that full balanced order will take an equally long time to achieve. Stay vigilant and life will always do its utmost to help you...

We can do anything we wish with this life of ours – anything at all. There are no rules or regulations. There is no guidebook, or 'completely right' path to follow. Life is made up of equally good and bad things, but it is up to us as individuals to find the mixture that will balance our life in the way we need it to be.

Taking Stock

Only we know the true content of our life, so only we can hold it by the reins and help it flow in the manner that it should. It is up to us alone to keep it moving in the direction that we need to always achieve the highest outcome and highest good. Only we can make the decisions that can take us forward to where we can find peace, balance and happiness. Stress and dis-ease, arguments and anger are merely signposts to warn us that things are not sitting quite right. When we take heed and look further (probably within rather than without), we will often find that the culprit is a train of thought or a belief that is out of synch with the truth of the matter. Once the cause is determined, we can work steadily towards a favourable outcome.

We must also learn to keep our tempers at bay. Anger is like the valve on a pressure cooker. Slowly our temper simmers until it reaches boiling point, then poof, off we go like a rocket into space and there is no turning back. Once we let rip, woe betide anyone or anything that stands in our way. But so often this is the last thing that a situation needs, and once said or done, words or actions can never be taken back.

Only we can know when anger threatens to engulf either ourselves or the situation at hand. For those who fail to notice the signals that build up beforehand, anger can be triggered without warning. So they believe that their anger is justified and that it stems from the actions of people around them and from the situations they find themselves in. They totally blank the possibility that it could stem from within themselves first and foremost. They are oblivious to the fact that they might have any control over their behaviour at all, but even instant anger can be traced back to a mood or thought pattern you were previously in. I, too, had to learn this lesson, not because I was shouting out and directing my anger onto others but more because I was keeping it simmering inside. I directed it at myself more often than not, without knowing or understanding that I was doing so.

Only we have access to the thoughts that whirl around in our head. Others see only the little bits that we allow them to see and often wonder why we do the things we do.

All that we are stems from thoughts and opinions that were first born in our mind. I, too, am a product of this and so is this book you are reading. Once upon a time it was a thought which was part of a daydream, a little hope that perhaps one day I might like to accomplish something, and look at it now. It is here in your hand, giving you the strength and encouragement that you need to go forward to your next stage, your next level. I, too, must realize the power of my own thoughts in action.

Balance played an important part in helping this book to come about, because without it, many things could not have been successfully accomplished. Each and every day many things that threaten to take up our time come onto our path. In fact, the harder we try to concentrate, the more disruptions we have to face. I, too, could relate to this every time I sat down to write, but when you are balanced you can still manage to do all that you intend, as long as you really desire to do so. An interruption is often the excuse we need not to do what we ought. It is the reason we give ourselves to take a break from what we are doing. Interruptions occur naturally as part of the flow of life, but it is up to us to try to keep them to a minimum. I, too, am still in the throes of practising this and so far I am winning.

Only we can keep our life moving and flowing in some sort of order. Chaos is not order, but neither is vegetating. Life must constantly flow and change, move and grow, in order for us to feel fulfilled, energized and at one with it. That part of us which is us, our spirit or energy part, needs constant stimulation and love. It needs us to love the life we are living and it needs continuous feeding with new experiences and interactions. It needs us to live, really live, and to enjoy every moment we are doing it.

You alone bear the consequences of the stress, sadness and worry you carry inside, because only you can feel them. These things stem from your being because of thoughts and situations that occur both within you and in the outer world itself. Worry is a product of the happenings you are experiencing. Life can never be problem-free. We have already discussed that problems have their purpose and their place, and we could not evolve as a species without them. Problems are brick walls. They are the end of a particular path we are following and in order to go beyond them we have to find the key to their solution. We have to alter something. They are a natural part of growth and only we can decide what needs to be done to solve them.

Life moves at its own pace, to its own rhythm, and even the best-laid plans can be torn apart by circumstance and other people. This will always be the case, as others will demand your undivided attention, but what they don't always know is the importance of your present job in hand. Only you know that. Providing you are true and fair, there is no reason why they will not let you continue, but again weigh up the odds for yourself. Sometimes it is better to stop for a moment to deal with them than to push their own shouting issue to one side. Life's flow needs your interaction too. It cannot stop just because you don't have time in your schedule to fit it in. Instead of getting stressed, make an educated choice and deal correctly with the flow of the moment as you know you must.

Only man can choose what he will do from moment to moment. All other species act on instinct. Man is the only one who can choose the direction his life will follow. Yet too often we forget this when we are tied up in the course of everyday life. We feel that we are at the mercy of the world itself. We feel that time and everything else are running against us. How often do we sit down at the end of a day and count the things that went right? Most of us would answer 'Not very often.' We go to sleep on a negative note, thinking of what we must do the next day or going over the problems of the day that's just finished. Instead, why don't we thank our lucky stars for all the good things that have come about, no matter how small? Every day 100 things can go our way, but we are too tunnel-minded to notice. It might be that we were on time for work because the traffic worked with us. It might be that a meeting or reprimand went better than we thought or hoped it would. It might be that we finished the day much as we began it – a little better but definitely not any worse. The things we recall might be small or monumental, but they are still issues that went in our favour. Send your thanks out and be glad. I, too, do this every day and if you do it regularly it's surprising how many good days you will find you have had.

When people operate from the time bracket they are in, they automatically take life as it comes. There is no need to look either too far forward or too far back. All that needs to happen for you or to you will happen at the time that it should, not before or after.

It is easy to look forward when an event is approaching in anticipation of either joy or fear. I, too, do it, because patience is not something we adults are good at. We forever tell our children to 'wait and see' or 'be patient for a while', but how often do we fall short of this ourselves? We can't wait for this evening, let alone next week or next year. We want everything yesterday, then we wonder why life goes by too fast or the event was not as good as we thought it would be. It was because we just couldn't wait for it to happen. For ages our thoughts had been wandering and we had been planning just how we perceived it would be. We had built up a whole scenario in our heads, so is it any wonder that reality bears no resemblance to that when the time comes and the events actually take place?

Each time we look ahead we think about what will occur. Remember, thought is energy in motion, so every thought will place energy ahead of you on your pathway. If it is positive energy, it will be excitement and pleasant anticipation that you feel as you move into the energy you've placed ahead of you. Sometimes this will be fine and the occasion will be all that it should, but at other times you will have built up such a crescendo that the event can't possibly meet the high expectations or energy hype you have placed upon it. You can prevent this from occurring in the future by quietly drawing your attention back to focus on the events happening right now – here today – on the task that you are now undertaking. By doing this as often as you are able you allow time to take its natural course, so when the events or issues finally arrive, you have placed no more than perfectly normal balanced energy upon them. I, too, had to do this for the birth of this book and when you are excited it is no easy task. But over-excitement is itself an unbalanced state, so when you feel that way, ask for your excess energy to be recycled and rechannelled to where it might be needed and for you yourself to come back 'down' to Earth.

The opposite applies when we dread a task, a day or an event that is looming ahead. It is irrelevant what the issue might be or when it might take place, because the effect is still the same: the energy that we produce is negative. It is this that we now place ahead in our path. It is this that stops the easy flow of life and places grey matter around the time yet to come.

Every time we think a negative thought, the energy that that thought produces is bound for somewhere. It will either attach itself to the life of the person about whom you were thinking or it will cling to and gather around the issue you were thinking about. When we have a task that we really should do, we know it needs doing, but we dread it. It seems that the task looms larger and larger in front of us, and we dread it more in the process. We almost have to psych ourselves up just to face it. Yet how many of us know that we have made it ten times worse through our own negative thoughts? Because of our dread of it, we have placed nothing but heaviness ahead. I, too, am a culprit and, worse still, I should know better. I know that all I need do is recycle, yet sometimes even this cannot stop me from venturing down that negative avenue. It has become normal for us to behave this way and because of that it is a habit. Habits can be very hard to break, even when we do know much better, but the thing is not to give up. If we keep on trying, sure enough we'll get there. We have the whole of our lifetime ahead of us, so we have all of that time to practise.

Life is good and it can be fun. All we need do is remember and relearn how to live it. Since we were small we have been stumbling along its narrow path. It is now time to relearn much that we really already know. We just need to remind ourselves how to do it.

CHAPTER FIFTEEN

Clearing Old Debris

(I am I) Only man can clear the debris he has left in his wake. He alone is responsible for things both done and undone by his hand. Only he can go back and place the pieces of his life back into the order they should be in. Only he can come home with a clean slate. (I am I)

We are the only ones who can forgive ourselves for the mistakes we have made in the past, both in history and in our own personal life. We can look back with greater understanding to see that we were no more than children. This is not fantasy, but fact. From the moment we are born we follow. We follow the lead of anyone who seems to know better than we do. Sometimes we are forced to follow because that is the way life should be and at other times we choose to, either by instinct or by desire. But who has taught the people we follow what they know? How do we know they know any better than we do ourselves? The truth is that we don't really know at all. We just assume. We assume they know better because they are older or happier. They appear to be better at life than we are or have been. Yet do they really know all that we think they do, or even that they think they do? The answer is probably no. They mostly know what they have experienced or have been told along the way. They are neither better nor worse than we are. They are just people, much like us. Yes, they have different likes and dislikes and their outside shells and lifestyles might be completely individual, but at the bottom line they are the same, exactly the same, as we are. I, too, began to see this at a very early age. We are all the same, whether we are a pop star or a pauper. There is no difference of any kind except money, and this would be a chapter all by itself.

All of us are trying to live life successfully in the only way we know. We are all the products of our life experiences, and the sooner we can see that, the sooner we can learn to see past the obvious differences between us. Life for other people is the same as it is for us. They work, they sleep and they play. They might move in different circles and do different things, but they are simply doing the same as we are. All over the world, people are still people. They are all looking for the same personal reward. They spend money, they eat, they work and they sleep. They use the bathroom and they look for fun. They are happy, sad and inquisitive. They, too, are living for the easier time they imagine is up ahead and they, too, are hoping that a better place awaits them after the rigour and turmoil of life. But unlike you, they are probably not aware that they can take up the reins of their life and change its course to a smoother path. If we are not happy, it's up to us to make the appropriate alterations and shifts until we are to the corner of the world in which we live and interact.

Life can be what we make it. Those who ruffle our feathers and give us grief are merely stuck in their own problems. If you are the cause of their difficulty, however, the matter needs some attention. You need to talk together to find out where the problem lies. If you are not the problem, understand that things will right themselves in a while. Send thoughts out for help. Ask for justice to reign. Ask that both you and the other person or people to be as small as a grain of sand. Ask for all illusion and negative energy to be recycled and ask for love, light and truth to surround you both – or all. Ask for the situation to calm down and for the truth to come to your rescue. Even if you are partly to blame, ask for help in the same way. Ask to communicate better. Ask for all that you need and you will get it. When you expect a row, it will sometimes fizzle out into nothing. You will communicate on equal terms with the other person and an agreement will be reached far more easily than it would have before. By asking to be made small you have been placed on an equal footing. There will be no difference or distance between you. You will be able to communicate as two people should, without fear of misunderstanding and wrongful blame.

All we need do is ask for the help we require and it will come to our rescue. There are no requirements or restrictions that will stop this from happening. You should not feel silly or stupid, because the thoughts that you think are only for you. No other person can hear them. Help is always available to us, because that is our birthright. All we ever need is available, but to access it, we must ask. Just as it is impossible to speak to a person in another city without first picking up the telephone or making a computer link, by asking you are making a better connection to those who are about you. You are sending out your thoughts and connecting to that other part of yourself and to God. It is not a fairy tale and it is not fantasy. Try it for yourself. Just because we do not see the air we breathe does not mean it's not there. It is. And so is God.

God is not a person but an intelligent energy source of which we are all part. You are not your finger, yet your finger is a part of you, and so it is with us. We are part of the whole and are still connected to it. We are energy and matter beings who are always connected to God. We can be nothing else, ever. The system is unchangeable. We were energy before we came into this life and we will be energy when we return home once more. Now we are in a physical body having a physical experience in a physical world. We need our body to be the vehicle that helps us experience and move and live this life, because without it we would be spirit once more.

This life is ours to live, to enjoy and to explore. We are here to live and have fun, not to live and worry and fear. Only life can fill the void in your being, but to live it to the full takes practice. We can come to terms with our life and rearrange the parts that are no longer fulfilling their purpose or function. It is up to us to fix the areas in our life that need fixing. We are the only ones who can ultimately please ourselves.

The life we have charge of is our own affair and the path we tread is ours as well. It is up to us to take charge of our destiny and to live a life that we would be proud to own up to. What we do, and when, is up to us also, but the fact that we must choose is clear.

CHAPTER SIXTEEN

Signals and Signs

There are times to go forward and times to retreat. There are times to grow and change and times to take stock. It is up to you to find out which category you are currently in. I, too, must learn to recognize the signs better than I do and it will take practice. In the world today we are used to charging forward at all times. We are used to pushing and conniving to achieve the desired results. How often do we sit down and wait a while to see what will transpire? It is more likely that we will rush ahead in case we miss our chance.

Only we can know the truth of that statement for us, because only we can know the thoughts and plans that whirl about in our heads. We alone know where we have been, where we are and where we intend to be in the future. We know the course we would like our life to take. Every day we look at the day ahead and read it like a book. We know exactly where we will be and what we must do, but in reality how many of those thoughts leave room for life to take over? How much room do we leave for life to open up and show us its colours? We don't. We do what we have to do when it needs to be done and for the rest of the day we wear blinkers. We are tuned in to what we expect to happen, instead of what could happen or actually is occurring. We are on automatic pilot without even realizing it.

I, too, am guilty of this, because of the things that I know I must achieve in any given time-frame. Part of this is natural, because without focus we cannot hope to continue in the way we should. To be organized is a good thing, but it also keeps us bound deep in the throes of busy life. We get too rigid and inflexible, so that when other opportunities arise, we feel unable to partake of them. It is hard to go with the flow, because the guilt of what we will not achieve in the meantime takes hold. Only we can help ourselves by staying on course, regardless of the hiccups and blips that occur all around. I, too, am in the midst of this every day.

Only you can make up your mind, once and for all, to keep on going forward, even when the pathway looks blocked. It is human nature to despair and fear when we find ourselves in the midst of unexpected problems, pains and doubts, but it is at exactly those times that we are being helped and led along the way.

At these times we don't know the way. We don't know how to move in the direction that will serve us best, so it is then that we need a little more faith in the powers that are working around us. We are never alone, even when we think we are. There is always someone who knows what our next step should be. When we are full of doubt and our way seems blocked, we must have faith that the situation will change and the way forward will be highlighted to help us see. I, too, have had to have faith in writing this book. I, too, have had to learn to sit tight, even when my instincts were telling me otherwise. We are used to solving our own problems, or attempting to solve them. We spend hours, days, weeks trying to get out of the place we are in, when really if we had only stayed put for a time the solution would have presented itself. Just like children we must learn that when we are lost we must stay where we are until help arrives. And only we can help ourselves by asking and then allowing the help to get there.

We are taught at a very early age to ask for help when we need it, and indeed we do. We ask anyone who will listen to us. Only in asking the people around us we often make things worse. How can they help us? They don't know which way we are going. They know their own way, the way they have travelled, and they have perhaps seen a little of our journey, but the things that they have experienced were for them on their own journey, not for us on ours. The steps that we need to take might be completely different from theirs, even though they might look the same. So in asking our friends for their thoughts we are merely taking ourselves in a sideways direction instead of on an upward and outward route. We even know this inside, after asking. How often do we feel that even though those around us did their best, they didn't really understand where we are coming from? How often do we still feel alone, even after the advice has been given? We feel that when we make our final decision, we are still on our own. Yet we are not. We so are not. We just think we are because we are unaccustomed to the influence that stems from within.

At your most turbulent time, sit down in a quiet place and go within. Quiet your mind and wait for your thoughts to calm down. Only when we are still can we allow our thoughts to lead us forward. Only then can we learn to listen to the ever-ready influences that surround us.

Learning to be still in the midst of confusion or conflict often goes against the grain. Man is used to making his own decisions and then enacting them by all means available to him. Man has free will. This is his birthright. It is his by the laws that govern the planet and because of this only he can ever make the final choices that he needs to make. If this right were removed, then there would be no free will of any kind. But man is bound by the very thing that offers him his freedom. He looks to others to show him the light, to lead the way or to show him the guide rope. He looks to others, because he feels that at some level he needs reassurance or needs to be given the next step to take. He looks to others for strength and support when all the while all these things and more are within himself.

Man is taught to stand up and fight for all that he needs, yet the opposite is a more effective approach. This does not mean being a doormat for all to walk over, nor does it mean wimping out. Instead it means that in the face of adversity, it is better to stand still and remain small until the storm has passed. It means that two conflicting energies can only create havoc. So wait until things have calmed down and review the options available to you once again. It is up to you which you choose. Life is yours for the taking, but you must be clear as to the direction you wish it to take you in.

The problem is that too often we are unclear. We travel halfway down a certain path and then the doubts set in. We doubt that we have made the right choice. We doubt because we allow others to sway us. We even doubt our ability to see things through to the end. There could be 100 different reasons why we change our mind and all of them as valid as each other, but the bottom line is that we doubt at all. But only we can ever make the choices that we need to choose and once we have we should stay put. Only then can the universe come to our aid.

Only we can access and reassess the situations and predicaments we find ourselves in. There will be times when we choose a course of action and then the circumstances that surround us alter. I, too, can relate to this, but at these times the course we were set upon was only a stepping stone, even though we did not know it at that time. It was not to be a permanent fixture, just a vehicle that took us from one point to the next.

Life is like a long-haul journey. We begin at one point with the aim of reaching another. Along that route are many highways, A roads and little lanes. There are by-passes, diversions and accidents to encounter, but once we begin we have to check and recheck the best roads to follow. We have to choose and rechoose once we hit problems or traffic jams, until eventually we arrive. We might be late, very late, we might be tired and fed up, but we always get there. We know we will.

It is the same with life. *Life is a journey.* It will not always be plain sailing. Sometimes it's easy and sometimes we get stuck. We get snarled up in stuff – other people's stuff as well as our own, but stuff all the same. Only by standing still and taking stock can we get a clearer picture. We can rise above the place we are in and view the whole area from another perspective, another angle. Only we can do this, because only we know the way we are going. Only we know the truths we are living and the illusions that pull us back.

Be honest with yourself. Cut the maybes and could or should haves. Find the bottom line, the truth. Look at where you are. Only you can do this, by yourself and for yourself – and for those you love.

Don't wait any longer for someone to fix your problems. Don't wait for someone to give you what you are lacking. Don't push and shove to get where you need to go. Go within and find out how to do it properly. This may be the harder way, but it is the only way just the same.

Only you can fix your life. Only you can bring the happiness back into your stride, because only you know the parts that are lacking. It's all up to you.

CHAPTER SEVENTEEN

Freedom

(I am I) Only man has been misinformed that the world starts and ends with him. Only he believes that he is alone on this Earth and that all he does he does alone, by himself, under his own steam. But he is mistaken. He is not alone and never was. He is just a drop in a large ocean of life and activity. He is just the vehicle that keeps the world turning and its energy moving as it should. He is the manifestation of a physical being that is only a part of who he really is.

Man is love and life in motion. He is capable of birth and of destruction. The story of his life is but a chapter in the history of existence and it is this he must come to realize. His life does not begin and end with his present form; it extends an eternity in either direction. He had life before he was born to his parents and he will continue that life after his breath has left his body. He is the manifestation of a living God, capable of all he desires. He alone has power over the universe that is his life. He alone pulls the strings and plays the notes that he dances to the tune of. He holds more power in his own right hand than he could ever imagine in many lifetimes. He is all he could ever want to be. He is all I intended him to be and much more besides. (I am I)

You Are in Charge

The whole world is in the middle of a major shake-up and the trauma we all feel is a symptom of the crisis that we're facing. It's time to wake up, to step away from the darkness of the wrongs we have caused and to return to the light that can help us. No one is immune from this shake-up. We are living the cause and effect of past actions and of the imbalance we ourselves have placed upon the Earth. Yet we are more than capable of pulling things together. Life is dictating that we must if we are ever to save our time-frame and our species from destruction.

Where you are now is not a mistake. It is not an error; it is by design. We are living the life we are living to find out who we are *and* who we are not. To experience both sides is the only way we can learn. Just as parents who love their children must allow them to learn from their mistakes, so we, too, are living a similar exercise. We have learned that life is hard, that we must struggle and stress to keep it under our control. We have learned that no matter how hard we try or how kind and good we try to be, life still throws stuff in our path. We move two steps forward and three steps back just as often as there are weeks in a year. Many of us look around and wonder what life is really all about and whether there is any point to it. We have had enough and that is why the cavalry – spirit, guardians, angels – have stepped forward to help. It is time to begin afresh – from today.

Each new day is a gift. It is a blank page that's waiting for instruction, a chance to redraw, to rechoose and reconnect. It is also a chance to let go of old grudges and to turn things around. For too long, too much has been taken for granted. We assume that all we have had will always be there and that everything's ours for the taking, yet this is not always totally correct. So each day we experience is a new day. It's a fresh chance to redraw, to begin anew. All the things you have ever done were part of yesterday; today, this day, rechoose, realign whatever you will, with a clear mind and a firm decision to make life work. But know that every change must begin somewhere and that somewhere might just as well be with you. In fact, it can only begin with you because you alone hold the keys to your life – to use however you choose, as your right, as your birthright given by creation itself

The Earth is a living entity – just like man. It was born, it has grown and has evolved to the point we all witness today. It is completely self-sustaining – unlike anything upon its own surface, including man. We are foolish to believe that the Earth's healthy condition is timeless, because it is not. Time has played the most important role in its growth and sustainability and it is this that mankind forgets. Man only visits for short periods at a time – yet we devour its resources much more quickly than can be replenished. We need to wake up to the reason why we have life before we irreparably damage or remove more than Earth can healthily give.

Nothing upon Earth will last forever. This is a fact of life. Just like man, the Earth must replenish what it uses to refuel itself. This has to continue for the Earth to remain healthy and forever the thriving planet it now is.

(I am I) Life is not a game. This is not a rehearsal. Everyone chose to be here today, now, not just to live a lifetime on the planet but to help Earth sort many things out. (I am I)

We hold the key to everything. Each one of us is responsible for the energy we direct straight to the Earth's surface on a daily basis. Too often we are blocked, negative or needy when we should be clear, positive, open and channelling. How can the Earth function in the way that it must when thousands upon thousands of necessary live working parts are misfiring, unreliable or broken? And worse still, we are stripping it bare and working against its life forces in the meantime. Based on our current track record, humanity is growing at a rate that's completely unsustainable for the planet to possibly keep pace with.

The way forward is to change the way we think and interact with Earth planet. We must realign much that we usually take for granted in our daily lives and alter our approach to life. We must be honest and take stock of *ourselves*. This is our life, our own time-space and chapter, therefore it's our own personal responsibility to make sure everything we touch stays in balance and that we leave nothing unnecessary or broken in our wake. Nothing upon Earth controls us, apart from the obvious forces of nature. We are the masters of everything we become and perceive. How else could we be independent? How else could we all have free will? Everything we are we discover, choose, learn and integrate all by ourselves – daily. Thus life has no choice but to follow and to try to keep up with our pace. Nothing and no one can stop us. If we are ever to be able to turn things around, we must wake up to the price we are collectively making the Earth pay.

You rule your own mind – it does not and should not control you. You rule your thoughts and you are boss of yourself and your actions. You make all the decisions and choices that carry you from A to Z.

(I am I) Fear is the only thing to overrule man – the fear he puts upon himself, the fear that is sometimes placed there by others. Fear is his life's lock – with truth and trust being the key. (I am I)

Trust and fear are distinctly opposite. We choose between them each day and each moment. Thoughts that trust, positive thoughts, assist life and help it flow, whilst fear can only block and achieve the opposite.

Life and people can only hurt us when we let them, when on some level of our conscious or subconscious we think that it's deserved or that they can, when we believe they have the power to overrule or override us, when we think they have the right to behave as they do or when we take on board their bad moods or beliefs. Yet in truth we are all the same. Not one man/woman/child is more important than any other. Yes, we might have different levels of need and responsibility at any one time, but at our most basic we are all exactly the same. We each have a life and we must each choose and create how it will be.

Change always starts first within your own mind, within your thoughts and your usual thought patterns. Be strong yet kind and patient with yourself as you begin this journey. This is the beginning of a completely new chapter of self-discovery, with many chances to rethink, redraw and rechoose. For man to perform a task such as this one, alone, would ordinarily be nigh-on impossible; indeed, that's how and why we all became stuck in the first place. Whenever we let down our armour we felt vulnerable and weak, so we kept it up and learned to make it thicker. Yet remember we are not alone and never have been. We are surrounded by energy, by the Earth's life and living forces, and working with them makes us confident and strong. Change might not always be easy, but all of us have a task to perform, a talent that lies hidden until we find it.

A living God is here, by our side, every waking day of life, communicating by thought, listening to our needs, integrating, helping and guiding every step. Nothing that we think falls by the wayside.

(I am I) I have always been with man, but now I need him to know that for sure. I need him to turn once again back to Me. (I am I)

Ask silently for strength and courage when you need it. Ask for protection, love and guidance in the same way. Ask for the energy you need to see you comfortably through your day, especially when your reserves feel low or depleted. Ask that God remain in charge of all you need to do, that you may follow instead of struggling all alone. Help and the answers that you need are always close at hand. The hard part is staying calm enough to realize it.

Evidence of the Earth's living consciousness, a living God, is erupting all over the place, in every walk of life. Doorways and avenues of exploration and wonder are opening up everywhere. Science up to now has adequately explained the *hows* of life, but only spiritual investigation will explain *why*. Long ago, when communication was at its lowest level and only few could read or write, before newspapers, radio or television, men of power decided that science and religion should not touch, that they should remain separate, that they were contradictory to each other, that both were equally powerful and should not mix. The Church was to lead us forward in matters of spirit whilst science would explain everything else. But man and Earth are more. Both are scientific and spiritual entities. Neither can be separate from the other. Life cannot be explained by science alone, nor can it be explained by just the Church. Its essence lies far outside man's current understanding. It goes beyond anything we usually explain, touch and see.

Only recently have we had the freedom of thought and speech that is widely evident, and even this is still localized in terms of Earth's scale and size. We have never been so able to source the reality of scientific and spiritual truths for ourselves, yet we have never been so lost and alone either. The whole of the life you have lived until now has only brought you as far as you are, so it stands to reason that making it better will take a little while too. But don't panic and give up before you begin. Things are not as black as they might outwardly seem. Step by step, little by little, you will be able to make a difference – almost immediately in many cases, but the more deeply rooted your problems, the longer they will take to resolve. Rome was not built in a day, but it was built, and it still stands tall and proud today. So don't give up – just go slowly but surely forward towards the future that is awaiting you and your family.

We are children until the day we die, each living our own life experience, our own interpretation of life. We can look back with pride or we can look back with sadness, but the point is that we do look back. Don't be too sad or worry about what was done yesterday; we all make mistakes and do bad or wrong things. Yet wrong things are only wrong choices. Would a good parent ever turn their back on a child because of things they did before they knew the truth? A good parent would not. A loving hand would always be extended. And for us it is no less the same. We did all we did before today, for whatever reasons we found ourselves doing it, but now it's time to let go and start over. We can live each new day as though it's our last, with a clean slate to write upon as we wish, or we can carry on the same as before. Don't waste this opportunity, this chance that we have. Open yourself up to allow the truths that are yours to manifest. If you don't, they will wait quietly within until you can, but be sure – they won't go away.

We are completely separate entities, joined only through Earth and through life. No one knows our thoughts, our burdens, dreams or goals. We are good at carrying problems from days to months to years and because we do it so well others assume that we are fine, that we are happy with our lot and with life. Often their first inkling that something is wrong is when we become ill or blow a fuse. They then look up in amazement and wonder why. Yet we could have been on overload for months, even years, in one way or another. People are simply used to seeing us the way we are, the way we have always been. They don't notice our pressures building up, because they are busy dealing with their own. Have you noticed how when disasters strike, everyone experiences the same thing or has the same symptoms? Everyone suddenly says, 'It's funny you should say that, because…!' We are all in the same boat; we are all expertly carrying on with things regardless…

When we have reached the end of our line, only we can know it, be that in business, finance, love or family affairs. Often our children are so used to seeing us struggle and strive that they believe the whole world is really like that, or they see the alternative, where everything is hidden away, and they think life is easy. But it is not – for anyone. Problems and troubles are problems and troubles, no matter how we dress them up or how they are presented. Only we can break the confines of the moulds we operate in, by staying in life's absolute truth as it occurs.

Often we are far happier living a lie than we are facing reality, so we bury our head in the sand and wait for something to change by itself or through the actions or non-actions of another. We don't like change because it makes us feel uncomfortable and we don't like confrontation either, so we sit and wait and stew in our thoughts and our minds. We leave signals and signs all over the place that we think are as clear as a whistle and when no one notices we get hurt or mad because we believe they don't give a damn. We falsely believe they don't care, that they are unfeeling or hostile towards us, but again the truth is often the opposite. They have probably got their own head stuck in the sand as well. They, just like us, are refusing to look at the issues they must, so both of us are caught in stalemate, both are snapping and moaning at one another, feeling perfectly justified, and yet both have got completely opposite ends of the stick. The only way forward is to talk, to recognize that we are on the same level and probably want the same thing.

Two wrongs can never make a right until someone puts down their blame. Just ask God that illusion may be recycled and that truth, light and love may prevail overall. Ask that the words and understanding you both need to speak be given to you and then simply watch and wait. Very quickly, without effort, all will be out in the open and all you need do is speak kindly to each other and listen to the words being said.

In every conversation where two or more people speak at once, they are fighting for the same 'now' space, all fighting to be heard. It is far better to just speak one at a time and hear each other out. Often this is all a situation will need. If tempers start to flare or hot up, walk away for a moment, go and blow your nose or something, break the cycle, and when you resume, it will be on equal ground once again. Even if you don't agree with what is being said, mentally ask for guidance and help. Ask for love to prevail, even if it seems a long shot at the time. Ask and wait and see what happens. You may be pleasantly surprised. As long as you have spoken your truth, the truth as you know it to be, then you should have nothing to worry about. Don't retaliate with anger, because anger can only feed the problem with negativity, just as you can't put out fire with fire. Patience, truth and love are the keys that work best, regardless of the situation at hand.

Communication is a difficult thing and it is open to infinite interpretation and misunderstanding. Given the individuality of each person and the infinite thoughts and words available to us at any one time, trying to make a connection is a very tricky business. Billions of thoughts cross our mind every waking hour. These, combined with the moods we feel, produce the words and actions that we present to the world. The words we select are totally dependent on our interpretation of the moment at hand and this is itself open to variation, mood and debate. This is how we fall prey to misinterpretation, illusion and mistakes. Only by chance do we ever get the connection completely right.

Communication is an art. It is an art that we learn from infancy, providing the setting is correct at home and around us. Many people are afraid to voice their opinions for fear of reprimand or reprisal. They are scared to go their own way and do their own thing. They find it far easier to follow the opinion of the majority or the crowd. They are used to following instead of exploring and leading themselves in their thoughts and actions.

Life for many is a game of follow my leader. Providing this is your choice, then that is fine. Only you know whether you are a leader or a follower, whether you like to make your own decisions or follow along the route that others have trodden before you. You know if you are good at reading people and situations or if you prefer to shy away from the hustle and bustle of mainstream life. Only you can make the necessary adjustments that will allow you to go forward your own way, regardless of the opinion of the people around you, unless they have reason or validity.

This is your life. You are here to live it to the very best of your ability. When all is said and done, only you will stand up with pride or regret as you look back on opportunities that could have made a difference, times you let slip through your fingers. We are not only responsible for the bad things we do and cause others to do, but for the good we leave undone – the times we miss. No one will stand over you with a whip or an axe in punishment; you will do that yourself, metaphorically, as you view what you've left in your wake. You will regret things you could have achieved but did not. You will be sorry for missed opportunities that came your way. No one will punish you, but you will surely kick yourself very hard…

This life we have here is a gift. We chose to come. We came not only to live the experience as fully as we saw fit but perhaps to achieve a few things along the way. We alone will be responsible for the life and time-frame we have spent and for the loose ends that we will leave behind.

The world would not be a better or a worse place without you being here, but the fact is that you are here. You are living in this space and you have a function to perform. Man is the manifestation of God himself. We are not meant to be perfect because we are human beings and it is in our nature to get things wrong. Being perfect is the function of God, but we should come as close to perfection as it is in our nature to be. Yes, your past is probably a mess, but it is what it is. A child without guidance would never become what it could, or should, become, and so it is also with us. We have had free rein over our life and look where it has got us. So ask now for guidance. Ask for all the help under the sun. Ask… Ask in the silence of your mind, with all the love that exists in your heart. Only you can feel the difference when you do. Ask and you will be given. Seek and you will find. These words are taken from the Bible, but they are not without meaning. They are truths that have been buried for far too long. Only you can take the hand that in truth has always been extended towards you. You need only recognize that it is there. You can make the life you have finally work for you. It is your right to be happy – and all the powers that be will help you – if you can learn to let them.

Now it is up to us to take the next step that is applicable to us on our journey because only we know the truth of the situation we are in. We can show any face we wish to the world, and nine times out of ten we can get away with it, but we can never fool ourselves or our maker.

The blueprint of your life stays with you for the whole of your life. It is who and what you are. It is all you have ever been and only you can grow into what you are likely to become. It is all up to you and you alone. And it is here that all things physical must begin and end. It is here that the world we interact with is born. All thoughts begin and end in each of us, from the first one to the last, and it is because of those thoughts that we do all the things that we do. We are the authors of our own scripts, our own lives. I, too, am still in the throes of this lesson each and every day. Life has a way of letting you know exactly what your failings are, and if we can't learn those lessons ourselves, we have to learn them through watching others suffer through their mistakes. Life places us exactly where we need to be at any given moment because there is always much more to it than we know.

Only we can make this world better through love and through greater understanding of the world both within and without ourselves. We have travelled through eons of time and science has explained a lot, but now we must look at a different picture. It is time for us to recognize and understand our part, the part we play on an individual level, to pull all life's pieces together in the way that was intended by God. God is not fiction, not some fantastical religious raving by a society of Bible bashers. God is real and really does exist. Once upon a time we did not know of the existence of radio waves and sound waves. We could not detect them until suddenly we could, and it is the same thing with God. Remember God is just the name that is given for identification purposes and Buddha, Allah, Mohammed, etc. are all names that relate to the same.

There are many paths that go up a mountain, but there is only one peak. All paths take you there and though they may differ slightly in ease and terrain, yet they are still all the same. They are all routes that will get you to where you need to be. And it is the same with us. We are all parts of the same thing – the all that is. We are all energy beings in a physical form, having a physical lifetime experience. Our bodies are individual and our own, yet fundamentally they are all the same. Our energies are interconnected with the planet and with each other. The air in a house seems different from room to room, yet where is the split? There is none. It is all the same. It is all part of the air in that house. And so it is with us. We are energy beings in individual bodies, but ultimately we are all part of one big whole and can never be anything else. We are joined without even realizing.

Life is not a game of chance, of haphazard events and blunders. It is for real. It is very much a piece of living art in motion. We do not drift along in our daily events at the mercy of all and sundry; it is instead a well-planned, well-thought-out affair. We are like symphonies in motion, where each word, each thought and deed must play its part in the weaving of the final sound sequence. We are not disconnected and isolated from each other, but very much a part of a whole. We interact together every day of our waking lives. It has always been this way and always will be, only now we are learning to notice life's rules.

In order to know the part we play, we must first understand one another. Until we do, we will remain exactly where we are, doing what we always have done and being who we have always been.

In order for your life to get better you must first understand where you're at, and to do that you need to come back to reality. The truth is always plain to see because it is the bottom line. It's the 'what is, without question' in your life.

You must take a look at where you are now from behind the scenes. Go to a bookshop, to the self-help section. Have a browse, see what takes your fancy and go home. Kick off your shoes, get a cup of coffee, tea or juice and sit down and read. This book is not just a book. It is the start of a journey in words that will lead you to discover who you really are, why you are here and why you react the way you do to life. It will begin to tell you truths about yourself that you have not even considered and the best part is that it cannot argue with you – or you with it. Only you can understand the deeper meanings behind what you read and in the process you will put away ghosts that have been with you forever. You will open up like a flower, or a seed in sunlight, as understanding will course through your veins, and slowly, slowly, you will begin to rebuild what years of hardship, and struggle, and lack of love have stripped away. You will get back to the person that you really are and always were – only most of the world did not know it. You might not even have known it yourself…

Wherever you are, you owe it to yourself to take another shot at life, to start again with a better understanding of why you are where you are, where you've been, where you've been stuck and where you would really like to go. If you keep on doing what you've always been doing, you will always get what you've always got. For something to change, you must change – not outwardly in appearance but inwardly in insight and understanding. Life is what you make it, so unravel the chains that have kept you precisely where you are.

Only we can make the decision to make life work with us rather than against us, so it is up to us to take the steps towards a greater understanding of it. How can we expect to be happy when we give so much of ourselves, our power and our lives away unnecessarily? We almost invite misfortune to our door every day, without even knowing. Yet how *can* we know we are doing this until we learn? How can we expect others to treat us with the love and respect we deserve when we are our own worst enemies?

Life will always come to our aid, but first we must learn a better way to connect with it. Force, fast change and panic are not necessary. Just do what you do the way you always did, but in the meantime get some advice and learn about yourself and about how others interconnect and interact around you. Instead of picking up a chat magazine, read a book. Instead of staring blindly out of a window, read a book. Before you go to sleep, read a book for five, ten, fifteen minutes. We can never know all there is to know and we are never too old to learn.

Life is ours for the taking. There is no magic formula, no quick fix and no easy ride. But there is a new day, a new page to write our life history upon. With a new perspective and the knowledge we have gained, we can make educated choices rather than haphazard guesses and mistakes, but above all we must never forget that we are never alone. Even in our gravest moments there are always help, strength and love standing by, and all we need do is let it all in through our mind, through our own private thought structures. Pain, worry and stress serve no purpose at all. They just make you irritable, miserable and ill. If you don't want to keep them any longer, then learn to let them go. Ask that all you don't need be lifted from your shoulders and recycled. Ask for love, light and energy to replace it. Just ask.

Life will not always be plain sailing, because that would be boring and make us stale and stagnate, but with each passing day it will get smoother and it won't be your imagination. I, too, have had to go through this. It is hard, as life keeps coming, yet it can be surprisingly easy. Just allow the changes to happen. You will be helped if you ask – and only if you ask – every step of the way.

Only man can help himself. So it is written and so it must remain throughout his life.

CHAPTER EIGHTEEN

A Conscious Effort to Evolve

Man is a physical being. He is also an energy one. The two must combine to produce life within his body of matter. The physical body is grown in the womb for this specific purpose. It is the same for all things on the surface of this planet. All things must grow into the final shape that we see and all have their purpose, apart from decoration and existence. Man is no different. He, too, has a function, a purpose upon Earth – it could not be otherwise. Man is designed to be a keeper of this planet. He is the only species with intelligence beyond what he was born with. He is capable of lifting himself far above his original state to become anything he can possibly imagine. He is king of the whole world he surveys, not by presumption and greed, but by design. He was specifically made to fulfil this role and it's yet another reason for his being here.

Every man is lord of his own castle, ruler of his own affairs. He has intelligence, choice and free will. He is programmer of all he may ever wish to achieve, born to live a physical life and to experience any part of that life he could wish for. There are no rules, no boundaries and no regulations that can starve his own need for growth. He is capable of anything his mind can imagine or desire.

In fact, everything in his life up until now has first been desired by him, first as a thought – no matter how fleeting – then as a dream, then as reality. This is the nature of life.

Only man can pursue the route he would like his own life to take. He can make a million different choices and he can try them all, but only he can have the final say in the directions he settles upon. He does this many times during the course of his life. He can see evidence of this all around him and has already lived it in the years he has been here, but the questions that face him now are whether or not he is happy with his choices. Is he happy within his very being? If he is not, then he needs to reassess the life he is currently living.

There is no reason why he should not be content, given the fact that his life has always been his creation, his choice, but how often do we make choices and regret them later? How often are we disheartened and unhappy with a life we have worked long and hard to achieve? We believe we are at the mercy of others. We often blame them internally for the fact that we are where we are. Only we forget that nine times out of ten we chose to be there ourselves. It is not others' fault that things are not as we expected them to be and vice versa. Similarly, you cannot be blamed for the unhappiness of other people, providing you are not directly responsible yourself – but that is another matter entirely.

Only we can stand our ground and work steadily towards what we believe in. It is up to us to stand up for ourselves and for what we think is right – but not to the point of nastiness, butchery and war. None of these things is ever necessary. They symbolize everything we are stepping away from. They themselves represent nothing but a total lack of self-control and respect for fellow men.

Only kindness, truth and love can take us forward to the place where we now need to be. Not the sissy, hearts-and-flowers, wimpish love, but the solid love with respect and understanding that stems from a place deep within us all. Only we can tap into this connection. We are the only ones who can do whatever it takes to get us where we need to be.

Each one of us must unlock the truth and happiness that exist within the chambers of our heart. In the past we shut those doors tight to keep ourselves safe from any harm we came across, when we were young, innocent and still learning that the world was not always a kind place. We learned very early on to keep parts of ourselves locked away for safe-keeping, out of harm's reach. We learned to read situations and the people that we interacted with. We learned what we could and could not show the world, for the sake of peace and quiet, for others or for our own self-respect. Only we can know the truth of those statements because only we know the different aspects of ourselves that have been pushed away out of reach – out of view of the world and ourselves.

The problem is that we are who we are. We are *all* that we are and we cannot remove any part of ourselves without affecting the person we will become. We are all that we are *because* of the past and *because* of the life we have lived. Other experiences would have made us completely different, so everything we experienced was necessary.

We are human and it is our nature to be both good and bad at some time in our life. I, too, have been my share of both, but we learn our greatest lessons from pain and sorrow, tears and anguish. Life will lead us in many directions, but it is up to us individually to discern which will have the best outcome.

Steps in Time

Life comes to us in stages. It is built up gradually, little by little and stage by stage, over time. Distinct patterns are visible when we look for them but only we can decide if we have been fulfilled during these phases or not. Only we can honestly state if we have achieved what we sought to achieve or if when we got there all was flat, different and empty. Only we know our truths, but we must be open and honest as we look back. We are the only ones who can pull ourselves out of the pits we have dug, whether they be financial-, emotional-, character-, family- or friendship-based. Life is not over at any stage, whatever our age. From any moment in time we can begin again, with a new day and a new frame of mind.

Only you can make the difference that your own life is crying out for – even if at this time you are not sure how. Don't worry any more. Just calmly pull yourself up and out of the place you are in at this moment in life's cycle. Take charge and recognize this chance that you have to make your life and things work for you. Be quietly resolved to stick with it and don't repeat things you normally would do. Many choices are open to you at all times, providing you go out to find them.

Life is not all doom and gloom even when it looks completely that way. Place your trust in the help that surrounds you on an unseen level and ask for guidance to come. Don't be too rigid in your expectations of what that help will look like; remember, you are open to suggestion and new ideas. Sit tight for a while; allow life to unfold a little more before you decide to take your next step. Only you can do these things for yourself, and for the majority even this will be a huge transition.

We were energy before we came to be born here on Earth and we will still be energy after our time here is spent. That part of you that is you is not in your arm or your leg. It is not your hand. If you were to lose a limb you would still be the person you are at this moment. You might be incapacitated, but you would still be completely yourself. The part that is you is your consciousness. This is your life force, your soul. This is the essence of who you are and it is everything that you are. It is made of pure energy. It cannot and will never die. I, too, am pure energy, as is every living creature on the planet. We are all living energy. We are all part of a living whole, a living Earth.

Because of this only you can fulfil the role that you play during the course of your lifespan. You are individual. You are unique. Throughout the world there is not another soul such as yours. There is no other with the same intelligence, life experience and expectations, no one with the same past or the same destiny. Only you can take your place in this present scale of time. Only you can make the choices that will take you further towards your destiny, towards your future and the rest of your physical life. You are an individual son/daughter/child of God, but you are also an important, intelligent part of the whole, of the all that is and ever will be. Only you can come back to find the peace and quiet that await you in the corners of your own mind, to claim the peace and happiness that you have searched lifetimes to find.

Now you must decide to find out who and what you are. You can look forward to where you want to be, but you should look back as well to better understand where you have come from and to recognize strengths and talents you have developed along the way. Even if you believe that your life has been total doom, gloom, sadness, pain and hardship, you will be able to find surprising hidden strengths that you have gained only because of those difficult circumstances. You will be able to read the past differently and with greater understanding than perhaps you do now.

Life is not always all you think it to be. There is a host of activity invisible to the naked eye that continues in a constant stream of fluid movement. You can begin to see this for yourself when you decide to open up to some truths that lie before you. Nothing ever occurs for nothing, therefore everything always contains a reason, for either you personally or for the other person/people concerned. There is no such thing as a chance meeting, a chance conversation or a chance decision. Because life is a symphony in motion, everything is orchestrated to occur at the exact time it was destined to do so, not before and definitely not later. You are at this point in your life's infrastructure because at this time it is where you should be.

Only we can decide when we have had enough of the life we are living, and in doing so we are not giving up, quite the opposite: we are opening ourselves up to attract and receive all the necessary help that we need. We are asking to be thrown a lifeline that we may use to bring ourselves back to reality and grounding. When we have had enough of life's troubles and strife only we can choose to step off the merry-go-round of daily monotony, to return to the basics, to the reality of our life and our lot. Peace of mind, happiness and love have never left us – instead it is we who have distanced ourselves. We have herded ourselves down a one-way street until we have now reached the end of our tether. Is that where you want to stay for the rest of your life, living hand-to-mouth, week-to-week, year-in and year-out? Is that to be the sum of your achievements, the result of your hard life of long labour? Decide this for yourself, by yourself, and if you have had enough, then down your chains and get off that never-ending cyclone. Clamber back to reality, look at where you are now and what you're left with. Make the choice to find a better, easier way to live your life, to be your whole self, with all and everything that that decision entails. This book can help you sow seeds. It will also be a daily tool that will help you, but only you can put in the necessary time and effort to get you where you need to be.

Life is good; it is hard, but still good, a joy to be lived every day. But first you must remember how. You have to be open, honest and above all truthful with yourself. Only you can know whether you wake up with a spring in your step or if each day is a chore, if it's hard going. We have all been stuck in a loop of behaviour and reaction, and now it is time to break free – to smash the moulds and the nets we are caught in.

Only man can make the necessary connections that he needs to help mend his life – not outwardly, but inwardly. He must reconnect his self with his own inner dimensions. He knows the world around about him inside out, but knowing and approving of his self in this way is a different story. He knows too well all the times he has let himself down. He often forgets the many good and courageous things he has done along the course of his life's chosen path. He connects far more easily to the negative side of his personality than to the positive. It is far easier for him to take an insult on the chin than a compliment, no matter how sincere. He believes on some level that he deserves everything he gets, but the truth is quite often the opposite: he deserves a good clean break in his life, a lucky streak. He needs to reconnect with the 'all that is' once again, to help his life run more smoothly than it does.

Only we can love ourselves enough to allow each new day to evolve. Instead of rigidly sticking to the things you must do, categorize them and allow a little chance to take over. Step back just a pace and see what happens, even though you are now moving against your usual grain, it will not always feel right or comfortable. When you begin to stress out over something, anything, just hand it up. Silently hand it over to all spirit/guardians/angels that surround and work with you. Ask humbly that they recycle any problems that you have and give them back in a way you can handle. Ask that you yourself be made as small as a grain of sand, so that all unnecessary energy fluctuations bounce right off you, and ask that your day may flow and work better. Ask for negativity and stress to be removed and recycled, and ask for peace and love to lead the situation instead. Almost immediately the knot that was building up inside you will disperse. If another person is involved, quietly ask the same for them too. Ask that all things be as they should be and quietly get on with your day. You will often then forget about what you just did, but when you look back again later, the effects of the exercise will be apparent. Life will become sweeter and easier to handle, the more we ask for the help that we need. Do this as often in the day as you find necessary – remember, you alone feel the symptoms you have. We never can do it too much. The help that waits quietly by our side is ours by right of birth. It is up to all *now* to use it.

At birth, each and every person is allocated a guardian angel, a spirit protector. This is someone who has previously lived their own life, their own journey, here on Earth and has proven their worth in the realm of spirit as a trustworthy character. This is not the same as a higher-realm angel, but is instead your lifelong companion and guardian. The two of you will travel your time-frame together until the moment comes that you will both separate. Your guardian angel is neither judge nor jury nor instructor to you in any way, because the life you live is yours by free will and free choice, just as theirs was for them. The guardian you have is your lifelong protector – your friend.

Man will have many helpers and inspirers during the course that his whole life will run. These will also be beings who have lived their own time on Earth. They will have gained valid experience in their own specific fields of knowledge, understanding and expertise. These beings will come close from time to time on man's right-hand side to inspire and help in times of need. They are inspirers who can help only when their help is required or when it is called for. This is the work that they have elected to undertake and it is only through their input, combined with man's own, that new inventions and ideas are born as if from nowhere. This combined effort will take physical man forward to a more balanced future and peaceful existence.

We are energy in motion. Our thoughts have more power than we can ever imagine. We will see the huge difference that recycling the negative stuff will make to our mind space. We will notice how situations and arguments will be greatly reduced when we purposely bring our mind back to peace. The endless chatter and turmoil that we usually allow to churn over in our thoughts will slow down and we will remain more alert in the truth of the present we are experiencing. Only we can do this for ourselves because only we know what thoughts we are thinking. The human mind is like an arena. It should be clear of everything except what is actually occurring right now.

Very often it would seem that we are victims of others and of circumstance, but that is not always strictly correct. Circumstances that tie us down are regularly born of our own lack of attention to detail in specific areas. Usually we are given many clues, signs and signals that all is not well, but often we choose to ignore them or simply don't see them. I, too, am guilty of this. Sometimes it seems easier to bury your head in the sand and continue as you are than to bring situations and truths in to light. But putting something back into its rightful order means that we must stop what we are often unknowingly doing. We must reassess our situation or expend our energy in another direction. Often we again choose to wait, believing that tomorrow will be equally good. But often again, it is not. How many times do we wish we had tackled something yesterday because it would have stopped or changed an issue that was coming to a head? It is not always easy to keep on top of everything in life, especially when we are nervous or fearful or life is busy.

To get life back into better working order, we must bring our focus of attention back from where it has been – to operate fully in the time-frame we're in. Aim to do what needs to be done at the time that it needs to be done. Life is precious. Time runs through our hands like running water. Once it is spent, no amount of wishing can bring it back. We are so busy that we often miss out on life itself. It is not always easy or convenient to take time out of a busy schedule, to do something a little different, something for ourselves. It can be easier to work, and to work hard, because work will always keep coming. It is harder to prioritize and keep a little time free for life's intervention, especially if this is something you would normally not do. Don't let it be that you look back in old age to see all the opportunities you could have taken or achieved a little better, if only you had made time and effort enough to grasp them...

Only you can rearrange your schedule to allow a time slot for living. We are used to there always being a tomorrow, but it is today that counts the most. If we learn to make today work for us, our tomorrows will suddenly free themselves up. That backlog of stuff that stands blocking our path now will be gone. I, too, am guilty of leaving things until tomorrow, but tomorrow holds its own challenges and it would be nice to greet them with an easy, open mind.

It is easy to slip back into past patterns of behaviour, especially when you must live your life or plan around other people. It is hard to realize that they themselves are probably stuck too, but you are already one step further ahead. You can choose to free yourself up because you realize that there is a problem. People will always place demands on you, both in work and in pleasure, but it is up to you to stick to your guns, even when it might make them mad. At these times ask mentally for help. Ask to be helped to achieve your objective. Don't be too rigid, but instead try to remain as flexible as you can. Be able to do what needs to be done but remain also aware of the needs of others. Follow your inner guidance systems and you won't go far wrong. Providing you keep yourself small when you get up each day, you will not feel the onslaught of anger and negative emotions that others emanate. At all times keep yourself balanced and protected.

> Close your eyes and imagine a large old-fashioned set of pendulum scales in front of you. Look at them for a moment. They represent a state of balance that's inside you.
>
> Notice whether they are level or lopsided. If they are balanced, then fine, but if not, place the necessary brass weights upon

the scales until they sit with both sides swinging in perfect balance.

This exercise should take only a few seconds to do, but immediately you will have recentred yourself. Now carry on with your day. You can check from time to time that the scales are still level, especially if you work in a stressful or public environment. I, too, should practise this exercise a little more often than I do, to remember to calm myself, especially when I become snappy towards others.

Being out of balance or out of synch with yourself can happen at any time. You can start your day very well, then for no apparent reason things can change and the world will be clamouring and shouting for your attention. It is easy to fall prey to over-aggressive tendencies in retaliation, but don't give up. As soon as you recognize the fluttering of anxiety inside your stomach, your neck, back or chest, simply bring yourself again inwardly to peace. Imagine yourself as small as you can possibly be and check the position of those scales.

Because we are energetic as well as physical beings we are susceptible to the mood swings and energy fluctuations of those around us. We have already said that in reality there is little difference in the air from room to room in any house – it is all part of the same, it is joined, there is no break-off point. Well, the same rule applies equally to us. We are pure energy housed in a physical body or form. It is the energy part of us that houses our actual body, not the other way around, as we would imagine. The part of ourselves that is energy extends at least a metre, if not more, beyond our physical shape. It also enters or permeates inside our whole physical being. The part that is energy exists at its densest inside our body and gets finer as it splays away from our form. It is like a gobstopper, the little black seed inside being our body, or form, while layer upon layer of energy exists round about us in different colours and varying thickness. We are in effect intelligent, walking energy, and this energy part of ourselves is our soul. It is the blueprint of everything we are, all we have been and may become. It is like a black box on an aeroplane. It is the energy record of all our movements, everywhere, all through life. It shows where we have excelled and where we became stuck. It shows our state of bodily health and state of mind. It shows just how far we have progressed in the time that our soul has been in existence.

This energy has no boundaries or barriers. Just as the air within a room is not contained by the room, so it is with the energy of each one of us. It, too, has no definite cut-off point. Just as clouds in the sky have their own shape and size but also become part of the whole sky as they intermingle with one another, so it is also the same with each of us. We permanently intermingle with everyone and everything. We, too, have no defining line other than our bodily form. As our energy pattern splays further away from our physical body or shape it gets finer and finer in density.

We think that nothing exists in the space that we see between people, objects and all other matter. We think that our life cycle ends and begins completely with us, and that we alone control all that we do, but this is not so. We are part of a much larger scale. We wrongly believe we must scream, shout and badger our way forward to get where we need to go, but this is just what we have grown accustomed to thinking. We have believed all we have been taught to believe by people who, in this respect, knew little better than us. Throughout history we have been taught to believe in only what we can see, touch and feel. We were punished for believing or even proving that other things could and do exist. Yet man has been searching for the meaning of life throughout the whole of the time-frame he has been here. That is why – deep, deep down where it matters – nothing has really sustained him, because somehow he felt something was missing

Man holds much more importance than even he can begin to grasp. This is not a 'pie in the sky' statement or idea; it is the truth. Man little understands the role he must play in the scale of the Earth and the universe. He is not a pawn that the universe plays with but a single part of a much larger picture and everything he does is timed to perfection. Nothing will ever be completed before its time is right. Everything must occur in correct order, yet man does not always determine that order. A force greater than he leads him on.

We are used to running our own show. We are used to making all decisions for ourselves, by ourselves. We think that we alone have control over all things we say, think and do. We believe we alone are responsible for all that we do and to a certain extent we are – through personal responsibility we are completely responsible for things we do personally, to other people and to ourselves – but we are not completely alone in the tasks we undertake and the routes we then choose to follow. We are part of a greater whole and once we have decided upon a course of action, the universe collaborates to help us attract and achieve it. We get help from all sorts of directions, although until now most people have been totally unaware of this fact.

Man is not the be-all and end-all of all that is; he is an integral part in the workings of this planet. He is one cog in the workings of a well-run, well-oiled machine. Before we are born we exist in a pure state of energy. We return again to that energy state after physical death has occurred. In between, we are energy having a physical lifetime experience.

We each came to Earth with an outlined life plan of what we would hope to achieve. I, too, had mine and this book is part of it. We also each have a destiny that was agreed and allotted before we were born, before we were even the twinkle in our own parents' eyes. We can fulfil that destiny, whatever it may be and wherever it may take us, but one thing is certain, that because only we know what our deepest hopes and desires are, only we can take up that challenge.

Many people are part of a larger life plan as well as their own individual one and that is why some people seem to excel more than others. But we are all here to experience life in all the ways that we can, to enjoy everything that this world has to offer. We are here to look after the planet and to deal with those things that fall into our pathway or life. We are here to do all that we can, in any way that we can, both for others and for ourselves. Only we can know what that will entail for each one of us. It might mean nothing more than the fact that we love and look after our own family, but to others it can mean a lot more. There are no limitations upon the many things that we can do or be, but we are so often faced with the problem of our life getting stuck – long before we even get to that point. Man is stuck in a loop of behaviour that no longer serves his life purpose. I, too, have been there and in some ways still am. It takes years of practice and focus to undo all that we have become so good at doing automatically, but then we do have the remainder of our life to work these things out.

We are not perfect and we probably never can be (not in this lifetime anyway). I, too, must remember this because I, like many other people, am often far too hard on myself. We have already said that we are far more tolerant of other people than we are of ourselves. We need to set the balance straight, but it will take honesty, time and patience with ourselves. It will also take practice and focus. We have to remember that life does not control us, it responds to us, to our thoughts, needs and unconscious signals, whenever things move through our mind. This is another reason why we must learn to control the many thoughts that chatter uncontrollably around in our head. I try to practise this as often as I can, but it is easy to forget and to slip firmly back into old habits. So aim to catch yourself out as frequently as you are able, and the more you do, the more you will focus upon the tasks and decisions in hand.

Your thoughts are not as private or as silent as you think. It is only here on Earth that words are necessary; everywhere else thought is used for communication instead of voice. Generated thoughts are heard like Tannoy announcements on the spirit plane. Nothing is ever wasted, hidden or lost. Only you can curb what you actually transmit, and perhaps now that you know that others hear you too, this will begin to help you settle down. It may be just the ticket you need to wake up to yourself, to the truths that surround you and always have done. Don't just believe in that part of your life that you already know and have used; go and search out some of these truths for yourself.

Today we have never been so free and able to find out whatever we wish. We are not punished for our beliefs or for everything that we do. Instead the world has never been so open, so tolerant of people's individual needs. We are free to move in whichever direction we choose and in the West virtually nothing or no one ever stands in our way. This time-frame is ripe for us to explore the mysteries of the universe more deeply – not in a historical, scientific sense but in a truer deeper, spiritual one. However, until we can learn to understand and accept ourselves, we can never achieve a true understanding of the rest of the human population. So all our journeys should commence from within.

Once we begin to trace the truth of our species's evolution and understand it better than we do now, we will be able to trace the course of our individual unrest right back to infancy and beyond. We have been brought up on patterns that run distinctly through our family trees. These patterns are forms of unconscious behaviour that have been passed down from generation to generation. Most of this we would deny, given the opportunity, but history can plainly show us the opposite.

It is time for us to begin anew, not in a materialistic, technological way, but in a gentle, more understanding manner. Are we willing to see where this new opening will take us or shall we again close our eyes and our ears? We can choose to stay exactly as we are. We can deny everything as much as we like by burying our heads in the sand, but the world will still keep on turning around us. It cannot and will not stand still just because we might choose not to play ball, and sooner or later it will give us cause to catch up. I, too, have learned this many times along the course of my path. I, too, must watch and understand every step I take to get myself safely to where I will eventually be.

Life comes in stages of change and fluctuation, of clearing out old habits and beliefs that no longer serve us or their purpose. This millennium is a period of new growth and all we see around us is a mirror image of the truth of this fact. It is not for us to run away from our responsibilities and obligations but to live up to them in a more realistic light. We are simply taking off the blinkers that we have worn since our childhood and, in many cases, that have been handed down through past generations. We are weeding out that which we no longer need or want and will eventually feel a lot better for doing it.

CHAPTER NINETEEN

Intervention

(I am I) Man is not born to simply live and die; he is eternal. He is eternal – because I am eternal. He is an individual – working part of Me. (I am I)

Only man can decide that he has had enough of the pain and turmoil that surround him, both in his personal life and in the world at large, and that it's now time to move life forward to its next level. We have to give a little back of what has been taken out, not in monetary terms but in love, understanding, peace and knowledge.

The truths that we shall find are not brand new. They are old truths of the universe, as old as the planet itself, yet to us, as we discover them, they'll be like diamonds. We will wake up as if from sleep and see the world the same yet different, we will see others without the masks they have often learned to wear. Because nothing will be hidden, no one can cheat or hurt us, we will recognize life's real truths at a glance. All things will seem quite different, yet the same, as we grow up and out of the old ways that have held us back.

We alone must make the choice that we are ready to understand more, that we are willing to break old patterns and so move on, because until the time we do life will carry on the same as it always has. If life today suits all your needs, if you wake up every morning feeling happy and fulfilled, then carry on, you will wake at a time that's right for you. But if, just like the rest of us, you are struggling, worn and stressed, then maybe it's time for you to explore a new alternative.

We can alter our surroundings as often as we wish, or our work, our home, our partners and our life, but we can never run away from our own selves. We are stuck with all we are until we learn to look much deeper, until we find the flaws and errors that keep us bound.

Man is not born to live and then die. Neither should he live in pain and turmoil forever more. At his death there will be no one pointing fingers at him or at his failings. There is no distinct and final chapter at his death.

At the time of our birth an angel/guardian is assigned to us to protect and guide us. They do not take decisions that control or interfere, but instead support and help us through the journey that lies ahead. This is not an angel with wings, as we might imagine, but someone who has worked hard to attain that position and right. There are many ranks of angels with their own professions and assignments, just as there are many people at different levels with many jobs and roles on Earth. The guardian assigned to us was elected for the job before we got here. Not necessarily by us, but for us, for the specific talents they had to offer to assist us, depending on the route our life journey was to follow. We are placed or joined together because we are in harmony on some level, they may already own the skills that we ourselves need to develop. This is a labour of love, of choice. If we don't wake up and grow, neither can they. If we grind to a halt, so do they. We hold them back. This two-way relationship has stood the test of time and once we understand it and accept it, we can open ourselves up to the help that's quietly waiting to come in. The life that we ourselves have lived until this present day is living proof that we don't always know what's best for us, even though we will often swear we do.

There is always someone by our side who knows us better than we know ourselves. They have been with us our whole life through. They know our weaknesses, our strengths, where we're heading and where we've been. They know also what we need or want to achieve whilst we are here. They are not myth, but fact, and more and more in real time this is being proven.

Only you can decide if you believe this or not, but then belief is not a necessary requirement. You cannot ever alter truth by refusing to acknowledge its existence. Your guardian will always be with you whether you want them there or not. This is how it is – there's no alternative. They are not judge or jury – they never could be. They too made their mistakes, just the same as we do now. But this is *our* time and *our* journey, not their own.

Your life is for you to live in any way that you see fit, because it is your journey – it's yours alone. You are here to do all you want to do and to be all that you want to be, to achieve all that you want and need to accomplish. You are here to use this time-frame in any way you choose, but when you go back home to spirit there will be cause to look back in hindsight at your pathway. There is no good or bad – just what is, what was, what could have been, and so on. You will discover if you have lived up to your pre-birth expectations and whether you have met your life's requirements or not.

We can choose and rechoose the many things we want to do better, maybe not completely from scratch but at least with the empty page of each brand-new day. Each new day brings forth new opportunities, new choices and decisions. We can continue as we are or try again. Instead of feeling dragged along, we can set a brand-new beat. Instead of being life's victim – take the lead.

Life is not always against us, even though it may seem that way. Very often we give others power and let our own just drain away. Do you know or even recognize that you do it? Probably not. Is this yet another pattern that you need to break?

Wherever you are now is where you are supposed to be – good or bad, but where you go from here is completely up to you. You only need the tools that would better help or serve your purpose, and the self-help books that you might read are just one way of gaining these. They will place truths in front of you that family and friends could not; they will reach buttons and switches that may not have been flicked for years.

When you understand what has happened to your own life, you will find strengths that the pain and traumas have left you with. Wisdom born from pain is the strongest lesson of all and if you can get beyond all that, life will again start to unfold beneath your feet. Be ready and be able to read it correctly when it happens. Don't wait for time and others to lead you on, because most probably they don't know how or what you need. They, too, are looking for answers to their own life's tasks and questions. They, too, are waiting for the time their boat comes in.

We are at a stage in life where we can look behind the surface of human behaviour. Throughout history man has been more in tune with his material success and progression than he has with his emotions and feelings. It was necessary for him to gain all things he possibly could before concluding that it didn't give him the happiness he thought it would. You can't know where you're going until it is clear where you have been. You can't be who you will become until you're clear about who you're not. You can't give something up before you've possessed it in the first place. Man needed all these opposites to find his real self.

Life will always give you cause to challenge your ideals, regardless of whether you want it to or not. But by looking at it in a different light, you will be calling all the shots. You will be saying that from here things will be different. Maybe take a few weeks or months to do some soul searching. It will be worth far more to you than you would believe. You cannot switch your life to pause – but you can give this all your free time, and if you do you'll begin to see it is worthwhile.

In the beginning the world was created. It formed, grew and developed over billions and billions of years. It was good. Man was also made, again over many years, and he has progressed to where he finds himself today. He has surpassed and overruled all that he ever was. His boundaries are pushed and stretched to bulging limits; he is at a point of crisis, with himself and with the world, with a technological explosion around the corner.

When the world was created, all life was balanced and in harmony and order. All things lived together, not always peacefully, but as they were supposed to do to uphold life. But as we look around us now, we can see the world that man has made – man's creation. He has made it how it is and, because of his free will, he will take it forward to whatever heights he dares to climb. Yet he has forgotten that there's more that needs attention. He has forgotten that there is another side to physical life…

Man has a lot to live for. He is up against the world, but more importantly he is up against himself. He is his own worst enemy and it is he who instils the most fear, doubt and negativity into his being. He knows very well the things he has done wrong, the things he could have done better. He knows his failings and shortcomings inside out and never forgets to remind himself of any of them. If he is given a compliment, he shrugs it off. If he does something well, he believes he could or should have done it better. He can look at others and sing their praises, often from the heart, but when he looks at himself his eyesight begins to dim. He is the only one that needs to learn to forgive himself in this way. Everyone around him – God, spirits, angels, guides and guardians – have long seen past his faults. They see him in the light of his true colours. They know the person beneath the behaviour and activity on display. But man himself does not see what they do.

So many people are totally or blissfully unaware that anything exists other than their own daily strife. They become that strife... They are not happy, but they have resigned themselves to the fact that they probably never will be. Their shoulders are drooped and their days are long and heavy. If only they knew the truth. If only they understood that they hold the keys to their own happiness in their own hand.

Finding Your Way

Only those who are willing to learn will find the truths they seek, according to their needs and their beliefs. The content of our findings will be tailored to suit our needs, but the bottom line is that the truths are the same. Each person has their own preferred method of discovery.

Some will read, some will listen to music or watch films. Some will walk and think. But along each route that's taken, personal triggers will be sparked off. You will be guided along the path that's best for you.

Children grow and learn every day. They learn of the past as they look to the future and live in the present. They can see the world as it is now better sometimes than we adults. They can listen to stories of the past and shake their heads at the stupidity of it all. They will embrace the future with their own ideas and ways of doing things, just as we did. But wouldn't it be nice if they did not become as bogged down as we have? Wouldn't it be nice if by clearing away our own rubble, we could smooth their path and help them go their distance to meet their goals?

Life is crying out for love and understanding, peace and normality. I, too, keep getting caught in the crossfire of events that are occurring all around, every day. It is time to slow things down so that we can catch up on an emotional, spiritual level – not spiritual as in 'Allelujah, praise the Lord,' but in a realistic down-to-earth sort of way. Instead of racing through life with our feet constantly on fire we should learn to walk properly once more, to enjoy life's little things as they occur, before we miss the lot. Life is short and we will be a long time on the other side, in the world of spirit, wishing we had used our chances better.

Many moons ago a wise old man told of a dream he had. He told of things yet to come. He told of things gone by and he told of the bit in between. He told of bridges and of ladders. He told of mountains high. He saw the shape of things to come, but first he told of our ability to get there. We are a race of intelligent beings. Nothing is too tall or far or deep for us to cross. We can go the distance if we choose, but choose we must, for ourselves, by ourselves. There is no knight in shining armour coming to our rescue, only plain old common sense and a new way of thinking. But this 'new way' is not new in any way at all. It is as old as the hills, but we have forgotten it. We have forgotten our own roots, our own origins. We are so good at striving forward, at achieving all we want, that we have not realized that we crossed the start/finish line long ago. Our race has been won – it is all over. All we need do now is find ourselves once more.

We can break the cycle that we are caught up in. If we are sincere in our efforts, we will get back on track. The world seems to be falling apart, but we can stop it if we want to – if we all try. At this moment in time many of us just don't know how. We are fighting for our wellbeing, holding on for dear life. We are not quite sure where and when it is going to end. I, too, am at the same juncture, but I know that I am lucky. I already have hold of my lifeline. I already know where I am going. And you can be the same, if you try.

Only you can shake yourself out of the place where you have nestled for years. Your life might not have been working properly, but you, too, have played your part. You have been happy to remain there, even though you may not have realized it till now. How often do we prefer to face the hardship we have grown to expect rather than face the uncertainty of change and the unknown? How often do we moan and groan but still do the same things over and over again? Only you can step out of habits you have acquired along the way, but to do so you must first recognize their existence.

Don't make any rash alterations at the moment. That is not what this whole exercise is about. It is more about waking yourself up to the little things you do, day in and day out, automatically. It is about recognizing how you keep yourself exactly where you are. We all do it and our parents and grandparents are probably still doing it too.

We have a new page to write upon every day and whatever we choose to put there is up to us. Just because life has dealt you a rough ride does not mean that you have to curl up tight and take it. You are probably not living to your true potential. Life has a habit of moving you slowly into positions you would rather it didn't. But life is not a game and we are not its pawns. We are the masters of the life we have, not in a commanding, domineering way, but in a quieter, more refined way.

Only you can decide where you go from here. Perhaps this book has engaged a hitherto sleeping connection within you. Perhaps you have an unexplained excitement waking up. That is normal. You are being shown a window of opportunity – a new lease of life. At this moment in time probably nothing has changed in your life at all, but you have. You have already begun to change the way you look at it. Perhaps you could use this new-found freedom to search more deeply into yourself. If you keep on doing what you have always been doing and thinking the same thoughts, you will soon be right back where you were before you read this book. You will just get what you have always got before. So don't waste this change, this energy fluctuation that you can feel inside. Take the next step. Keep on going forward. Don't slip back into familiar old patterns. Be more aware of the things that are going on within and around you. Take time out to read a little, to explore new depths, find the keys within yourself that make the difference.

There is another twist to this, too: what about our children? They only know what we have taught them and what they have seen and put together for themselves. If we do not offload the baggage we are carrying around with us, we will end up piling it onto the shoulders of our offspring.

How many times do we hear the expression, 'The trouble with you is that you are just like your mother/ father'? We repeat the patterns that we ourselves have been subjected to, even when we try our utmost to stop. This is the way it has been for generations, all the way back along our own family lines. As each generation grows up they are either the same or the opposite of what they have experienced for themselves. Then as the next grows up they, too, choose the same or the opposite. Eventually we all get back to where we were. We are stuck in a loop of behaviour and response that we are oblivious to.

The only way to break the cycle is to make your own changes from choices that are born within you. By learning more about yourself, you can make more of a choice in how you now respond – not react – to the world, to your world, the one that you live and operate in. You can make educated choices instead of worried, frightened, hurried ones. You can drop your haphazard approach and work out what is really best for you. Only you can make these choices from decisions that occur every day. It is not for your helper/angel/guardian to make them for you. The life you are living is yours alone.

We have a free rein over every word, every thought and every action we undertake. We alone must take our life forward to its next stage. This resolution is always ours. We can stay as we are for all eternity if we choose, but the point is that to do this is not necessary. If we are true and kind in our dealings, in our hearts, then there is no reason why we should remain in pain and hardship until our death. Lessons not learned here simply await us as we cross over into the next life. Yet there is no next life – only a continuation of this one. It's not another life but another level. So we may as well use this opportunity to grow and to reassess some choices that we have passed over or not been ready for before. And in allowing ourselves to put our life into better order here, we are also helping each other. The more we open up, the more open people can be with us. There are no holds barred. Life is ours for the making, not the taking.

To make the choices that will take us to where we need to be, we must first relearn the basics. It is surprising how our thoughts, especially misshapen ones, can falsely colour the things that we feel, hear and see. We do not always hear things in the way they were meant. We sometimes see what we want to see rather than the truth as it really is. And our feelings – how often do these get mixed up due to bad news, sad films, music, hormones, etc.? How often are the things we feel overwritten in an instant by the deeds of others? How often do we fly into a rage at the drop of a hat and let it spoil something we have been looking forward to for weeks? Which of our senses always shows us the truth? None of them does. They are capable of taking us a million miles away from reality, without us even knowing. We can simply be living a truth that does not exist, except in our head. How often when confronted by a real truth are we ashamed? How often can we hardly believe the things we have said or done, simply because we saw life in one way and not another?

We hurt ourselves as well as others by simply following wrong feelings. Now we are being given an opportunity to begin again, on a surer footing. Yes, there may be repercussions for some of us as we let old forms of behaviour slip away, but what about our own peace of mind and our own self-respect? How much does it mean to you to sleep soundly at night? To know that you are living life to the very best of your ability? How much does it mean to you to be offered a new way forward? It meant a lot to me and I took it, because I was fed up with feeling hurt and down. Life was cruel and I didn't want it to carry on that way. There were people who needed me and who depended on me too, and I knew that if I cracked up it would affect their world and my world too. I felt that I owed it to them as well as to myself to pull myself up and out of the place I was in – on the inside, not the outside.

Life should never make you feel small or worthless. It should be a pleasure to know that because of you this world is a better place. And it will be.

Each of us has a special function. We all matter and the way we feel matters much more than we know. We can never know all there is about ourselves, at least not in this lifetime. The more you learn, the more you realize how much there is yet to learn, understand and grow. We are all in the same place – the same boat... We are all living works of art that have not been finished yet. Do you want a say in the finished article or are you fine with others calling your shots? When you stand up in front of your maker will you be pleased with the result or will you try to hide away from most of it? No one will judge you. You will do that for yourself, by yourself.

When we are children we make mistakes because at the time we don't know any better. Then, when we learn, we stop doing the things that we did. But when we grow up we still often act as children. We do not learn by our mistakes, we repeat them and repeat them over and over again, even when we know that really we ought to know better. Little by little, if we are lucky, we grow and learn along the way, but only in the directions we are moving in and only if we are open to the experiences that cross our path. For the rest of the time we continue as we are until we meet a hiccup. Then we get round it in whatever way we can and continue as before. At what point in our life do we actually grow up? And who determines that we do and when it will be? There is no trumpet call or drum roll. There are no exams to take. It is just assumed that at a certain point we know how to look after ourselves – but do we?

How do we ever know that we have finally grown up? The answer is that we don't. Many people are like children until the day they die. They have the same tantrums, the same moods. They have the same likes and dislikes and do or don't do the same things.

As a race, we don't welcome change very easily. We prefer to stay with the devils we know rather than face those that we don't. It is hard to see past a looming obstacle. It is hard to know which path to choose for the best, but a little more self-understanding, time and patience will always give a clearer picture. Then we can learn to read the signs from another viewpoint and move forward. With a little time and effort, we can make the difference that our life is crying out for. Not by blame or force, but by understanding how and why we are again back at this point, why others behave as they do and what the motives are that drive them. What others say is not always what they mean, just as you yourself colour your words to suit the understanding of the people you speak to. The signals we think we are giving are not always as clear as we think. They are often completely misunderstood and then we wonder why…

Only you can look to see if all is as it should be in your life. Do those around you appreciate you as they should? Do they understand all you are trying to achieve? You can only be who you really are, but do others see and understand that? Do you let others pull your strings and push your buttons? Do you dance to the sound of your own tune or are you caught up in theirs? Only you can answer these questions and more besides. Are you true to yourself? If not, then it is time to explore why. It is time to know how you got to where you are and then how you can move away. Life has as many positives as negatives. Which do you attract? Do you know how or why? I did not know. Life was calling more shots than I was and I was always on the not-so-sweet receiving end, but not any more… Yes, life is still a mix of good and bad, but the lows are never as deep as they were and I can pick myself up far more easily when the need arises.

Looking Within

Only you can look into the workings of your head. I, too, had to do the same.

During youth we set the basic behaviour modes that ordinarily will take us safely through life. We learn how to act and interact around others. We learn how to behave and how not to behave. We put together all the building blocks that will help to make us who we are. But even in a loving family environment mistakes can be made. I, too, should know this. Every member of every family will view the world in their own unique way. Even when children are treated the same, even when they're twins or triplets, the very fact that they came in a different order will play a huge part in the development of their outlook, a much larger part, in fact, than most of us understand. Parents ordinarily do their best to give their offspring all the love and support that they need, but, as we have discussed, they have never been trained or assessed for their abilities for the job. Mistakes are made left, right and centre and most of us just have to live with the end results through adolescence and through early adult life.

As parents, out of too much love (or loving too much), we, too, get most things wrong. We hurt our children and our families without realizing it, sometimes almost every day. So how do we stop? How do we find out where repetition and mistakes are being made? Most of us don't know how – that is, unless we are lucky.

Only we can ever love our children enough to find out the mistakes we are making. Is it fair to simply try our best and hope it works out? It is they who must learn to live with our mistakes or painfully put them to rights themselves in adulthood.

Many things that go amiss lie in the way we view daily life, in the way we act and then react within it. Children not only have to face their own lessons in growing up, they have to live through their parents' baggage and emotional crossfire as well. They spend a lot of time ducking and diving through the mood swings of the adults that surround them. Is this completely fair on them? They love us and because of this all-complete unconditional love they are led in many directions they really need not take. The sincerity of their desire to please takes many forms and it is up to us to channel that to the best advantage for the children themselves, but how many of us realize this? How many times do we use this desire for our own ends instead? Our children end up moulded into little versions of the adults they look up to. Either that or they pull away and become the opposite. Is this what we want for them or would we prefer them to grow up into complete individuals in their own right, to follow their own dreams and creativity?

We owe it to the children we love to get ourselves and our parenting techniques in order. We all make mistakes. That is part and parcel of being human, but it is up to us to find how deeply serious these mistakes are and put them right. Only we can do this for ourselves, for our own peace of mind and for our own future.

Life, as we know, is not always as straightforward as it may seem, or indeed as we would like. Even when we are ourselves in order, it is easy to get knocked back off course by the troubles and anxieties of others, especially when those others live or work closely with you. I, too, can vouch for that nearly every day. It is difficult to remain centred when fear and anxiety are knocking their loudest to come in. I, too, am there more often than I care to be, but you cannot stop life from turning and being all it will.

The only thing we can do at these times is to remain small and attend to that which must be done. Try to let the storm pass as painlessly as possible, especially if it is not really in your nature to do so. People have the right to come and go through life's interactions as they will. Sometimes they will create havoc around you, but if you remain small and calm, against all the odds, you will not be caught up in their wake. We know inside ourselves if we have contributed to the distress of someone or not, but whether we did or did not, we must ask for help. We must ask that the storm pass as easily as possible for all involved. We must ask that all negativity be recycled and be replaced once more by love, light and understanding. We are the only ones who can do this when the need occurs, and it has more effect than we could know or realize.

In times of stress it is easy to let the strength of our emotions take over and toss us onto a wild and turbulent sea of fear and worry, but this is self-perpetuating: we fear because we are worried and because we are worried we feed our fears. Notice when you are on this roller coaster. As soon as you realize you are, try to get off. Try to calm the storm that's raging within and bring yourself back to the moment you are in. Try with all your might to let go of your negative thoughts and feelings. Recycle the issue and once again face the task you are supposed to be doing. Ask that your worries be lifted and ask that they be returned if necessary in a way you can handle. Ask that the solutions be made clearer to you in the next few days, or sooner if possible, but above all try to keep yourself in the love mode. Ask that the worry be lifted from your shoulders and that you may continue as you must.

Negativity is a powerful force. It engulfs the unsuspecting. It can take a perfectly fine day and turn it upside down. It can rip you to shreds, along with your confidence and your peace of mind. Negativity is a product of the ego. It never fails to let you know how useless you are. It tells you that you are being used and that you are stupid to let it happen. It tells you a multitude of negative things that have no use other than to feed your self-doubt. The ego is what keeps you down when in reality you need to be uplifted. You need to be helped out of where you are, not pushed further into it. Recycle all these things as soon as they arise, so that you may no longer be held captive by those chains.

The truth is quieter, much less obvious: you are where you are because at this moment a few things need addressing. If you sit down quietly with an open mind and stick to the task in hand, slowly the thoughts that can help you will filter through. No one is deliberately pulling you down. You just need to reassess your life, to change a few of the things you do. Perhaps some of them are out of date. Perhaps a lot of them are out of date. But you can be sure that *something* needs addressing. Stay in the love mode, not the stressed one, and it will become clearer to you.

The future stems from the present, not the other way around. When we become fearful, it is because we are looking too far ahead. We are worrying about what might happen and trying to fix it before it occurs. This in turn puts the present out of kilter, because we then alter what would have taken us to a better place had we not altered it. When we worry and fix problems before they arise, it is like trying to set a bone before it is broken. We are doing something that does not need doing. We are interfering with the flow of life and are chasing our tails for nothing. We cannot get to where we are going until we get there, and before we do, many more steps must be taken in the middle.

Life does not go from A to Z in one fell swoop; it takes days and weeks and years for time to do its work. By trying to pre-empt a problem we don't always take into consideration natural progress and growth. Things alter their state with time and it is easy to forget this. Yes, there are specific instances when it is necessary to plan for further ahead, but in those cases that is always obvious. When we keep on moving our goalposts because of fear, we alter a whole array of things that will actually draw us closer to that which we fear. In all probability if we had left things as they were, natural progression would have taken us closer to where we needed to be.

Nothing can occur before its designated slot in time. But because we are running so fast to keep up we forget that time must take its own course and role as well. If we are trying to run before we can walk, we are upsetting the apple cart in the meantime. In order to put things right we must slow down the whole process of life a little. We want everything quickly, but that just does not always work as well as it should. Everything in life must take its time to manifest and our greatest role model is nature. Nature's timing is always perfect, yet we are even altering that today with science.

Be Positive

Only we can bring ourselves back into step, back into line with the universe, and that must begin within our own selves. If it does not, then we will never get any further forward than we are right now, and right now the world is in crisis.

Only people who are positively balanced can take on a new lease of life. Those who despair will only drag negative energy with them wherever they go. Life is for living, for enjoying. I, too, must take each day as though it were my last and live it to the full.

Life is a gamble. It is not always a sure thing. The news every day merely confirms this fact. The world is a big place. Each person is on their own path. Some will be stuck and some will not, but ultimately we all have the same potential for happiness and contentment. And nothing else should matter.

God is with us all. God is the body that we live upon, the intelligence that is part of us all – every one of us. But it is up to us to pull ourselves out of the place into which we have fallen. God cannot do it for us because we have free will. And no one else can do it on our behalf because they do not have the correct combination of answers to fit. They are in the same predicament. Each and every person, no matter who they are, is trying to make their life work, to meet their own ends. Only we can bring all the pieces of who we are, where we have been and where we go from here back together. Only we can complete the picture of our life. Whatever we miss, we pass automatically on to our children. We are giving the world we have made to them in their innocence to clear up. We expect them to do what we ourselves have not been able to do. Is that fair? Is that why we invite our children into this world?

We need to look honestly at ourselves – at the things we do and have done, and at the world we are creating, not just for now, but also for the future. You must be completely sure that the person you see yourself to be today is the person you want to take with you to the next level. Only you can decide. But if you can put yourself back together, it will automatically affect those around you. Lead by example and you won't go far wrong.

If we were completely alone, the things we have yet to accomplish would be daunting, but, as we have already discussed, we are never alone and once a decision has been made, we will be helped every step of the way. Ensure you remain open enough to recognize that help when it arrives. Only you can take that step. You know if you are happy with where you are now or not. If you are, then fine. Well done. But the majority of us have done our best and are still failing fast, not necessarily because of our own mistakes, but because of circumstances that seem out of our control. Yet they are not out of our control. We have simply given our power over to them. We can get it back whenever we wish. We can stand up and start to rebuild, from within. We can look at how we always get back to the same place and can learn to change and fine-tune our direction. I, too, have some course corrections to perform. Just like everyone else, I am far from perfect, but these things will take time and patience.

It does not matter how little or how much we achieve in our time here; the point is that we start to make the effort. What we begin will be continued by others in their time, on their journey. I, too, must play my part in this, as should we all. I, too, have little desire for my children to be left with the world as we see it today. However, I, too, must take my time. As urgent as it is to make changes, they must be carried out slowly, precisely and with care. I have tried to hurry when I should not have done so and found that this only created more turmoil. A job cannot be finished before it is destined to be complete. Everything has its own timescale. And as important as the task of setting ourselves straight is, it will take time, patience and self-understanding to complete.

Sometimes mistakes play a very necessary role. They help us get things out of our system. We need to pass through them to hit triggers and buttons that rest on the other side. So if you make a mistake, don't worry, just pick yourself up, reassess where you are and go forward. The universe will place in front of you exactly what you need at the time that you need it. In actual fact you will find that you need look for very little. As you open yourself up to the truths that surround you, all that you have already learned will be put into action. All you need do is face the issues that confront you and make your choice, depending on the thoughts you have at the time. There is little more to it than that.

Simply operate fully in the present moment, the one you are experiencing right now. The past is past. Each day, each hour and each minute will bring you all that you need to address at the time that it needs addressing.

Don't go spinning in directions you have no call for right now. Everything that is necessary will present itself at the time that is right for it to do so.

Life is not a game of chance. It is well thought out. Every instant has its questions and its answers. Every word we say, every thought we think and every deed we do will make a connection somewhere with someone. We are constantly feeding others, just as we, too, feed off them.

Life is a stream of energy connections. It is always on the move. But when we are stressed or worried, we are like live wires that have broken free from their moorings, or like mainline cables that are waving frantically in the air from side to side. We flop about in all directions and unsettle others in the process. We have outblown our energy field and we are interfering with everyone else's. This is not good because we're out of control. We have been knocked off balance by circumstances, life or other people.

At such times the first thing to do is to regain your balance and to bring yourself back down to size. Bring yourself back to the size of a single grain of sand. Imagine you can become that small. It will help you feel more secure in yourself. You will stop attracting adverse attention and you can settle your problem in the peace of your own mind, not out in the open for the whole world to see. It will also be easier to think with less interruption. I, too, bring myself to this point whenever I feel anxious inside.

Once you are practised at it, then you can work out if it is your own anxiety you are feeling or someone else's. It is surprising how much garbage we collect in the form of other people's stresses in the course of a day, especially when we work with the public. Life in our own circle can be fine, then for no apparent reason we become grouchy because we have picked up on someone else's negativity. Always recycle what you are feeling. Ask that it be lifted from you and from the person who owns it. That way you have killed two birds with one stone, so to speak.

With patience and practice you can get so far in tune with yourself that you will begin to feel things you never felt before. You will be able to talk to a person or walk into a room and feel the energy that is at play there. You will feel comfort or negativity. You will feel warmth or adversity. You will know if someone is working with you or against you. You will know if someone is happy or sad, pleased or mad. All these things and more are very much at work every day in our lives on an invisible energy level, but presently the majority of us are oblivious to everything. We think the day holds no more than the little that we see, hear and say. But how wrong is that!

We are the only ones who can learn the lessons that matter, who can understand the things that really make us who we are, not by how we look but by how we are inside. We are used to changing our clothes, our hairstyles, our whole outer life, but the changes that will make the most profound differences are inside, and these can only be accessed with a willingness to learn and understand. I, too, had to learn this and I went through many tribulations before I did, and in some ways I still am doing so. We have already said that we can never know all there is to know, at least not in this lifetime.

Only we can lift ourselves up to the heights that await us. Life is changing by the day and it gives all of us a reason and a chance to reassess the situation. Rubbish is falling down on everyone, everywhere. It is up to us whether we give up and drown or stand tall and fight –

not with words or fists, but with knowledge and a greater understanding of how we got into this predicament in the first place.

Stepping Back

Many things come to try us in life and it is how we handle them that determines our strength of character. I, too, can vouch for that. Life is never smooth all the time for anyone, but trauma helps us keep our life in good working order. It usually pre-empts a period of change, of alteration. I, too, am in this place even today. I work hard to keep my life in order but then something happens that throws the whole thing into chaos once more. Actually not the whole thing, but it often seems that way. Usually a problem occurs in one specific area at a time, but we automatically feel that all the good work we have done for months has been wasted again. This is not always the case and if we were to look down from a higher level we would see that much of our life was functioning normally.

Problems usually occur in one place at a time and are a clear indication of where our attention needs to focus for a while. If we look at a car engine, once any part is broken it renders the whole thing unusable until it is mended. We are lucky that that is not the case for us. We can still function when one part of our lives is not working, and indeed most of our life continues to tick over quite nicely during those times. The largest problem lies within us, in the way we over-explode. Any problem, whether large or small, can throw our equilibrium all over the place. We think our world is falling to bits – but we forget it's probably caused through a knock-on effect and the way we react now will mean everything.

We must clear our heads of excess worry and deal with the situation at hand in the way that it dictates and at the time that it arises. Problems are merely areas that need special attention. They need dealing with. They highlight things that are not functioning as efficiently as they need to be. They show areas of life that need updating, for whatever reason. That is all. There is no gremlin making your life hard. Problems do not arise because your life was made to be difficult. They are more the result of a lack of care and attention, not always your own but sometimes other people's. It is easy to let fear take over and allow your emotions to run riot, but it is precisely at these times that we must look to God once more. Make yourself small. In your mind become as small as a seed or a grain of sand and stay that way until the storm is over. Ask that all illusion and all negativity be recycled. Ask that you may be helped through this situation in the best way possible for you. Ask that you be surrounded by peace and love and light. Ask that you may be given the strength and courage that will get you from where you are to where you ought to be.

The solution may be clear or it may take a little time to find and to put into place, but the point is that you will succeed. In the meantime look at areas in your life that are working well for you and draw strength from those. Look at all that you have achieved and take pride in that.

Life is not a battlefield. It is a well-run body of cause and effect. It is a game of survival. Only the fittest and the most vigilant will come through with flying colours. Not the fittest in body, but in mind. A good frame of mind can overcome anything. It is our minds that need attention at this moment in Earth's history, not our bodies. Our bodies have never been so loved and pampered.

Many of us just don't realize the power of thought and what it is capable of in terms of doing, achieving and attracting. The mind is the most powerful force in our body. It can raise us high above the mountains or can bring us crashing down deeper than the ground. It is the cause of world wars, death and destruction.

(I am I) Man was given a mind so that he could experience and enjoy all that he surveyed, all that he mastered and encountered. He was given a mind so that he could know himself and his function, so that he could be more than his wildest dreams would allow. It is the mind that can take humanity from strength to strength, to heights far greater than the original symbol of Adam and Eve. Man has superseded all expectations in every way, but to all intents and purposes his mind is still closed to much that it can do and much that it has yet to achieve. Man does not realize that it is the collective mind that he controls as well as his own. Each thought that he ever thinks has a knock-on effect somewhere, especially the negative ones. Life really is a struggle between darkness and light; the dark being negative and the light being positive. All the worry, stress and fear that man produces, not just individually but collectively, has an effect that is far greater than he can imagine, and it is this that often keeps him where he would rather not be. It is this that is the driving force behind war and turmoil. The more things go wrong, the worse man feels and the more he worries and stresses and fears. It is this that adds to his load, as it attracts even more negativity towards him. He gets pulled deeper and deeper into his own worries and doubts.

Positivity has the opposite effect. It immediately repels the negativity and allows man to operate within a clearer area. It keeps him energized and motivated, so that he is able to go forward to seek the solutions that he needs. Positivity is what both man and the Earth are crying out for now. It is this that is the central requirement for life.

Man is more responsible for the condition of the world at this time than he knows. It is time for him to wake up not only to his own self but also to the effect he has on the larger one. He is not alone in the things that he does. Because he is joined to everyone and everything, the negativity he produces has a knock-on effect. Collectively, it is this that is making the world unstable. It is this that is attracting many of the bad things that are occurring. It is not the hand of God, because God gave man free will. It is the hand of man that is the cause, so it is only by his hand that things can be corrected. This is the turning point that this Earth is crying out for. This is the whole point of this book.

Man has gone as far as he can in many ways at this point in time. He is living the life of a king by many standards. Everything he could ever want or need is at his disposal. He is the ruler of all he surveys, of all his wants and of all his dreams. He alone is responsible for his state of life right now, if not individually, then collectively. He is not alone in any way, shape or form. He never has been and never will be – ever. He is a living, breathing biochemical work of art. He is far more advanced than any machine he could ever make. Even the computer, man's favourite toy, has not the living capabilities of man himself. He is life in motion, energy in motion, intelligence in progress. He is either the thing that will take this world to its next stage or the tool that will completely destroy it. The choice is up to him, not just individually but collectively. (I am I)

It is so easy to get bogged down with chores and responsibilities that many people have forgotten how to have fun. Yes, there are always things we must do and places we must be, especially when others rely on us, but sometimes we forget about ourselves. We forget that we should allow some free time for ourselves, just to be. I, too, need a gentle reminder every now and then. I, too, forget the importance of this lifespan I am living.

Time is the most precious thing we have, yet we allow

it to run through our fingers like water. We forget that each minute spent is non-returnable. We are also experts at wishing it away. We long for things to be other than they are and fail to notice the space we are in now. How many of us can honestly say that we make the best use of each and every day? Not just for work, but for pleasure too. How many of us take our work and our worries home with us and spend much of our free time worrying about this and that? I would like to say not many, but in reality we all do. It is a habit. How many of us are creatures of habit without even realizing?

Only we can empty our minds and bring them back to peace, the way we empty our bins at home and the bins on our computers. I, too, have had to master this and even now my old ways try to come back. They are habits born of a lifetime of worry. This is the fault of forgetting – or in some cases not knowing – that we control our mind. It does not control us. How often do we allow our thoughts free rein to wander ceaselessly wherever they will, then when we try to relax, we can't? We are too busy trying to quiet our minds. We get stuck in a loop, when the only way out is to hand those thoughts and that turmoil up to those who can defuse them. We should hand up and recycle all that we don't need at the moment that we are in. Our thoughts will always come back to us if and when we need them, that is the nature of man, but there is no need to churn them over and over again before or after an event. The only time that truly matters is the moment you are experiencing now. All the rest belongs to past or future.

We are lucky to be able to look both forward and back. We are lucky that we can plan and practice a little way ahead, because it can be beneficial to set things into place, but sometimes we forget that the actual time of an event is the most potent. Each moment we experience is the one and only of its kind. It is these that we should pay more attention to, even if it means learning how to enjoy them more. How many times do we wish we had spent more time with someone or on doing something? How many times do people say the same thing to us? We have built a world that is so fast and so needy that our time gets eaten up before it even gets to us. At this moment even writing this book is difficult to fit into my busy schedule of life. But I am managing.

Pace Yourself

Only we can pull our time back into a more realistic and usable pace. It seems incredible, but all we have to do is ask and it is given. So ask that your day be in the hands of God. Ask that you may achieve all that you need to do and ask that you be protected by love and light. Ask that your perception of time be slowed as much as possible so that you may achieve all that you need and wish. Ask and it will be done. But first you must ask.

Only you can bring your life back into a better working order, one that works better for you. As soon as you realize you are not in it alone, the more help you can open yourself up to receive, but it must work the other way too. Not only is it good to open yourself up, but it is also necessary to close yourself down properly. Every night, once you are in bed, you should do this in your mind. Snuggle down first, then you can begin.

Imagine you can climb a ladder up to a roof. It may be only a few steps high, but this will vary with each individual. Close the roof hatch tight and pull across the bolt. Climb down the ladder.

Imagine taking a shower, but the droplets are not of water but of a pure and brilliant light. Imagine this light washing over you, and as it does, slowly from your head to your feet, the stresses of the day simply drain away. You yourself are transformed into a vibrant light, a much brighter shade of your normal self.

Imagine a towel being lovingly held open for you to step into, a white towel that goes from your head to your toes. You don't know how, but now you have been gently carried onto your bed and a breathable glass dome has been lowered over your entirety, shut down and zipped tight at the bottom to keep you safe. Inside the dome are little glittery bits of colour that sparkle and shimmer in exactly the colours you need at the moment for healing. Settle down and go to sleep. You will be safe and sound until morning.

When you wake you have slept like a log and feel completely refreshed. Wake up slowly and let the day come gradually back to you in your usual fashion, but this time you will feel a lot calmer.

Man is in need of a lift. He is tired and emotionally drained. All his time is spent doing what he ought until there is little left for the things he needs to do for himself. If this is where you are, begin to notice when you are granted the extra time you need to finish or achieve something. Ask that your day be slow and send the thanks you feel out towards God. I, too, must learn to recognize the little things that help us out each day. It is too easy to be channelled into the ordinary instead of noticing the extraordinary. Little things come to clear our way often, but the more we keep our eyes open for them, the more we will notice.

When we wake up to the things that occur ceaselessly around us, we recognize that we are not alone in our daily tasks. As well as our guardian angel and guides, those we have loved and lost are with us much more than we know. Our friends, relations, guides and helpers actually smooth our way. As soon as we really need something, they bring it to us. They are not here merely to prove their existence, but to tell us that they are still with us, loving, helping and supporting us in all that we undertake, especially when it is for the good and furtherance of life and others.

(I am I) I have made a promise to mankind that I will honour always. That promise is that I will never leave his side. I will help and watch him grow and I will never judge him harshly. The words that were written in the Bible such a very long time ago have put the fear of God into man for far too long. They were written by men, who a long time ago felt the need to instil fear into man for his own protection. I will not hurt man. I gave him life. I am his life, as he is Mine. We both need each other for survival in this physical world. (I am I)

Only we can learn to recognize the truth behind our existence. It is as though we have been in a long waking sleep, but the time is ripe for us now to wake up. This has always been a requirement of our being, but it is only now that it is necessary for our own happiness and self-esteem and progression.

(I am I) Man was given free will so that he could use it in whatever way he chose. The time is here for him to extend that free will in other directions. He must choose those directions for himself. I can give him the means and the support, but only he can reach out his hand to take them. This is not a dream, nor is it a fairy story. I am real and this book is living proof, as are others that I have also had My hand in. These are given as truths to help mankind back onto his path of 'self'-discovery. Man has exhausted much of the material world about him, but all is not lost. By turning

onto a more forgiving, loving path he can put back in energy much
that he has taken. He can pick up and live the life he has chosen
rather than live in sadness, sorrow and turmoil. I shall be here to
help man every step of the way, but first he must recognize that I
am here. He must wake up to the choices that surround him every
day of his waking life. (I am I)

Man is on the brink of a new wave of life. All his dreams are about to come to fruition but, just like a gardener, he must weed out the parts that do not belong there. Over the years it is easy to collect excess junk and baggage and clutter – mental as well as physical.

As we grow, we change, but how often do we clear the corners of our mind or refine the way we behave? How often do we continue doing what we've always done, simply because we always have? A new company boss is adept at looking around and removing what is broken, dysfunctional or out of date, and we, too, need to approach ourselves in this manner. It is easy to clear out our kitchen cupboards, but do we ever do the same with our wardrobes, or do we cling to the things we like in the hope that perhaps one day we might fit back into them or they might come back into fashion again? And in the meantime we buy new things, accumulating more and more until our cupboards are crammed. I, too, was the same, and I, too, find it hard to let go of things that I love, but we must if we are to move forward to the new beginning that is promised.

Only we can look at ourselves in the light of truth. We know all our quirky habits inside out. We don't need anyone to tell us about them any more, but it is exactly these little things that hold us back and keep us where we are. The older the habit, the more the energy that surrounds it pulls us down. The more the energy pulls us down, the more tired and lifeless we become.

We are energy in motion. All that we do has an effect somewhere. If we are not operating to our fullest potential, then slowly the air around us loses its vibrancy. Others will not feel the strength of a positive connection when they are in our company and slowly, slowly, we will find that we spend more and more time on our own. The harder we try to combat this, the needier we will appear in the unconscious minds of other people around. The only thing to do then is to clear our energy field once more and this can only be done by hard work – not in the way we are used to, but on ourselves, in understanding our ways and our habits, clearing the thoughts that we automatically think and bringing in a new and fresh outlook on life. When we have done so, we may think that nothing has changed. Indeed, the material life we lead may still be the same, but our mental blocks will have dissolved and because of this the life force that surrounds us will begin to flow freely once more. People will again enjoy being in our company and we in turn will benefit from theirs and the energy that they bring along with them.

Only you can choose your path and what you choose is up to you. Only you know what lies deep in your heart. But life is short and the older we get, the more quickly time seems to pass. So choose your path and give yourself the time to enjoy it. It is supposed to be a pleasure to live, to create, to experience and to love. Love is the strongest emotion we have. It can move mountains, but it can just as easily tear us apart and burn all our bridges. Love is our very essence and that is why we search for it our whole life through.

Only you can live your life and the choices you make are only part of it. The rest is building and labouring, or reaping and sowing, as the Bible calls it. Life is the whole package and it is basically the same for everyone. Some of us may be rich, materially, and some of us may be poor, but we all strive to find the true meaning of our life. That is the part we play at a planetary level. And we are all part of the same thing, the same Earth.

CHAPTER TWENTY

Hope

(I am I) Only man likes to believe that what he builds is permanent. It is how he has learned to judge himself – by his achievements. He has grown beyond his wildest expectations. The majority live like kings while the rest still struggle for the basics. Life is a balance and at this moment in time many things are off balance. The answer does not lie in finance and materialism. Nor is it in technology. Instead it lies in quality of life and in state of mind. Only we can bring peace back to our inner selves and at the end of the day, when our life is said and done, it is only this that we can take back home. All we have ever built will fade away with time because that is the nature of this Earth. Matter will always reclaim itself. Man is beyond that. He is eternal in nature. He cannot and will not fade into nothingness. All that he is he will always be, and much more besides. (I am I)

The essence of man is pure energy. *(I am I) He is made of the life force of the planet. (I am I)* I, too, am energy. I, too, am eternal. All that I am I will take with me and all that I can be I am not yet. I, too, am still a work in process. I, too, am still in a state of transition. We all are. The person you are now is not all you can be. It is not your final lot, unless you choose it to be that way. This does not mean you should rip your life apart. Nor does it mean that you should throw in the towel and run away from where you are now. Instead you are being given the tools to climb to a greater height, to change the parts that need to be altered and to move forward to a plane or a level where you might be happier.

Worry and stress are not the requirements of God. Instead they are the result of choices we have made in our past. They are signs that all is not as it could be and they indicate areas in our life that need to be addressed. Only we feel the stress we carry around, unless we pass it by anger onto another, so it is only natural that it will fall to us to redraw these areas. I, too, have been here, though not so often now. I, too, am still picking up the tools that I need to take myself forward and out of the grey areas of life. Happiness is there for all who wish to attain it; it is not an impossibility, but a promise.

Only we can make the life we are living run smoothly. If there are things that need to change, we should do them gently and with love. Don't change anything on the spur of a moment. Be sure first. The only way to do that is to learn a little more about yourself. Open your eyes to the life that surrounds you – not the version you want to see, but the bottom line. Look and learn. Get some advice from books or from others who have been there – not necessarily your friends, but professional people. Always search within before you change without. You are like a baby who is not sure of what life will hold. It may be necessary to relearn some of the things that you thought you knew. You are not at the end of your life, but at the beginning. This is your fresh start, your new page, and how you choose to approach it is up to you. This is your life.

Only we can change the direction in which our family, our life, our society and our selves are heading. The chaos of the world is a symptom of a deeper unrest that is coursing through the veins and the thoughts of man. There is much negativity in the form of debt and fear and pain. Many people have dug holes so deep that they pray things will not change in case they are buried. They are afraid of every day and every delivery of their post. They are afraid they will get ill. They worry and fret their lives away, all in the name of progress. Is this what we really want? Is this what we have worked all our lives to achieve? Only you can know your own answer. Only you know where you are and what the truth of your life is really like. Only you can scale things down to a more realistic and suitable level.

Only we can grow into our future. It is not pre-written, although many things would appear to be so. The world is our oyster. The only person we must answer to is ourselves – to our own conscience. God gave us all the right to learn and to grow. It was known that when we searched things out for ourselves, even though the going might be hard, we would value them more. So God gave man the will to survive, to move beyond his limitations and to fight back against all odds. He gave man self-preservation. He gave him instinct and intelligence. He gave him the essence of himself so that he could fulfil his highest expectations. He gave him the power of determination and of love. He gave him the ability to choose and to rechoose when the life that he chose failed to fit.

All we are, we have chosen to be. I, too, am the product of my past, both good and bad, but given that there is no such thing as bad, I am simply all that I am, born of my past. I am my mistakes and my triumphs. I am born of my mother, as she was of hers. I am part of a long bloodline that goes back further than I could ever trace, but my spirit is unique. I alone have access to that. Nothing and no one else can be blamed for the person that I am. I have lived my life according to the choices that I thought were best at the time that I made them. The same is true for us all. We are the product of our own life, and our own destruction will be no less, unless we choose to rethink the route we are following. There is no one in our past to blame, even though we might believe otherwise. There will be no one in our future. We are the result of all that we chose to do throughout the course of our own life, and that is all there is to it. So, only I can make my life work. People can say all they want to say. They can try to help me or try to hold me back, but only I have the final say in the outcome of my time here on Earth.

Life will always be tough. That is in its very nature, but out of ashes the best roses can grow. When we think our life is over can be when it really begins. Stay with it, wherever you are, and learn to see past the events that engulf you. Look for the meaning within and beyond the difficulties that face you. Realize that stepping stones will be placed at your feet and take each day, each decision, as it comes. Don't look too far ahead, because fear will always be there to engulf you. Stay calm, stay focused, stay small and stay in the moment. Then everything will fall into its proper perspective and place. It is the very fact that you are not alone that will help you. Try to remember this as often as you can and look for the light that will show you the way – always.

Remember that only you can bring your life back into well-balanced order, especially when things are not quite as they should be. I, too, still struggle with fear as it sends doubts and criticism towards me. For many it is far easier to accept these are true than it is to accept a compliment. So we tear ourselves apart for no reason. We point the finger of prejudice at ourselves far more than we realize. Only we can retrain these thoughts onto a kinder, more forgiving level. There is enough criticism already apparent in life and we don't need it to seep from us as well. I, too, must be more aware of when illusion, doubt and self-criticism lead me astray. I, too, must have more confidence in the things I do.

The seeds of doubt take root from a very early age. They are hammered home extremely well during the course of childhood and adolescence. Even as adults we still dance to their tune. Only we can learn to recognize when we are criticizing ourselves and whether those criticisms are just or not. Whenever we make a decision we choose the best option at the time, yet so often we look back later and beat ourselves up. We wish we had chosen better, but we always had good reasons for our choice at the time.

(I am I) I, too, had decisions to make at the beginning of creation. I, too, could beat Myself to pulp because of the way history has turned out, but I also must stay in the love mode. I must have faith in My own creation. I must believe that in the end all things will correct themselves and that the planet will be revitalized. I, too, could let the seeds of doubt and pain take root, but if I did it would not take long for negativity and fear to take over. Like running weeds in a garden, the bad thoughts we have are all-consuming; that is the reason for the seeming original split in the Garden of Eden. In actual fact there has never been a split at all. I would never and could never separate Myself from you because you are Myself. I am Myself and I can never separate from Myself. There has never been a separation between man and God. Man just allowed his own mind to enter the bin of fear and doubt and negativity. Man lost confidence in himself, because he believed that he was completely alone. He thought that struggle and stress were necessary requirements for life. But they are not.

Problems help you grow, as they require your attention to check certain areas of your life that are malfunctioning, but that is all. Problems are not given to break the confidence of man. They are merely signposts that will lead you on to a smoother runway once more. Problems highlight trouble spots that need to be sorted out. Whether it is a pain in your body, a spot on your face, an industrial dispute or the stirrings of war and unrest, problems need attention to stop them escalating further. (I am I)

Only we can bring about the changes that we desire. There is no one else that can. Only you can take the leading role that leads you back to happiness, harmony and success. The point is that you are not just stuck with your life. You do have a choice – maybe just a few or perhaps many. Each one will take you closer to a happy future and life. All you have ever been is not all that you can be. The real you might lie in a completely opposite direction from the one you are moving in now, but don't worry and don't be afraid. Take life as it comes, day by day. Take it one step at a time, even if that step seems to take you off-course for a while. Detours happen day by day, but you always get to your destination eventually, if you persevere.

The only thing you must stand by is personal responsibility. Only you can turn yourself around. No one forces you to do the things that are making you mad, sad or irritable. The life we live is far too short not to live it well and it may be a long time before we come back here again. Every day we have here is precious. It can never be repeated, never be copied. That's why we should make the most of our time here and use each day as though it were our last.

Only we can get ourselves back into order, and that includes our emotional closets. Only we can dump the rubbish that in many cases we have been dragging around with us for years. The old stuff is past. It cannot hurt us any more. We just have to learn to not let it. Every time we dwell on something painful we are feeding that pain with our thoughts. We are keeping it alive. It is possible to drag issues out through a complete lifetime if we don't let them go. The old pain is brought forward by our attachment and can become even stronger over years. And pain from the past can come crashing to the present when we least expect it. It can bring us thundering down and ruin a perfectly happy occasion. But we can re-learn to let it all go.

(I am I) I can take it away. I can lift all you no longer need off your shoulders. The day you are in should be free of all that does not belong there. Choose to let go and go forward. (I am I)

Only you feel the hurt that you keep locked inside and it is because it is locked inside that you feel it. It may have been there for a long time, but you can choose to let it go.

(I am I) There is no pain or negativity that we cannot let go of. All these things serve no purpose other than to keep us under their control. I, too, have let Mine go. But before I did, in many ways the past ruled My life. I was beholden to it even though I did not want it. I had to let go and step forward or I would have lost My battle. Life is for living, not for regrets. I, too, have had to learn this, and those lessons are rarely sweet. All that we are, we are because of our past, but buried within that past and pain are the strengths that can take us forward. Find those strengths. Find all the positives that you can, no matter how remote, and place them under your belt. I can help you let all the rest go. Recycle all your litter back to Me.

Imagine you can see a five-bar gate in the arena of your mind. Open it, go through it and close it behind you. You find yourself on a meadow path. A lake, tranquil and rippling in the warm summer sun, is to your right. To the left are tall green trees, healthy hedges and meadow flowers blowing gently in the soft breeze. Walk along the path, enjoy the sensation you feel. You are at peace – and all is good. The path opens up and ahead of you is a cottage. The gate is closed – yet you see a sign that says 'You are welcome – please come in'. Open the gate, walk through and close it behind you. The garden is picturesque. Flowers, shrubs, fruits and garden seats are everywhere. You feel comfortable and at home. Wander around – take in the sights, smells and sounds. Relax a while by the stream that runs through the plot. Relax.

Let all your cares and stresses fall away. Partake of the tranquillity this garden offers you. Remain as long as you like.

Now you may take one flower of your choosing – from any bush, tree or bed that you wish; notice its colour. Accept it with love from God and from Spirit, say thank you – then respectfully leave.

Close the gate firmly behind you and stroll back through the meadow once more. Notice how light you feel and also the spring in your step. See the five-bar gate up ahead, go through it, then close it and notice the sign that says 'You are welcome to visit whenever you wish'. Feel yourself back in your chair and this time frame. Open your eyes and continue with the task presently at hand. (I am I)

Only we can learn to control our mind and its thoughts because only we have the ability to be in on the action. We can catch ourselves out when they go spinning off on a tangent, and the faster we do, the quicker we can stop things reoccurring.

The thoughts we think depend on a feeding system that link in with what we see, hear, taste and smell. Our thoughts depend very much on our senses and feelings at any given moment. Because only we know what is rattling around in our head and because we only show a small fraction of what's actually occurring, it is up to us to put ourselves back to rights.

Life should hardly ever be automatic. Each day should be a day in its own right and by remaining too rigid we risk losing out on spontaneity and not making the most of it.

How can we judge in advance what we should or should not do on any given day when we have not been there yet? Yet most of the time we do. We judge future events on our experience of past ones, of similar situations we have been in, when in truth we should take each day on its own merits. Only people who love their life can be like this, for the rest just follow the leader. You can break away from this circle of behaviour by living completely in the moment, by focusing on the job in hand and by not worrying about past or future until the need arises.

Only people who care about themselves will ever begin to look deep inside for the answers that are needed in their life. Those who believe more exists for them will reach out their hands to attain it. Where you are is probably only a fraction of where you will be before your life-frame is over, so if you can believe in yourself, then go for it. Do a few of those things that you have always wanted to do. Don't let your work or stress and strife rule your life. It takes patience and time to form a new way of thinking, but every small step we take along the way will bring us closer to our destination. Start by putting small things in order first. Life will present you with more soon enough. Just take each day as it comes and look for the sun that will start to shine through.

Man is not used to staying in the positivity of the love mode. We live most of our life in fear, even though we do not realize. It is natural to wonder about the future, but more often than not we worry about it. We also worry about our own failings, about our shortfalls. We worry about things that should not be worried about. We worry when we don't have anything to worry about. I, too, am worrying even now about this book, so I must again hand that worry up to the love and guidance of God.

(I am I) I have made a promise to help man in any way that I can. I shall stand by that promise through all eternity, but man must allow Me a look-in first. I can do nothing without his approval and his consent, because I would be violating the very gift I gave to him – free will. Many times I watch life from the wings and I wish someone, somewhere, would invite Me in – not in an 'Allelujah' manner, but as a person, as a friend. I am real. I am here. I am with each of you every day of your life. Not judging, just with you. I can never be anywhere else. I am you. You are a part of Me. This is your life, your time – to enjoy. I am here to experience it with you. When you are stuck in pain, in sadness, in doubt, or in negativity of any kind, you separate yourself from Me. You stand alone and you carry these things alone, like burdens on your own back. Only you can let Me in, into your life as a confidant, as a friend. I can recycle many of the things that burden you down, but not without you first giving them to Me.

I have made a promise to do My best. I will stand by you your whole life long and I will bring you safely back home after it is over. There are no exceptions. Would a mother disregard a child for making a mistake, even many mistakes? She would not. And neither would I. I have given you free will, so how could I admonish you for then using it?

The atrocities that occur on Earth are driven and fed by the hand and the mind of man. They are not of Me. I will take you home and place you where you can do no more harm, to yourself or to anyone else.

Each man has his own pathway to follow. There will be many opportunities to do bad as well as good. The path each will travel will be his own choice. It will never be too late to begin again, to change course to a better route. I have given man free will to choose, to use and to go forward on a surer footing. He alone is in the driving seat. He alone is responsible for the world – for his own world even more than the larger one. He alone is responsible for the thoughts he thinks and the deeds he carries out. I am here to help him whenever he chooses. This book is proof. But he must first choose to allow Me to guide him before I can. I am here. I am for him. But first he must realize that I am his friend, not his judge, or his jury, and definitely not his executioner.

Only man can help himself but first he must recognize the opportunity and the need to do so. All that we achieve here goes to help us on the next level, the next plane of existence. This life is not all there is, neither is it a school or a firing zone. It is a world that was created for love and for life and it is this that man is crying out for. He is love. He is the essence of love itself. All he surveys was made by love. I am with him now – and I always will be. (I am I)

Man is his own boss. Whatever he decides to do with his life he can. There has never been anyone standing over him directing him, except in his own imagination. Throughout his infancy and childhood, adults and superiors wield their rules and rods of iron, but when he grows up he can choose which of those rules to keep and which to stand by. He can work out for himself which rules are useful and which are hindering. He has the intelligence to make his own decisions and to stand on his own two feet.

Yet only those who believe in their own self-worth will ever push beyond the boundaries that were set, either rightly or wrongly, in childhood. During infancy rules are put in place to keep us safe or to teach us right from wrong, according to those who set them. Rules keep the world in some sort of order, but too many can lead to rebellion and the need for extreme behaviour. Sometimes rules hinder rather than guide. Sometimes they bring happiness and sometimes they lead to heartache, but whatever they do it is up to us, as individuals, to work with them or through them. It is up to us in adult life to become our own finished article. When we stand in the next life, what are we going to say? 'I couldn't because so-

and-so said I couldn't / because I didn't know I could / because I thought I couldn't do that...' The list is extreme and endless. But this is your life, so live it in a way that you can be proud of, that your ancestors can be proud of. Make them pleased to be associated with you. Make their struggles worthwhile by taking your own life forward on good note into the future. Make every day count for something, even if it's only something small, even if it's only the fact that you were completely focused on your actions on that day, even if it's only that you had a smile on your face and were happy.

Life is full of people who are searching for their own answers, their own way forward and their own happy-ever-after ending. But no one can give us these things until we first find our own peace of mind. I, too, was here years ago. I, too, had to put my life on hold while I did some soul searching. I, too, am finding my own self and it's not over yet. Becoming our true selves can take our whole life long. It is not possible to shed all our ghosts in one fell swoop and neither would it be good for our health. Time itself must play its own part, but we must set our course. It falls to us to put the past and its lessons into a perspective that will work better for us. We also need to use the strengths that have been afforded us by the experiences we have had, been given or been subjected to. Life is not a bed of roses all the time for anyone, and if people say it is, then perhaps they are not being as truthful as they would like to be. Life is as full of pits and snares as it is full of music and love.

(I am I) I am here with you to carry you when you need to be carried. I have the strength and the ability, but I can only do this if you turn to Me – if you let Me in. I can laugh and I can cry. I can experience all that you can, but I cannot override your decisions or your will. I cannot step in and stop the cause of man's sorrow

before he stops it himself. I can move mountains, but I cannot interfere in the laws of cause and effect. These are driven by man's will, not by My will. (I am I)

Many years ago man was born. He knew very little. He learned how to eat, to drink and to grow. He learned how to dress and to find and build shelter. He learned how to make a family, a community and how to band together. Little by little, his knowledge about himself and his world grew. He learned what he needed to learn to live and function as he does today. Now he knows his history and his roots. He lives life to the full and he takes advantage of the situations he finds himself in. I have taken advantage of a situation or two myself, but I have never hurt anyone in the process. Still, I have done things that I perhaps should not have done. I am human, like everyone else here on Earth. I have been to breaking point and back, but I have come through it. I have been broken by life and by circumstances that were beyond my control, yet now it is a distant memory. Life has been tough, but I have come through it all. There will always be things that will bring you down but there are just as many to lift you up high. Life cannot and should not be a smooth ride for anyone. We need our challenges, even if we can't always see that at the time. We are human beings, not mechanical machines. Just as the tide must ebb and flow for all eternity, so life must ebb and flow for us.

Only you can look at your life, both past and present, in the full light of truth. Only you can judge your actions, your responses and your decisions, not to punish yourself but to assess what you have done and learn from it. Only you can see where you were 110 per cent correct or completely and utterly wrong. Life is often able to show its colours better in hindsight than in the present. Looking back at the tracks we have made, only we can decide if they were worth it or not. Are we pleased with the outcome? Are we proud of the part we have played in our lifetime?

This is not about guilt. Nor is it about reprimand. It is more about recalibrating and redrawing our life's plan. It is about taking personal responsibility for the deeds that we have done and either taking stock or changing our route altogether. I, too, have been here, and not always by choice. I, too, have made decisions that perhaps in hindsight I should not, but I have learned to view life from a different perspective. Things are not always what they may appear to be at the time. There are many angles of approach and consideration. Often we see through eyes of illusion and doubt rather than truth and reality. The thoughts we think and feelings we have at the time play a huge part in what we think we see and hear and understand. I, too, have been there, so I know what I'm talking about. I, too, have had to redraw the shape of the thoughts that I produced and in the process have learned much more than I ever thought possible.

Life can never be a bed of roses, at least not without some growth and pain, but there is always a way out of situations. There is always a time when enough is enough and that time is now. The rubbish that is happening in your life is not unique to you, even though it may seem that way. Everyone everywhere is going through a shake-up of some kind or another. The circumstances may vary, but pain and trouble are still pain and trouble, whatever label you care to stick on them. Everyone everywhere is being asked to reassess, to take stock and to account for their life's achievements – not in material gain, but in emotional satisfaction and happiness. We are being asked to look at the sum total of who we are. We are to assess ourselves and look at ourselves – not our situation. We are to look within to see what we will take home with us when the time comes. We are to look at the legacy, not financially but emotionally, we will leave behind. Only we can see if we will leave peace and harmony or stress and worry. Have we lived life to the advantage or to the disadvantage of those who have crossed our path? Have we been an asset to this life or have we been a drain? Do we weave flowers or scars into the time we possess? Only you can tell what is true for you, because only you can see the life you have lived, not from an external viewpoint, but an internal one. Only you can look at yourself in this manner and now you don't have to wait until you die to do it. You are able to do it now. And every day that will now come before you.

Life will always try to lead us away from the place where we think we need to be, but if we stick to our guns it will also help us out. It is up to us to make a stand. It is also up to us whether we go with the flow or swim against it. I, too, can relate to this. I, too, still struggle against the tide more often than not, but there are also occasions when everything seems to flow as it should.

Life needs our attention everywhere in equal bursts. When we do not comply as we ought, life has a way of ordering our attention by placing obstacles in our path. When we recognize this, we can move beyond those obstacles quickly and smoothly; when we do not, we tend to get stressed. Stress is a negative emotion that only serves to feed the commotion that surrounds us. The sooner we can learn to recognize this, the sooner we can let it go and get back on track once more.

When things don't work out as they should, there is no point getting cross. It is far simpler to get over it as soon as possible. The less fuss we make, the smaller the obstacle and the more quickly we can get on with what we should.

This is important because life will not stand still and wait for us to catch up. Instead we must catch up as well as keep on top of the life we live. We must see the full picture and make our life fit accordingly. I, too, must juggle and strive to fit in all that needs to be done to keep things ticking over as they should. Even the people who are helping me write this book find that they must do the same.

(I am I) Even for Me, things get in the way before a project is complete. Even I must contend with life, and not necessarily in the way I would plan. Life is like a roller coaster. It takes you up, but it brings you back down, sometimes 100 times a day. But it is up to us to try our best to keep a balance within ourselves. Anger is as natural as laughter, but only in the required dosage. Too much of either at the wrong time can cause a problem that soon escalates out of control. Negativity attracts further negativity and the opposite is true for love, light and happiness. The vibrations that surround us always have a knock-on effect. It is up to us to make ourselves small when necessary, especially when the going gets tough. It is up to us to recycle the negative stuff when we think the situation calls for it, and it is up to us to ask for love and light in return. It is up to us to balance our frame of mind and to make the most of the day we are in. (I am I)

Only a few people will ever attain total peace and harmony within themselves. For the rest of us, the best we can hope for is to remain relatively happy within our chosen field. Many of us, however, accept stress and unhappiness too readily. Many forget that it is they who control their mind. Many forget that they have a choice. It is easy to become so busy and bogged down with your own life that you forget there is more to the world. Only we can bring ourselves back into the life that surrounds us. Don't let time pass you by as you miss the little things that matter.

It is easy to get stuck in a loop. Because we think we need so much in our material life, we must work hard to maintain our position and feed the demand. Then, because we work so hard, we feel justified in treating ourselves to whatever we think we want. Even when the purse says a definite *no*, the head overrides its decision. Then credit becomes more a problem than a lifeline. Again, it serves to keep us working and buying beyond necessity.

The only way to stop is to stop. Take a look at your life. Do you really need to buy and replace all that you do? Man gives away more new things than ever before. Hardly anything becomes worn out. The charity shops are brimming so high that they too throw an awful lot away.

Only we can step off this merry-go-round, but it must start within before it can filter without. Only we can alter the course of this trend, but not with the idea that we are being heroic and depriving ourselves. This will only serve to feed the illness at a later stage, when we think we have been good for long enough. The only true way out is to wake up to reality and look at how you keep yourself where you are, working as hard as you do. I, too, have been there and I still wrestle with myself. We are combating a habit that for many has stemmed from a lifetime of wanting.

(I am I) Man has all he wants and certainly much more than he needs. Man is like a computer program that is locked on a course of action. (I am I)

Only we can break free of this cycle. Only we can decide that our buying has reached beyond the scale of necessity. This does not mean that we buy no more, but it means that we wake up to the truth. At the moment, even with everything we have, we want more. Everything we do, we do to the extreme. We buy all the necessary equipment to master a task or skill, then before we even get going with it, we change our mind and quit. Our dumps have little to do with rubbish but more and more to do with dumping.

(I am I) The Earth is My body. Why do we treat it as we do? Is it because we don't realize or is it because we really don't care? The truth is probably that we didn't know. But now we do.

Man is My creation. Whether you believe this or not is irrelevant; you cannot change that fact. Only man can learn the truth of his existence and alter the course of his life accordingly. This is not a command, but a natural outcome of the truths that are here to be discovered. Only man can look at life and learn to see beyond what his eyes relay. Only he can engage his own powers of deduction. He does not have to wait for the majority to lead him. He is capable of doing his own research. He has a perfectly equipped mind of his own. Finding the truth that lies all around does not take major intelligence, but an open and truthful mind. (I am I)

Only we are responsible for the little corner of the world that is us. Only we have to answer at some point for the life we have lived.

(I am I) I will not stand in judgement, but perhaps more in sadness, just as man does now when he looks about himself at the real world. What he does not see is the part he himself plays in keeping the world exactly as it is. But that does not absolve him of guilt for not seeing the truth. Man can never be a saint, but he could live his life better than he does now. (I am I)

So often we don't see below the surface of life. In truth we don't always see clearly at all. We see what we choose and want to see. Our eyes see only what our brain tells them they are seeing. Learn to look beyond and behind the shop window. Learn to look at reality instead of what you usually accept as reality. Only you can do this for yourself. Only you can wake yourself up from the automatic state of existence that is normally apparent.

(I am I) I gave man life so that I could experience physical life Myself. It is only in solid form that I can know all that you do. (I am I)

Only we as individuals can turn this life around. *(I am I) Each man does matter. He matters more than he realizes. (I am I)*

Only we can make the changes necessary within our own life. Only we can make the part we play more functional and positive. I, too, must reassess continuously, otherwise my life would become stagnant and stale.

The nature of life is to keep moving in forward rotation. This pattern applies to most living things, so it is only natural that it should apply to man as well. But because we have become locked in our ways and habits, we try to keep things as close as possible to how they are. Many of us have learned that change is sometimes a bad thing, so we try not to rock the boat unless we have to. We prefer to remain safe but stagnant instead of carefree and unsure of what the future will hold. This is the way life has taught us to be during the course of the events we have lived through, but without risk there can never be any growth. We have already said that sometimes it is necessary to shake things up in order to allow the dust to settle in a different order.

(I am I) I also can verify this. There have been many events throughout history that have appeared to signal the end of a cycle as we knew it, but clearly when we look back we can see how far we have come in their wake. (I am I)

Only we can look back upon our own life to see the distance we have travelled. The world has changed tenfold in my lifetime alone and it certainly is not over yet. Periods of time need periods of change and periods of rest in between. We can make these into positive or negative experiences, and the choice is really up to us on an individual level. Each person really does make a difference, because collectively we make a force and a force is a power to be reckoned with.

The choice is with us on where to take our lives. Only we can learn to be proud of ourselves once more. Only we can take this life into the future on a positive note. This does not mean that we have to abandon everything that we did before, but that we understand why we did what we did on a deeper lever. We need to find the scars that are buried deep inside and lay them to rest once and for all. No one can take away the experiences we have lived through, but we can pick ourselves up and move forward *despite* those things. Let's go and find out what we can be. Every day is a new opportunity.

(I am I) As the sun rises, so must it set. What man does in between is his own affair, but he must understand that it is his own conscience he will wrestle with when the time comes for him to do so. It is up to each individual to be the very best example of a man he can be, despite his history and his background. He lives in a society today that welcomes freedom of thought, speech and action. There has never been a better time to come out and live for all you are worth. Man has never been so free yet so stuck by his own life. Take each opportunity and live it in the best way you know how. Find out more about the workings of your own mind. If parents are but children themselves, how can they ever be parents? How can the blind lead the blind? They cannot. (I am I)

Only we can step down from the treadmill of excess and indulgence, overwork and over-stress. Only we can change from living automatically to living in light and happiness.

(I am I) Only man can come back to a more realistic level of life that will be kinder to him and to this Earth he lives upon. While he continues to indulge in excessive obligations, he will continue

to drain the resources of his fellow man. The West is bleeding the East dry, while the Middle East is killing one another. Balance can only be restored one step at a time and whether we realize it or not, this balance must come from within each one of us at home. It will have a gradual knock-on effect that will reach far beyond anything we can imagine. (I am I)

Man has come a very long way in his evolution. In fact he has come further over the past 50 years than he ever has before. He has left behind animalistic senses of greed and barbarism. He has grown both mentally and technologically, yet emotionally in many ways he is still a child. He has the same wants, needs and expectations that he had while at home with his parents. He still thinks that the world owes him.

I have also had to shake this belief from my own psyche. I have had to wake up – and grow up as well. We look to others to feed us with the love and fulfilment that we need when it is really in our own emotional banks inside. How can another give us what we are looking for? How can they share what they have yet to find themselves? Again you can see how easy it is to be stuck in a loop of behaviour that you don't even realize exists.

Man has become adept at providing all that he needs for his material survival, but as far as his emotional self is concerned he really does not yet have a clue. He still has much to learn. At birth he was equipped with a brain and a heart. The brain was to keep the body functioning and to process his experiences in a way that he could comprehend. The heart was to pump his life force around his body and to experience all that it could in the name of love and emotion. Man has gone extremely far with the use of his brain, but if in infancy misinformation and misplaced emotional building blocks were apparent, then his feelings will lead him astray. The heart can feel love and pain in an emotional fashion, but it is the brain that computes and transmits what those feelings are. Very often misinformation is transmitted and the heart does not know, but because man is used to reading his heart, he follows behind on a wild goose chase. So anxiety can be mistaken for fear; fear can be mistaken for love. Love can be disguised in any number of means, but the point is that many of these emotions have become muddled.

How can we follow what has not been labelled correctly in the first place? How can we go forward when our emotions are misleading us and pulling us back? We can travel all over the place when in reality what we are really looking for can be right under our very noses. How often do we realize things when it really is too late? How often do we wish we had seen more clearly both the negative and the positive aspects of life? How much do we allow ourselves to take in the name of tolerance when really we should have pulled in the rope months ago? All these things and many more are the direct result of our emotional mix-ups.

How can we tell if this is happening to us – if we are the victims of our own illusions? It is easy. Just look back over your shoulder at the life you have lived until now. Has it been a happy one? Are you living your 'happy ever after'? Is it even in sight? Are you as understood as you think you deserve to be? Do your parents fully know and understand you? Can you communicate both pro-fessionally and personally as well as you think you can? Or do you find yourself in unwelcome situations again and again without really knowing or understanding why or how? Are you giving life your best shot and is that best shot providing you with the peace and happiness that you think it should? Look at your answers. All these and many more besides are indications, signals, signposts that all is not quite as it should be in your emotional life. Your physical, material life may be functioning quite nicely. You have probably got that down to a fine art, but your emotional self may be another ball game entirely.

(I am I) Man is clever. He is intelligent and he is resourceful. He is adept at taking his life and moulding it into whatever he seems to need. But how often when he gets there does his life measure up to his expectations? It is easy to pin anything we wish onto a future event or date, but how often does it fall short of what we think it will be like? The new millennium is a good recent example. Up to the event man was building himself up to a crescendo. He had his life practically wrapped up in expectation of the good things it would herald. He knew a change was coming, so he placed all his dreams and hopes and desires on the forthcoming event, then when it came and went like any other new year, he felt almost cheated. He soon saw that not a lot was going to change at all. His balloon, blown up over months of expectation, deflated.

The changes that man desires are possible. In fact, it is up to him and him alone to make them into a reality. The date is just the date, the time is just the time, but in him, now and always, there is the potential to do and be all he could ever dream of being. Instead of pinning these hopes onto events and other people, the time is now ripe for him to instigate these changes within himself. Not without, as he learned in his childhood.

From a very early age man has looked to others to fulfil his expectations. Indeed, that is the role of a loving and caring parent. But somewhere along the course of his life man should make the switch. He should wake up to the fact that really he must only rely on himself. All he ever needs in courage, strength and love is in overflowing abundance inside him. At this moment in time that will possibly be hard for him to believe, because he must learn to access this resource, to tap into it. If it were easy he would have done so already and the world would not perhaps be as lopsided as it is today. This is a skill he must learn to acquire. He must first understand that there is another side to life, another lake of tranquillity that he can tap into. He must learn that he is not as internally alone as he thinks, that his thoughts and his heart are an open book to another level of life, of existence. He must understand that the struggles he sometimes must face are not always the course of providence, but due to his own lack of understanding. He must learn that he is not struggling against the world completely alone and he must learn to open up – not necessarily to others yet, but to himself, to his own understanding. Life is falling at his feet, but often he just does not notice. (I am I)

Only man can hear his own inner voice. Only he can look at his life in the true light of what really is, in the moments when he is completely alone with his thoughts. The majority of the time we can feel fine. We can ramble through life quite nicely on automatic pilot, but every now and then we have cause to ask ourselves what it's all about, why we live the way we do. We ask ourselves if it is worth it – worth all the sweat and the worry. We ask whether we are reaping the joys and the rewards that we deserve. We wonder why life is flying ever faster, why there is so much turmoil and sadness around us, even in our own social circles.

I, too, have had cause to re-examine my life and the route it was taking. The sun would rise and then set once again without my having seen it at all. I was not locked up in a room, but I was so involved with my life that the outside world just passed me by. Days would roll into weeks and then it was nearly Christmas again. I, too, had to check whether I was using my life to its best advantage or whether I was simply allowing it to pass.

This experience is not unique to me. Many others experience it in one way or another, some to a greater, some to a lesser, degree, but it is a symptom that is widely spread across the modern world. It is a state of mind that is instantly recognizable when you are busy and concerned with the necessities of life. Many of us squeeze so much into our waking day that we forget to take time out to rest. *(I am I) Even I had to take time out for a rest! (I am I)*

But the human body is not like a mechanical machine. It requires periods of rest in order to keep it uplifted and in full working order. When we push ourselves too hard, all we want to do is sleep. It can be an effort to go out to have fun. But without fun, life can quickly become a chore.

Is this the lesson we want our children to follow? They will copy our examples long before they heed our words. At this time they do not necessarily have a good track record from us to follow. Again, it is up to us to reassess the way we live and to put things into a better working order.

Life must be balanced in almost every direction for it to work smoothly and efficiently. We can do anything we want, whenever we want, but the rule is that it should be balanced.

(I am I) I must also keep the world in balance, and given today's erratic behaviour by much of the human race, this is not always an easy thing to do. (I am I) 'Balance' is not always a word that is prominent in human awareness. We rarely think of it at all, other than in regard to our finances or perhaps our dietary requirements. Balance is a concept that is too often forgotten. Yet it is perhaps one of the most important.

(I am I) At the beginning, the world was made in balance and harmony and light. Man fitted perfectly and the role he was given was to retain that balance. Even in his own state of health a state of balance must be maintained. (I am I)

Life is pulling our attention in too many directions at once. We must do too many things at any one time to give each task our full attention. This is not necessarily bad, but it doesn't give rise to a good sense of balance either. As long as we can keep on top of the chores that are raging for attention, all will be well, but when we become tired or distracted, our world begins to crumble. It is hard going to keep up with the juggling we need to do. Yet only we can prioritize our time and our attention. *(I am I) Only man can look at his daily timetable and adjust it to a more flexible level. (I am I)*

I, too, have commitments, but it is surprising what you can achieve when you focus your energy as and where it's required. This book was achieved in such a way, it is a miracle all of its own.

Only we can bring ourselves back into the reality of the present. I, too, have to practise this every day. Sometimes I win and can remove a heap of backlog, while at other times I seem to get nowhere fast, despite my hard efforts to do so.

It is necessary for us to 'bend like the willow branch'. If we can bend and flex we are less likely to snap under the stresses of life, so at all times try to remain flexible – not physically but mentally. Whenever something or someone drags you off course, come right back to it after the event. Life will not stop and wait for you as you attempt to sort it out. Instead it will continue to march forward and all you can hope to do is to keep up. Life waits for no man. It must keep on moving because that is the nature of the planet's survival. Only man can get stuck and stagnant for a while, so he must learn to free himself and move forward.

If you can learn to keep an open mind, during the next few months you will be given ample opportunity to begin your own voyage of self-discovery. It is not boring, nor is it hard. Once you set your mind to it, everything will fall into place, piece by little piece.

I, too, am still in the process of working through my history. I mean the 'since I was old enough to have an opinion and make my own choices' sort of history. I, too, am moving forward, but am clearing my path at the same time.

We alone choose whether to be happy and content with life or whether to stay exactly as we are – at the mercy of circumstance and of all and sundry who cross our path. This voyage of self-discovery will stop others from taking advantage of you any more. You will be able to stop them in their tracks instead because you will see them coming a mile away. In learning more about yourself you will also obtain a better understanding of other people. You will spot the things we all unconsciously do to get life to flow in our favour. You will recognize things that have been going on for years, invisibly, for everyone. Life will present its colours to you in a completely different dimension, just like a child who suddenly wakes up to a new way of thinking. Once you learn to see beyond the vision of the eyes, beyond the feelings that lead you astray and beyond the words and actions of others, when you are spoken to you will hear for the first time what is really being said, instead of jumping to automatic conclusions. You will wonder how on Earth you did not know these things before.

Our function, as already discussed, is to allow the planet's energy free passage between ourselves and the sky and the ground. But this can only be achieved by keeping ourselves open. We have to connect in a clearer way than we do at the moment. Not just 'clearer' as in 'making the connection', but 'clearer' as in 'emptying our own emotional bins first'. The rubbish we have trudged around with since infancy is blocking our perception of the real world. The illusions that we keep fuelled by wrong thinking are keeping us away from the place we should be – totally present in the now!

Only we can bring ourselves back to reality with our feet planted firmly on the ground. Only we can take each new day as it comes and make it worth its weight in gold. Only we can live every day as though it were our last. We need to clear the backlog of tasks that we take forward with us with every dawn that breaks. I, too, have a mountain that follows me, but, one step at a time, I can say that it is slowly diminishing. This task cannot be rushed, but neither can it be forgotten. It is because of this backlog that our energy drains steadily away. So I, too, am working through my own trail of rubbish.

(I am I) Rubbish can take many forms and it can come in many disguises. It can range from a stack of half-finished projects to unfulfilled promises to cluttered cupboards and drawers. It can span decades of time and as you begin to wade through the pile you will see just how deep it is. Don't let this worry or dishearten you. It is natural. The bonus is that you are now waking up to yourself and your 'stuff'. You have made the choice to move forward and to clean up. You know now why you must and why it is actually worth it. In some cases these things have taken lifetimes to build up and they can take your own lifetime to clear. But the point is that as long as you attack the pile earnestly, then you are clearing it – one step at a time. A mountain in its totality can never be moved, but if you take one boulder, one stone, at a time, it is possible to move the whole thing.

Another point to remember is that you are not alone, not ever. All that you will do yourself will constitute but a fraction of what will be done on your behalf by spirit. (I am I)

Man could do so much to help himself if he did but know it. All the help and guidance he could ever need is right under his nose, but he is as an infant watching

TV. He operates within his own mental limitations and everything else flies over his head and beyond his range of knowledge, much as a child might watch an adult programme but can only understand a small part of it. Man needs to wake up in order to move up to the next level of survival. He operates too fully on the material/physical level. Yes, he lives in a physical world, but he is not completely of this world. He is made of solid matter but he is so much more besides.

I, too, am matter, but of a slightly different calibre. The energy we are made of becomes finer as we tune in to ourselves on a new level of understanding. Yet I am still only a fraction of what I will eventually become and as yet I do not know what that is. No one here on Earth can plug into their soul and see how far it has already travelled along the course of evolution, so it is only fitting that neither can we know how far we have left to go.

All souls here on Earth were born, or came to be, at exactly the same time – at the beginning. There are no new editions. We are born individually into Earth's physical sphere at the time of our choosing and we leave it behind at our physical life's end, when we cross back over the bridge to the spirit world once more. We have all done this many times before and we shall continue to do so long into the future, as long as evolution's need occurs.

It is our destiny to grow and evolve. We have come a long way since the time of living in caves. Even in our own short lives we can look back with hindsight and realize the distance we have travelled, despite any obstacles we have encountered along the way.

Life is a gift. Each life is individual. Each one is no more special than another. We are all travelling to meet the same end. That is all there is to it. We don't really have any choice in the matter, yet we have every choice under the sun. Life is ours for the taking. It is here to be lived, to be loved and to be cherished.

(I am I) I once spoke directly to every man himself and I will do so again. Each man everywhere will hear Me as plainly as he hears his own thoughts. This book is a living example of that truth. I will talk to you, as you, too, will learn to talk with Me. I am not a legend, neither am I a ghost of the past or the future. I live and exist only in the here and now – as you should too, because now is the only time-frame that exists. The past is time that has gone and been spent. The future is yet but an illusion, an idea. The moment you are now in, and every moment you will ever be in at the time of its birth, is the miracle of God. It is here and only here that you will find Me. It is here that all things are possible. All of life stems from this point and this point alone. Remove your automatic button and be fully aware and alive once more in the now. (I am I)

Man has the world at his feet. All the possibilities he could ever imagine are here in the now for his taking.

(I am I) I will help him just as soon as he asks Me. Not by lip service, not by merely mouthing the words, but when he pulls those words from deep within his heart. I will not judge him by his past actions, words or deeds. I will not do that ever. I am only here to love him as a parent unconditionally loves his child. How could I turn my back on Myself? He is a part of Myself. You all are. Could you disconnect your own arm and not feel it? The answer is no. So neither could I. Each man, each person, each being and living thing is a part of Me that I can never replace. How could I dismantle Myself and for what purpose would I do it?

I am not imagination. I am real. I am not a man, not a figure looming high in the sky that threatens to tower over you through eternity, but I am with you, quietly, now, and have always been so. I could never be anywhere else because you live upon My own body. You breathe in My life force – into your lungs, in through your skin, through every pore in your being. I am all you are and you in return are a fraction of Me. Go out into space and look down. All that you see is Me. And you are a part of that. Each man is as important as the next, because combined as one, we make the whole. (I am I)

Man is important. He is the conscience of a planet that can live, breathe and comprehend all that he will ever come across. He is a living part of God. He is part of the all that is and the part he plays is irreplaceable. There are both good and bad in him, but he was equipped with self-intelligence. He can recognize right from wrong, hot from cold, love from hate. The choices and rules he then lives by are his own affair. It is up to him to choose the best and to become the best that he ever could be. It is up to him to live his life in a way that he himself would be proud to own up to. The past is past. It is up to him to move on.

Only man can wake himself up from the waking sleep that has been his life. Only he can choose to do this for himself, by himself. Yet when he does, he will see that he is not by himself and never has been.

(I am I) I am here, holding his hand. I will carry him through the next few months and years if he so wishes, but first he must learn to recognize My presence. How can he know I am helping him until he does?

Life can never be plain sailing. The very nature of this planet is a cycle of life and death, life and death. Man, too, is part of this cycle. Pain plays as much a part in his life as joy, but out of pain come growth and understanding. I will not cause him pain. He does that alone by his choices – he and others around him – but I can help him through these periods of pain a lot more easily than if he were wading through them alone. Man is not lost; he is found. He is right back where he should be. There is no more deviation in his way. He is home if he would but realize it. He is home.

Only you can take yourself into your future. You are not bound by ties of the past. You are free to travel in the direction of your choice, not physically but mentally. The thoughts you think do matter. They matter very much. In fact, if you but realize it, they make matter. (I am I)

Only man can wake himself up to the divine presence that surrounds him in all things. I, too, have had to do this. I, too, walked for almost 40 years through my life as though blinkered. I, too, have had to wake up to the divine presence that walks with me and talks with me. I, too, have had to let go of past mistakes, both those of my own making and those that came about through the intervention of others.

Only we can love ourselves and this life enough to have the guts to begin again with a clean slate, to take up the chance of a new beginning that has been offered to us. Life is a precious thing. Only we can choose to live it. Only we can make the difference it will take to make it work. Only we can put back as much as we have taken out.

The Native Americans knew a lot about life and about living in harmony with God and with the planet. They recognized the importance of balance and of prayer. They bound herbs and tobacco to give back to the planet by way of thanks for all they received. They took nothing from 'Mother Earth' that was not absolutely necessary for their survival. They looked upon 'Father Sky' as the bringer of that life to both Mother Earth and to themselves. They recognized the importance of a circle as a cycle. They learned to honour all things for their own value and importance. They lived in harmony (most of the time) with life. They believed in living life to the full and that all things played their part. They recognized the many cycles life passed through each year, each season. They believed in honouring those who walked before them and they kept their life alive through tradition and through stories. They understood both the powers of word and of thought. They knew a lot that the white man is only now beginning to understand.

But for all civilizations, both past and present, life is the same. We are born of the same source and are made of the same stuff.

(I am I) I made a promise to man that I would live with him if he would live with Me. Through all of time I have kept my promise.

The civilizations of the past have not all gone. They are very much alive. They have left your physical world and you know only their remains, but they are all a part of life as it is today. Many of those souls have made the choice to be born again into other lives, whilst others have made the choice to remain here, as they were, and to experience life from this side.

All life is life, whether it is of the physical or the spiritual. In essence all life is spirit. It is energy in form, in motion. Only man can wake himself up and learn to understand this. I miss him. I want him back. I would like to walk by his side once more, to laugh and to cry and to love with him. Man cannot live for long by himself and neither can I. We need each other to continue. (I am I)

Man has got lost over the course of time. Only he can find his way back home, though he cannot do it alone. But he is not alone. Every living day of his life he will be helped, although the cry must first come from his heart. Not his mind or his mouth. It must come from his very being when he realizes his mistake. And it is just that. He was mistaken.

Only we can live the life we are in. Only we can take it forward into the future. Neither God nor spirit can do it for us. Only we can take this Earth and turn it around once more. I, too, must play my part and this book will play its part too. Alone, we feel small and insignificant. We buckle with wonder as we see the immense tasks ahead. But life will lead us along, one little step at a time, and all we must do is keep up. We must not falter and we must not fall. We will walk with the aid and love of God, with the strength and support of spirit and with the help and the knowledge that they bring. Together we will make a world. Together we will repair what is broken and together we will walk into the future.

CHAPTER TWENTY-ONE

Rebirth

Learning to Live Again

Only we can get our lives back on track. Only we can bring the spring back to our step and the laughter back into our hearts. *(I am I) I must help you. (I am I)*

Now is time for reflection and for thought. Only man can sit down to look at and understand where he is now. There is help wherever he looks. This journey of awakening has not just begun, it always has been going on. For years those who have awoken have tried to reach those who are still asleep. They have written books and songs and plays. They have tried any way they can think of to record their findings in the hope that someday they will filter through to help mankind. Alone, their works seem small. But they are not alone. Today they are binding together more and more to make a blanket of awareness that is reaching out to cover humanity. Together, they tell the truth of a life that really does exist.

A child can only understand through his capacity of awareness. Everything else passes over his head. As adults, we are the same. All these truths have always been right in front of our noses. But we have missed them because we could not see. We did not understand. We did not know.

(I am I) I must help each individual in his own area of understanding to wake up. I must reach out and touch every one of you until you realize I am real. I am here – in the now. I am with you and I am helping you. Do not be fearful or live in guilt. Neither can help. They will only distance you more from the reality that you must now face. You are as a newborn child that is looking for guidance, for instruction. Only you can learn to reconnect to the all that is, to Me and the richness of the past combined with present. The future does not matter. All possible outcomes are always available to man at any one time, like an interactive computer game. The only thing that really matters is the now, and it is here that you will find Me. (I am I)

Only we can make the connections that really matter physically – by ourselves and for ourselves. Every day is a new day, a new beginning. Take each as it comes and do all that you must do. But before that, ask God to lead you. Ask to walk behind him, to be guided by him, instead of walking in front, as you always do. This is your life to live, but to live it well you sometimes need help.

(I am I) I will help you to get back on track, with your feet on the ground and your head in the air. I will help you sort through the rubble and the ashes of your life and I will help seeds take root. Together we will go forward with one foot in front of the other. (I am I)

This book has probably rocked you to your core. It will have touched places that until now you did not realize existed.

(I am I) I will help you through the next few years, but first you must let Me in. I cannot reach you, cannot hear and feel you, when you are racked with pain and guilt and stress. I am love and so are you. It is only in the love mode that we can connect once again. Not the passionate man–woman love, but the joy and happiness

in your heart kind of love – the love that is born of peace and contentment, the love that first made you. (I am I)

Every person, everywhere, began in the same way. We all began with a spark of love and light and physicality.

I must help man to understand both himself and his life better than he does right now. I, too, must make some changes in my approach to life. I, too, have some catching up to do. It is easy to get hung up on the past – even the recent past such as yesterday and the day before. I, too, must stay focused in the now more than in the past or the future. All of life is happening here, in the now. All of life stems from this moment in time. This is all there is. This is all there can be. All of the future begins from this point and all of the past has led to this point. All you will ever be stems from now.

(I am I) I, too, live in the moment. That is the only place I am ever in. All of my life is the sum total of all of yours and when you look at the state of the human world you can see what a mess you are leaving Me in. There is very much left for us to do to rectify the mistakes of the past. This cannot be done in one go, or we would create an imbalance of a different kind, a different order. Instead, everything must be addressed one step at a time, at the exact moment that it occurs. That is the law of cause and effect. To effect a change, to stop an event, is to change its course entirely. This has its benefits, but it also has its downfalls. The only way to ensure correct precision is to instigate everything in the now – the time when it arises. (I am I)

There is an upside to this. It means that in the here and now we have hit rock bottom, and from now, providing we can pull ourselves together, the only way left to travel is up.

(I am I) I second this statement. Providing you are willing to help yourselves, slowly, starting with your own life, then I will stay with you every step of the way. I will show you the best way

forward until you are able once more to go it alone. I will show you, but you must learn to listen, to see and to hear. (I am I)

The journey you are about to begin is a solitary one. But listed at the back of this book are a few of the countless books that can help you in your studies. I will help you find the ones that are best for you at this time.

You are journeying within to find the workings and the essence of your true self and in so doing you will also learn to see others in a different light and understand them better. With understanding comes forgiveness. You will learn to recognize how those before you are stuck. Once upon a time they were as free and as hopeful as you are. They had their hopes and dreams and aspirations too. The world was their oyster, the same as it is for you, but then real life took over. It dulled the light of their inspiration. Don't let your own light flicker and fade into nothingness. Nurture it back to health, back to life. Find your own sense of vitality and wonder once more. Rekindle the zest you used to have for life and relearn to enjoy it.

'Stress' is the word of the moment. Stress overrides all other emotions when we let it and most of us have no idea how to stop it. Once it takes a hold, it is self-perpetuating.

(I am I) Stress is one of the main things that will draw you away from Me; it is one of the things that keeps you locked into exactly where you are. When you are stressed, you are closed to everything else. You have switched to imbalance and overload. Take a deep breath and think of Me. Ask to be given truth and light and balance once more. Ask that all illusion be removed from the situation and ask Me to oversee the problem. Ask it for yourself, 20 times a day if necessary, but ask. I am powerless to help you unless you do.

Don't despair if it doesn't work right away. It may be that there is a further reason nestling somewhere behind the stress, or there might be something else that you are missing. I will always do all I can to sort things out in any way I can. It is in my interest, too, to keep you free of illusion. How can you know which way to go when you only see half the deck of cards? To choose correctly you need to see the whole picture – the truth of the moment you are experiencing. By asking for My help you help to avoid further miscommunication and misconception wherever possible. (I am I)

This life is for you to live. Spirit and God cannot do it for you. Only you have brought yourself to where you are now and only you can lead yourself back.

Over the course of time man has given too much of his own power away. He has left too much to others and to automatic pilot. The time is now right for him to take his own power back, but before he can he must recalibrate and remember how.

At no time in your life will you be left flapping around, wondering what step to take next for the best. When you don't know which way to turn, simply do nothing until you do. Never make a choice out of desperation or impulse. Some of our best choices may have been made this way, but so were some of our worst. Before we leap into the unknown it is better to see where we might land. Life will always allow you to see the full picture, but sometimes you must wait for it to unfold a little further so it can do so. Time must also play its part in the game of life, but in our haste we sometimes forget that.

(I am I) I will always allow you to see the whole picture if you allow Me to. I will always allow you to understand all your options before you make a choice. Life is about taking chances, but it is also important to keep your feet firmly on the ground. To change too much too soon can sometimes leave you without roots. Only you can look at your life and only you can decide how best to pull it together once more. Bridges can be rebuilt between arguing relations, one step at a time, but it is helpful to remember

Me. Ask Me beforehand to help you where help is needed. Ask that old blockages and fences be recycled. Ask that all illusion be removed and ask that the words you and all will need be given to you at the time they are needed. Walk with love and hope in your heart instead of doubt or blame or fear. One small step at a time and a miracle can be achieved.

When you are faced with a mountain, again remember Me. I will hand it to you one stone at a time, so you will be able to deal with it. Ask and it will be given, even if you don't always realize it at the time. (I am I)

Only we can learn to recognize the help and the support that are constantly around us. Those we have loved and lost are never far away. They are rooting for us, helping us to see the truth that is ours to see. They pop in and out to visit us much more than they sometimes could when they were here on Earth. They don't remain with us the whole time, because this is our life to live and they have theirs too, but they do keep a watchful, loving eye on us. Help is always there for us.

(I am I) When a leaflet falls onto your mat at exactly the time you need it, it is I. When you hear a conversation by chance that contains exactly what you need, it is I. When you watch a film or read a magazine and a helpful piece of information jumps out at you, it is I. I will give you whatever you need whenever you need it, but you must stay alert and you must allow time for these things to fall into place. Sometimes it is necessary for you to follow a wrong path to the end before you can move over and make another connection. But everything will lead to something, somewhere. (I am I)

Only we can walk with our eyes and our ears open and expect the unexpected. Once you start to recognize the coincidences that are happening all too frequently, you will attract even more to yourself. Learn to say a mental thank you in acknowledgement of having understood or received them. Learn to remain focused in the moment as often as you can, as miracles can only occur in life's now. If your attention wanders too far you can miss any subtleties that are there.

Life is not a chore for you to carry like a millstone around your neck. It is a voyage of discovery and fun. Not all the time, but for most of it. Let go of your rigid timetable sometimes to allow chance to step in and surprise you.

You are guided and helped nearly every step of the way, but most especially when you falter and appear to fall. Never fear. Keep your mind's arena as clear and as clutter-free as possible. When your mind wants to race, bring it quietly back. Ask that your thoughts be at peace and your mind be still. Ask again and again if necessary, but ask.

There may be times when things just won't leave you alone. The same thoughts may come back or you may find yourself facing again a problem that you thought you had dealt with already. At times such as these you may be missing the point, or perhaps something else needs your attention, maybe a change needs to be made, or something else you have been avoiding. Again, don't worry. Ask for help to understand the problem and then to sort it out. Ask for illusion to be removed. Ask to see only the truth. You may be pleasantly surprised by how quickly and easily you can remove the obstacle. Even an argument that you had been dreading can fluff away into nothing.

If you do find yourself in a tense situation, always speak the truth, but with love and consideration, never with anger. The anger that you produce will always bounce right back to you. It will inflame the situation even further. If to speak will cause discomfort or pain, try to remain calm and say nothing. Wait for a better time or opportunity to come, and be sure that it will.

All of your life stems from you. You are its central pillar. You can make it work or you can mow it down. Only you can take it forward to work in the very best fashion for you.

The things that you need will not always come to you in the form that you were waiting for or in the way that you thought you wanted them to. Life has a way of showing its colours in an unexpected manner, so try to remain open and flexible through each day. Life will unfold before your eyes, but first you must send up your thoughts and allow it to sort itself out. Only thoughts sent with an open loving mind can be heard. The pain and pleas and fears remain with us. They block our way and consequently our actions, and that is why they must be recycled. Otherwise, they will only fester and hinder. They will add negative energy to an already negative situation. Fearful thoughts only send fear into your future. You feed your future with them. Let them go. Send them back to where they can be transformed into something useful. Don't keep them to yourself or pile them onto others. Recycle them instead and allow truth to always shine through.

Life is tricky. Once you begin to be aware of the things that you do that keep you where you are, you will be surprised at how often you do them. You will realize how you have added unconsciously to the situations you found yourself in and how often you thought or blamed it on others.

Once you start to help yourself, you will start to help those you love, not in monetary or material form, but in the giving of your own essence, your own truths.

You will stop feeding your friends illusions and you will help them to step out of their chains. Love and light will always win through. Light is infinitely more powerful than darkness, but the darkness will keep you there until you learn to let it go, until you learn to hand it up to your God, your creator. If this is too difficult at first, pass it up to someone you know in spirit, someone you are more comfortable with. They will know what to do to pass it on on your behalf, but the point is that you must learn to pass it upwards, not outwards to your present friends or relations.

Only you can do these things to help yourself onto a surer, happier path. Books you will read after this will show you other ways in which to help yourself further. They will click other things back into a more usable order. They will show you other truths that will help you along your way, perhaps on a more physical level.

No change can be instant. Any change often takes time, patience and practice. Be patient with yourself. Don't be too quick to judge. Wait for the truth to come to light as often as you are able. Every person is in the same boat you are. They, too, are hoping for their own life to fit as it should. They, too, are searching for their missing link. They, too, are looking to find peace and love and contentment on a permanent level. They, too, are searching for their guiding star, so be gentle with them. If a truth needs to be spoken, say it with love and with kindness. Ask beforehand that the words be given to you – to give to them, and ask that they be received in the manner they should. Ask again that illusion be recycled and ask after the event, regardless of its outcome, for it to now be handled by God. Ask and let it go. Get on with the day in hand. Only we can do this for ourselves and for each other.

(I am I) Ask and it will be given. Ask in love and it will be done, always. I am your father, your provider, your living God. I am not vengeful, but always loving. I am tolerant and patient. I will wait for you until you are ready to accept Me back into your life, until you are ready to believe that I exist. I will always stand quietly by your side, whether you believe it or not, but if you are willing to give Me a try, you will see the proof for yourself. It will not take faith any more, because you will know beyond doubt. I will be fact. (I am I)

Only we can push past the bouts of depression that can overwhelm us when we least expect them to. I, too, have been in this place and it can still catch me out even now. It can be hard to remain uplifted and positive when all that's stretched ahead of you is doom and gloom. At these times you must accept the inevitable and hope that its storm will pass as quickly and quietly as possible. Keep your head down and keep yourself small in all that you do until it is safe to venture out once more. Remember that life will ebb and flow, like the tides of the sea. Sometimes it will be rough and sometimes rougher still, but at other times not a ripple will be seen.

Life must be this way for a reason. It has a beat all of its own, though most of the time it is hard to detect. Everything vibrates at its own frequency. All the events we experience have their time and their place in our life-frame. Sometimes in our darkest times an unexpected glimmer of hope will emerge to surprise us. That, too, is the nature of life.

We don't always go with the ebb and flow of life. Because we don't really like change, we unconsciously try to keep things exactly as they are, even when we can see that change is necessary. I, too, am guilty of this. I, too, must become more flexible and open to the mysteries of life. I, too, must learn to dance with the beat of the time I am in and to not get too bogged down in the now.

Man has a tendency to expect what he expects when he expects it. He is altogether too impatient. He wants everything yesterday, even when that's not possible, and he will go out of his way to obtain it. Life cannot always be like that. Nothing can happen before it is destined to be. There is no use pushing harder to get there first. Man is too impatient for his own good. He sails through the good times without even noticing and he runs riot in the bad.

I, too, must remain more consistent within myself. I should take more in my stride than I do. I find it too easy to panic when things get a little wobbly for a time. I jump to the conclusion that I must be doing something wrong, even when it is clear that I am not. I find it too easy to take the blame onto myself. But then again, we should not blame others either. They are on the opposite side of the same coin, that's all. At times like these all we can do is recycle once more and sit tight until the storm has sailed past.

Only we can do these things for ourselves, but we must first recognize that we need to. Over the next few days and weeks you will begin to notice when you start to beat yourself down, or perhaps allow others instead. The point is that this will help no one. Negativity will only attract more negativity and it will make you feel worse. Hand it up to those who know what to do with it on your behalf. Hand it up and then take a breather. Carry on with your day and allow life to sort itself out. Providing you don't do anything you shouldn't, things should settle down once more to an acceptable level.

Only we can sort our daily life into a better working order. Only we can weed each day until life again starts to bloom.

(I am I) The day you are in is the offering you will leave in your wake. Use it wisely. Treasure all things that you do as though

they will be your last. Tie up your loose ends and never leave for tomorrow what you can do today. When tomorrow comes it will dance to a whole new beat of its own. And who knows, you might even smile and be happy. (I am I)

The place you are in now is born of the sum of your past. The responsibilities you have you probably chose along the way. Stand by your obligations whenever you can, but don't stoop to carry more than your load too often. If you are a doer, make sure that others are not letting you do their share as well. I, too, used to do more than I was supposed to, mostly because I wanted to at first. It pleased me to be that way. But then I found the balance could shift and others would expect it automatically. The balance of life should be fair and just at all times. If you are doing too much, then you can be robbing others of the experience of doing enough. Too much in either direction will cause an imbalance somewhere. I, too, had to learn this and it was no easy task, especially if it's difficult to speak your truth.

(I am I) Life will come to you in the way you most expect. So expect nothing and let it take its own course. Do what you have to do at the time you are supposed to do it and leave the rest to us. (I am I)

Only you can make the adjustments that will leave you free to be who you want to be. Only you can move beyond the normal constraints that you would operate within. No one else can take your hand. The journey into the self can be a solitary one, but if you remain in truth and light, then you will never regret another day that you live. Life itself will appear too short, too fleeting, for you to achieve all that you wish to achieve. A whole lifetime just won't be long enough.

The world *can* be saved and we are the only ones who can do it, one small step by one small step at a time.

We can move mountains if we wish to, but we must start from within. Only within will we be able to clear out our rubbish and clutter, and only then can we begin to move forward as we would like.

Only man can save himself because man is in the driving seat. He must learn to walk once more in the sun. He must move away from the stress that engulfs him and he must find his own inner peace.

(I am I) I will help him if he so wishes. I will lead him on in the way that is best for him. Each journey is an individual affair. Children of the same family are all on their own individual journeys. They are all striving to find their own life and their own way back home. (I am I)

Only we can make our own way back home, back to the peace that resides in our mind and in our heart. Only we can take our turmoil and stress and turn it around. It is up to us to pull ourselves together, to control the thoughts that we think and to step out of the mundane that we have accepted as our lot. Life is too precious to allow it to dwindle recklessly away as we play the waiting game. Don't let your days drift into nothingness. Take hold of each one as a gift, as a gem, and treasure it for all its worth. You will never get it back once it's gone. Once it's gone, it's gone forever.

Life is not always easy. Neither should it always be hard. If your life is difficult most of the time, then you are probably missing the triggers that would lift you out of where you are. Begin to notice what you do to unconsciously keep yourself there. Begin to notice how others keep you there as well. *Families and How to Survive Them* is an excellent book that could help you gain a better perspective. Written by John Cleese and Robin Skynner, it highlights many things that we often take for granted and is written in an easy-to-read conversational format. It may help many things slot into place for you.

We are lucky today in that when we realize a problem exists, the tools are there to help us. We can talk to counsellors and go to professional people for advice if we want to, but if not, a mountain of information and help is available in book form. If you are not a book reader, then you might prefer to listen to books on tape or CD in 'talking books' format. Your local library should have them available. If this does not appeal to you either, you will just have to keep your wits about you and your ears open. You will stumble across all sorts of things at precisely the time that you need them. Everything is available to us in the form that we need it at the time that we need it, but we have to remain open and in the moment to notice.

I, too, have been on this route. I read a dozen books in as many months once I began. I read what I was directed to read, and this came from my intuition. You, too, will be led if you allow yourself to be. Notice what grabs your attention. Begin to be aware of the coincidences that thread and occur quite naturally in your life and follow them through when you can. A whole new world is waiting for you to notice that it's there. Nothing happens without a reason, so that means that every little thing that happens does so for a purpose. Relax a little and enjoy the ride. Notice what circumstance and life are trying to tell you, and if you have no use for it now, place it in your memory banks for later, when you can link it together with something else.

(I am I) I will help you go forward from this moment on if you ask Me to. I will lead you in a way that's loud and clear, but you must help Me. I can only use the tools that are available to Me at the time, so you must remain vigilant, open and aware. If you are not sure, then wait until you are. Ask Me to recycle the rubbish until you are left with the truth. If a thought is persistent, examine it. Find out what it's trying to tell you. If it leads you on, follow it. If

it appears negative, examine it too and find out why it's bothering you. Look to understand what it relates to. It might even be your ego that is panicking unnecessarily. There is a part of you that does not like change very much. That part served its purpose in your early youth, because it stopped you from going too far too fast. It stopped you from hurting yourself by keeping you within certain boundaries and limitations. Now this part of you might start to panic and might throw you off course. It wants to stay in the familiar. It tries to bring you back to where you were, because then it knows, or thinks, that you will be safe, but it is wrong – it is this that has held you back. It is the ego that is responsible for your unhappiness. Learn to make your own judgements. Don't just slip into automatic once more. Your ego will scream and shout at you like a spoiled little child, but learn to see beyond it. Ask that its illusions be recycled and ask for the light to shine through. (I am I)

Keep your head up and remain balanced. Learn as much as you can about yourself and go beyond the constraints that would normally hold you back. Not your personal responsibilities, they are another matter, but your own internal doubts and fears. Don't jump recklessly into the unknown, but go forward slowly and surely into your future as it presents itself.

(I am I) All time stems from this time, from the time that you are in now. Look after this time and the rest will surely fall into place. It may be bumpy for a while or life may surprise you and be incredibly smooth, but it will be all that it needs to be as it takes you on with your life. (I am I)

You are at the beginning of your life, at the start of your next phase. Look at it and protect it as you would a newborn child. You will be that child for a while. You might feel vulnerable and unsure as the armour plating you previously surrounded yourself with slips away. But don't begin to worry and don't get bored with the task in hand. Look at the strengths that you have and learn how to use them.

(I am I) All you are, all you have done and all you have been will have left you with lessons and strengths that are unique to you. Learn to recognize your good points and allow the rest to fall away. It will not happen overnight, but it will happen if you let it. Notice the love that sits quietly by and accept it, as you should. You may become tearful and emotional for a while. This, too, must play its part. It is a symptom of the new that's coming from the old. Don't worry. It will pass. It may take a while, but it is just a stage. It is a little of what needs to come out from your past. It is a little of what you have kept locked away. It is a part of you that simply needs to 'be' for a while. Nurture that part and understand it as necessary. Learn to let yourself be all that you need to be, but learn to let yourself live. (I am I)

Only we can open the doors that we have kept locked against the world, and even against ourselves. Some were banged shut so early in childhood that we don't even remember they exist. Learn to be patient with the world and with yourself. No one means to harm you. They, too, are probably in the same boat you are. They, too, are just trying to live in the best way that they know how. They, too, are searching for their own happy-ever-after ending and they are probably as unaware of their actions as you were. They will wake up when the time is right for them to do so, but until then just let it go and concentrate on your own actions, on your own responses.

(I am I) Ask Me and I will transform the situation into the truth. I will allow the truth to shine through when it should. I will be your strength and your armour. I will be your guide. (I am I)

Man is at the birth of a new dawn. That is why Nostradamus could not see beyond this point. That is why he signalled the end of the world. It is the end of the old and the birth of the new.

(I am I) Once again I must second this statement. Man is very much on the threshold of a new understanding – of a new wave of life. (I am I)

The world as we know it had to get to this point. It had to exhaust its limitations in order to go past them. Just as a boil must achieve its full head before it can be lanced, so the trials and tribulations of man had to reach a certain point of crescendo.

Only we can take life forward now, to the next stage, the next phase. We made the pledge to do just this before we came back. All we have been through and all we now know have been vital parts in making the connections we need to make. The place we have reached in our life is exactly where we need to be in order to go forward. We cannot be who we are until we are certain of who we are not and as a race we are quickly coming to that point. The path of individuality is not always as clear-cut as we would like it to be. There are times when we can sail smoothly and freely with the wind and then there are other times when everything seems to go incredibly wrong. These are the seasonal challenges of life. These are things we have to work with and through. Only we can live through them, but when we understand the reasons behind them it is unlikely that they will trouble us further. Once we have learned a lesson we learn how not to let it happen again.

Only we can go forward as we were always intended to do. Take this time as a breath of fresh air. Do all that you are required to do, but use your free time as a learning starting point that will guide you forward onto a much surer path. Take this time as a gift, a chance to take stock, as the Earth does in the winter months. Make yourself small and let the dust settle. Allow this time to do some healing of its own. Begin to take notice of the things that surround you, the patterns that are most prominent in your life and your family. Use your free time to read and to digest what you are learning. Take it slowly and be kind to yourself in the meantime. Life will always throw challenges at you, especially when you least expect it to. What matters most is the way you then handle both yourself and the situations you are in.

As already mentioned, books are available to help you understand the changes that will be occurring both within and without yourself right now. One that helped me was called *The I Ching or Book of Changes* by Brian Browne Walker. The *I Ching* is an ancient Chinese book of divination. Treat it with respect and you will be linked with a helping guide that will tune itself in to you. This is not a game. It is a very real tool that will link you to spirit. You will receive the advice that you need. Learn to use what it is telling you, but remember, it is only a tool, a guide. You must do the hard work for yourself, but with a guiding hand it will be easier than fumbling around in the dark.

The way you choose to go forward is your own affair. I, too, have been here and have thankfully come out of the other side, but who knows for how long? Knowledge and understanding do not make you immune to life. They merely help you walk through times of turmoil and stress more easily than you did before. They help you to recognize the light at the end of the tunnel.

Only we can work through the issues that need to be addressed, but each time we do, we grow a little stronger, a little surer of the path we should follow.

(I am I) I am by your side to experience with you all that you do. Learn to recognize this. Learn to trust Me as you used to trust yourself. Until now you have done all that you thought you wanted, all that you thought would bring you happiness and love, but has it? Is where you are where you would like to be? (I am I)

Only you can learn what the missing pieces are in your life. Books and other information will help, but only you can fit the pieces of your own puzzle together. And that is exactly what this is all about. It is a coming together of all the pieces of your life that are useful to you. It is a throwing away of old worn-out habits and behaviour patterns that no longer serve in the way that they should.

During infancy, depending on our surroundings and the quality of interaction that was available to us, we built up an unconscious picture of life. Some of it we used to guide ourselves through our early years, but some of it was laid aside as building foundations for a later date. In adulthood it is necessary to draw upon those foundations. Problems arise when we have mislaid those stones due to wrong information or wrong interpretation of what was happening in our infancy. A computer needs all its programming to be in order so that it may call upon what it needs at the appropriate time. It must have everything labelled correctly and in a specific sequence. And we are no different. We, too, must call upon past experiences at a certain times in our life and use them as a basis to go forward. If we misinterpreted or misjudged things in our early years, then the information we have to draw upon will be flawed. It will not serve us as it should. We of course have no idea this is going on. We don't even know that a problem exists. Our life is just our life to us, and that is all there is to it. But just as a computer can be upgraded from time to time, so can we. We are the most brilliant invention that nature ever put breath into. How can we be so cocky as to believe that we are perfect? That we know it all?

We check our cars and motorized engines for flaws on a regular basis. We don't expect them to run forever without any thought or update to their mechanics and technology. Over the past 100 years, just look at how far they have come. We are magnificent in our inventions, yet when do we ever pay even a fraction of such time and attention to ourselves? Our bodies and our looks, yes, but otherwise, until a problem surfaces, we carry on pretty much as generation upon generation before. Yet the driving force pushing us is internal – it's our innermost workings, our thoughts and our mind, the thoughts we have put together over the course of the lifetime we have been here. Without reassessment, how can we ever hope to get over the last few hurdles of life when we don't even know they exist?

Man has reached a state where he needs to update his outlook and his learning. He has gone as far as he can by himself. He has surpassed all expectation – yet he also feels lost and alone. It is now time to put everything about him into some kind of balance and order.

(I am I) I have stood by man through all of his life. I have been witness to all of his ups and especially his downs. Until he turns to Me, even now, I cannot help him. Because of free will, I am bound to watch on and wait. But from the first word he utters in My direction I will help him. I will pick him up from his pain and his sadness and I will set him gently back on his feet. I will be as a parent that looks out for his infant. I will be that parent and man will be My child. (I am I)

Only you can help this to occur. Only you can open a window in your mind to allow God to step in. Massive belief is not an issue. The first tiny inkling of a spark from you will bring the light forward and all the proof that you need will come flooding to your door. You just have to be aware of it. Notice the difference when you actually ask for help. Be sensible about it, but notice the difference all the same.

You have learned to lock yourself up so well that the armour you began to place about yourself during infancy may now have grown as thick as the thickest steel. Until you let God in, it will remain impregnable. This may have helped to guard you when you thought it was necessary, but it has also stopped much of the love you've craved and wanted from filtering in. Now it is time to begin to break open those layers. Under the protection and energy of God and with your adult discrimination abilities, it is safe to finally emerge, to come out into the light and full bloom. This is what your life has always been about. This is the time of your fruition.

Trust in yourself. You have learned your lessons well. Right from wrong is your forte. Pick up the scattered pieces of your life and move forward to a happier place. All the help you need is right beside you – within you. You must simply recognize it and help it flow.

Chapter Twenty-Two

Plugging Back into the Mainframe

(I am I) I am the light. I am the love. I am the lantern that will guide you. (I am I)

Only man knows all there is to know about himself and the path he has trod. He can recall at will practically all of his life as though it were only yesterday. The mind and its memories are not bound by time, or by lock or key.

(I am I) I am the keeper of these records. All that you have ever achieved is kept in order by Me. I am the conscious mind that holds the blueprint of the whole of this planet. I know all there is to know about all that has been, but the future is yet but a dream. (I am I)

All that is yet to be is contained each day in the thoughts of man. All that ever was was first a thought, an idea, that was born into materialization by the actions of mankind. Even the thoughts that he discarded have played their part, and because of this the possibilities of the future are endless.

The thoughts we generate hold more power than we can ever imagine. It is not by chance that the things we need turn up. It is not chance that puts them there but the conscious and unconscious thoughts we generate ten to the dozen. Our thoughts are like radar signals that send out words of instruction to the realms of spirit. Just as there are hundreds of workers here, performing their daily tasks on all levels, so there are even more in spirit. When we think of something we need, that thought is received by someone somewhere, who then tries to put it into being.

Now you can see the problems of always changing your mind. Because we are usually ahead of ourselves in our daily thoughts, by the time the things we want are placed in our path, we have usually changed our mind. We have already moved on to the next project by the time the cavalry has arrived. It is our fault, not the fault of God or of spirit. It is because we are living in the future more than we are living in the now, the present. We have left the now – once again – on automatic.

Only we can bring ourselves back to the present, not only in our actions but in the thoughts that we think as well. I, too, have to catch myself out when my attention wanders from place to place. I, too, must remain more focused than I do. The time that is most important to our life is always the time we are experiencing right now. Yet our attention is hardly ever fully there. I, too, have a dozen things that I must think about at any one time and it is not always easy to remain fully in tune with the task in hand. It is not easy, but we should at least try our best. For a start it will help us finish our tasks more quickly and easily than we would otherwise do, but it also has an added benefit: energy flows where thought goes, so when we remain fully focused, we stop wasting our own precious energy.

Only we can curb our thoughts. Only we can come back to the now. Only we can slow our life back down to a walking pace. The world we are all part of is getting faster and faster in every way. This can have its benefits, but it more often has none. And we are creating a generation of children who will come to expect life to be that way. They will think that this is how life is and should be. They, too, will join that 'instant' bandwagon when it is time for them to take this world forward. They will come to believe that speed is of the essence – the faster, the better.

I, too, have played my part in an illusion of this kind. I, too, was on that treadmill, that conveyor belt, and I, too, have had to recognize that it was time to get off, to come back properly to Earth and to reality. The problem is that we are living too much in the expectation of tomorrow. We are living too far into a projected illusion of the future.

Even our wages are spent before they come. We don't buy just what we need, we buy things that we might use if... Our homes are cluttered to the brim with knick-knacks and goodies that have caught our eye. Our cupboards and drawers are bursting. The shops are full from wall to wall with things that they hope we will want and in the meantime production lines can hardly keep pace as they make more and more for a projected market. The whole of our economy is about making, buying and using products that we don't really need. We are stuck in a loop that is not only drowning our resources, but our energy as well. We work, we spend, we worry and we buy. We work some more, spend some more, worry some more and buy even more.

We are being asked to wake up, not only to ourselves but also to the part we play in the state of the world. We are creating children who really believe that life is the way they see it. The people of the developing world work hard. They use their bare hands every waking day to produce enough products to earn a few pence. They live on bare necessities. This is not right – nor is it wrong. It is simply the way their world is. In the Middle East children have been taught they must fight. They fight for their very survival. It is as natural to them as the taking of air into their lungs. It is the way they have grown accustomed to be. In the West we work hard to get up the social ladder. We have become driven by material success. The world has become too segregated – too black and white. Only we can create a better balance. But the changes that will make the most difference must start from within before they can spread without.

Only we can look at our life, our surroundings and our thinking. Yes, it is necessary to live, and it is nice to live well if we can. But once we reach that point, enough should be enough. Yet it is very hard for us to recognize this when the majority of society does not. We could have our heart's desire granted by a fairy and still we would want more. We have forgotten to check whether our greatest goals and desires have been met.

This is not all doom and gloom. This is more about waking up to the realities of life. Is it necessary to spend hundreds and thousands of pounds on all the things that we do?

(I am I) I must second that. (I am I)

We should curb our spending in order to work less and enjoy life more. The simple things that matter most often go unnoticed each day, as we carry on, locked tightly into a world of our making, of wanting bigger, better and faster than ever before. We are trapped by our own wants and behaviour.

Just for a while, try to step off the merry-go-round. Try to see behind your actions and why you do what you do. Think twice about things you usually would do automatically. Try to work out if you really need what you are going to buy or if it is a 'feel-good' item, or whether, like me and so many others, you have a heart that far exceeds the limitations of your purse or bank account. Most of us spend far too much trying to make others feel happier. We give away far more than we are able to realistically afford, so we must work harder in the meantime to catch up. Working harder means producing more products and producing more products means that there will be more to sell, therefore more to buy. More to buy means more to spend and more to spend means more hard work. Once more we can see how easily we can be caught in this loop. The only way to stop is to get off the bandwagon. So, curb your own actions.

(I am I) I, too, second this once more. The only way forward is to slow everything down and take life back to a slower, healthier pace that will have a knock-on effect for us all. (I am I)

But even this will have its problems. We will still have a surplus of products floating around. We will still have to look at environmental and social issues.

To change anything too quickly will cause and create panic, and panic in any way is disruptive. It only serves to take things to the opposite extreme. So any process of change must be slow and sure.

Your life is your own affair. The way you live it and what you choose to do with it are equally your own affair. The thing we must do now is retrace our steps. We must put ourselves into a better working order. Not outwardly, but inwardly. Only we can take the life we live and make it worth its weight in gold. We can learn to live in a better frame of mind for the remainder of the time-frame we have left.

In times gone by man believed that the world was flat. Then he learned it was round. He thought he was alone and would stand before God or the Devil, depending on where he ended up. But he will not. He is always with his maker, as his maker is with him. There has never been a separation. Indeed, there never could be. God is us – all combined. He is all that we can see and equally all we cannot. God is as much alive and living as we are. He is here in the now – everywhere, every day. Only we ourselves thought he was not. We were mistaken, misled by the teachings and writings of other men. God is lonely and wants us back. He feels our separation as a parent feels that loses a child, as a brother feels that loses his brother. He feels our sadness and our fear, but until we reach out to touch him he is powerless to help. It is we who must remake our connection. God's has always been there.

Only we can love ourselves enough to come back on track with life and all that we are. We are like children that have forgotten their heritage. All our life we have been searching to find out who and where and what we are and where we belong, but we have only had half a picture to do it with. How could we ever believe when we only had half of the facts and a lot of interpretation besides? But our God, our creator, is here. He always was – and is only – in the present here and now.

(I am I) These words are true. If you never believe another word, then believe this: I am here. I am with you and I always will be. (I am I)

Only man can rediscover his connection to the divine source. This is not fairy tale, it is fact. All through the ages, man has always known there was more to himself than was physically obvious, more than was outwardly apparent.

(I am I) I am made manifest in all things, in all of life, but most especially in man. I live life with him and through him; all that he experiences he does with Me and through Me. We are bound together as the sky meets the sea. There is no split. No dividing

line. All things are a part of the whole, and the whole is a part of all things. All that we are, we are together, forever. (I am I)

Man can no more distance himself from God than he can from the Earth of which he is part.

(I am I) Neither can he distance himself from any part of himself – the good or the bad, the past or the present. He cannot dismiss a single part of his life, but he can understand the mistakes he has made. He can allow them to be recycled so that he does not carry them about with him forever. Each new day is just that – a new day to live and experience in a better way. (I am I)

All of the past, in whatever form it has appeared, has led us to this moment in time. Without one single thing we would not be where we are now. Not everything has been for the best – in fact, many things could have been avoided if we had understood our connection to life a little sooner – but one thing is certain: we cannot turn back the clock. We can only go forward, one tick at a time.

Only we can make better decisions. The choices are ours. When we are born we are given free choice. We obtain experiences in the manner and form that we can. Next we go out into the world and we live. We draw upon our past and hope it will take us forward as it should. We make a life for ourselves through our own decisions. We experience all that we do because we want to. We do the things we would love to do at the time we would love to do them. We live life by our own standards, our own beliefs and selections. Yes, we interact with others along the way, and they, too, have an influence upon us. We grow and we change, we change and we grow. We live and evolve through our own life's interaction and the attraction of cause and effect. This is the very nature of free will. We are the masters of our universe, of our little corner of the world. We choose how we will use it and what we will do with it. We choose all that we do out of free will. We are the sum total of all we have ever been, of all we have said, done and thought. Now it is time to take stock, to reassess, to change direction if necessary, but to audit our life just the same.

It is time to look honestly at the person you are and the life that you live. Ask yourself some soul-searching questions. Only you can update your own program. Only you can realign the parts that you no longer want or need. You alone can take your life forward from here. By going within you can learn what makes you function and what is your main driving force. Only you can decide what it is that you are searching for. Only you can know what matters to you. When you do you can begin to see a different picture unfolding. You will see deeper reasons behind many of the things that you did. None of us are angels. We are not meant to be at this stage. We are all here at different levels of unfolding. We are here to learn and to grow in a personal, spiritual way. Not a 'Praise the Lord' spiritual way, although that may come as a natural progression of our self-discoveries, but by 'spiritual' I mean the wellbeing and happiness of the soul, of the self. Of that part of you that is you.

You are not your arm, or your leg, or both legs. These are limbs. Without them you would be incapacitated, but you would still be you. There would be adjustments to be made on every level, but the essence of you would still be you. That is your spiritual self. That is the part that is energy. It is the blueprint of who and what you are. It is this part that merely lives within your physical body, as you would use a car to drive yourself about. Your body is just the vehicle that will carry you through this life. It gives you a physical experience in a physical world, a world made of matter. It helps you to experience life in a physical way. But it is no more to you than that. It never was and it never will be. It is biodegradable. It is supposed to function for the whole of your life, then return in the form of dust or smoke back to Earth once again. But the part of you that is you will always be you. It can never die. It is a part of life that is eternal. It is that part of you that can laugh and cry and think and know and be. It is all and everything that is you. You are spirit. You are energy in motion. You have love as your essence, as your core. You are you.

Only you can wake up to yourself, and once you do, you will have a clearer understanding of where you are going, of where you have been and of what you have learned.

(I am I) I must say that all these things are true. They always have been. The problem has been that words and misunderstandings have got in the way. (I am I)

Throughout the ages there have always been some who have woken before others, though the majority has not woken up at all. Depending on the understanding in their time-frame, those who awoke tried to portray the truths that they found and were a part of, but words are too limiting. They do not always correctly express what we are trying to say. First we are limited by our own choice of them and even when a picture is correctly portrayed, understanding depends on the receptivity of the receiver. We can only take in the information that we can relate to; the rest falls to the ground like waste. Through the years, many have tried to tell us these truths, but we were not ready. We did not hear and we did not understand. We took the words that we heard and shaped them as best we could. We painted our own picture, with our limited understanding and beliefs. We led ourselves a merry dance.

Yet the truth will always be the truth, whether we understand it, or believe it, or not. Nothing can change it. Truth cannot alter. It is simply the truth. It is just what it is and what it always will be.

(I am I) I am the truth and the light. Before the world (however science may explain it), there was only darkness. There was only space, as you know space to be. There came a change, an alteration to the conditions that were, and over time, over hundreds of millions of years, the Earth was born. Then, over hundreds of millions more years, the Earth became as it is today. I am that Earth. I am the essence of this living, breathing, rotating planet, just as you are. All of life must move, must rotate and must grow. Nothing is ever stagnant, or it would be dead. All of life has a pulse of its own and, combined, we make up this planet.

It is not necessary for man to know the whole picture. It is not necessary for man to understand all things as I do, but it is necessary that he understands enough to know the nature of his connection to the world. He must have a clearer picture than perhaps he does now. When a child feels wanted, he feels loved and connected. Man needs to feel wanted, needed and necessary to this life. He has searched for his whole life to belong on a deeper level, somewhere, to someone, for something.

The nature of this Earth is that all things seem to live and die, live and die. Man has thought he was the same. He has lost his zest for life because of these thoughts. He sees himself as disposable, as insignificant. But by his very nature he is not either of these things. His existence could not be more vital than it is. He is the caretaker of this planet, this Earth upon which he lives. He is a living, breathing part of this Earth and all he does will leave its mark somewhere, for someone, on something, for the future and for all of eternity. The planet upon which he lives will be his home again. He will most definitely come back and he will choose to do so. That is why it is important for him now to pull himself together. It is time for him to clean up his act and to live in such a way that he can be proud to say, 'That was my life. That was the part that I played in shaping this world.'

Man holds more power in his thoughts than he does in the whole of his physical body. He is like Me. He is a chip off the old block. He could perform miracles, if he could but realize it. He can be happy and content for all eternity, but first he must learn to live his own life in the best way that he can. He must first master his own inner world – the world that makes him tick. Only man can do this for the love of this life, for his own self, for his family and for the planet that he is a part of.

Man is the instigator of all that he sees around him. He alone has shaped his past and he too will shape his future. Life for him can be all that he wants it to be. He can bow his head and let life lead him, or he can stand tall and grow under his own hand. He can make the rest of his life a happy one or he can stumble along in the dark. Life for us all can be anything we choose it to be, but the point is that we can choose. From now until the end of our days we can choose. We can walk alone as we believe we always have, or we can walk with our creator. I am only a thought away from you. (I am I)

Only you can choose where you will go from here. The books listed at the back of this book are only a few of the tools available to help you start your journey. (I am I) I will help you in all you undertake. I will help you. (I am I)

Take some time out of the rat race. Maintain your commitments and responsibilities, but use your free time to collect your thoughts together.

(I am I) I will help you again, but you must allow yourself to ask. It does not matter if you feel silly or strange. Confidence will come with time and practice. I can hear the smallest whisper of sincerity and love. I will come wherever I am invited. There are no restrictions, no limitations to My love. I have waited your whole life long for you to need Me, to recognize My presence intertwined with your own. There is nothing you have done that I will not see through, that I will not help you overcome. (I am I)

Only you stand in your own way – you and your thoughts of doubt and of fear, your thoughts of guilt and of failure. Do not be afraid that you will be judged. How can you be blamed for the things you did when you did them under false guidance and belief? The time is right for you to awaken. Here and now is the only thing that matters. Do not allow yourself to be bound by the past any longer. It is over. Take this day you are in and live it for all you are worth; use it in a way you can be proud of. Do this for yourself, do it for those you love. Only you can live it, so live it!

Only you can put the spring back into your step. But you will not be alone in your efforts, even when you think you are. Never again will you be caught up in the chains that held you before.

(I am I) Give all your fears and doubts and pain over to Me. I will recycle them. I will give you back only what you will need to work with. I will lift your burdens and your spirit. (I am I)

The rest of your life can be a joy to you, but first you must learn to walk once again. You must unlearn some of your old thought patterns and learn some truer ones.

(I am I) The life you have lived until now was through your free will alone. Now I will be your crutch, your support and your strength. When you have any doubt or fear at all, just call Me. Make yourself small and let the moment come back into truth. Allow all illusion to fall away. (I am I)

Only do what you need to do in the moment you are in.

(I am I) I will lead you one step at a time and I will only ever be one step away from you. Ask Me to be there and I will. (I am I)

With this help, we can pull ourselves together once more and wake up to the world that really matters.

(I am I) There will always be those who think you are crazy. Don't listen. Ask Me to shield you. There will always be pain and

violence and sadness. Ask that I may help the situation. Send Me
where you think I am needed. There will always be problems and
obstacles to overcome, of varying degrees. Ask Me to help you
through them. Don't skirt them any more. Face them as full-on as
you should and ask to be helped every step of the way. Your life
will turn around, in some ways instantly, overnight, and in others
more slowly. (I am I)

Wherever you are right now is exactly the place you should be in at this time. However bad your troubles, it has taken you your lifetime to get to this point. Therefore it is only natural that it will take a little time and effort to pull you out. Miracles can happen and regularly do, but they can only operate within the laws of the moment.

(I am I) I will help you through anything, but don't be too
closed in your thinking. Help comes in many shapes and guises.
Sometimes the way is clear, sometimes it is not. Sometimes we
have to travel the distance of a problem before it can be put to rest.
But if you ask for help, don't think you have not been heard, and
never think you are on your own. At all times I will be there. (I am I)

Life cannot stop just because you want or need it to, but a chain of harsh events can be softened with a bit of extra help. Negativity and illusion can be removed by recycling and truth. Light and energy will be your shield at those times. When you ask for help, you will be helped, but it is important that you help yourself as well.

At such times, it is important to make yourself small deep inside. Mentally curl yourself up and still your thoughts. Think of spirit and ask them to recycle all that should not be there. Don't allow yourself to be afraid or your thoughts to wander. Remain completely focused on the task you are doing or on the events that are happening around you.

You may feel a little strange, as though you are watching all the happenings through a window. Know that it is spirit protecting, shielding and enwrapping you in energy. You may feel disconnected. Again, don't worry. Remain small and in the truth of the moment you are in. From this time on spirit will be with you and you will know it.

Man is his own worst enemy. He thinks he can get away with a little bit of this and a little bit of that. He thinks that as long as no one is watching he can do whatever he wants, but he is wrong. There is no force towering over his actions, but there is the energy of the self, and it is this that attracts all things and all things cling to. It is this that mirrors man's true thoughts and words and deeds. This energy is his soul. It is his blueprint. Every little thing he does is amplified on this level. It produces either a negative or a positive reaction and in turn will add to his feelings of power or negativity.

So, as you clear more and more of the rubbish that has accumulated on your path, you will find you can get away with less and less. It will not be that others will look at you and notice, but more that you will become more and more uneasy with yourself when you do things that you know you ought not. This is your spirit self prodding you. It is your conscience and it will become stronger as you progress on your journey. You will not necessarily become good for goodness' sake but because you will feel uncomfortable when you don't. The little things you do wrong will prey on your mind like neon signals until you put them right once more. It may be that no one else will know, but you definitely will. Peace can only stem from peace and when you disturb it, you will know.

There are no eternal rules of right or wrong doing. There is only what is. Each person is equipped with the facility to judge for themselves. However, moral and social rules are a good starting point. They give us limitations that we can operate within, but we are also programmed with a finer judgement. When we do things that we really know we should not, we feel it on some other level within ourselves. Yes we can be, and often are, hardened to these feelings. We can choose to ignore our better judgement and hope that all will be well in spite of our actions, and often it is. Often we can get away with all sorts of things, but do we really? The answer is that we do not. Everything remains visible in our blueprint. The laws of cause and effect always come into play somewhere. All that we do is given back to us in one way or another. The form it takes might be completely unrecognizable, but we will always reap what we sow eventually, if not in this life, then the next. We can get away with nothing, so the sooner we realize this fact the better it will be for us all.

So often we set ourselves up as the judge and jury of other people, yet we forget to monitor so closely our own actions – our own thoughts and words. Very often we distribute nothing but negativity, even to our friends. How often do we backchat and re-enact scenes in our mind? How often do we replay events that have occurred and wish we had said this or done that? Little do we realize that we are simply making the whole matter worse. We are heaping negativity onto an already negative situation when in reality we should just recycle the whole thing.

We are as much to blame for the downs in our life as the people who inflicted them upon us. We are as much responsible for the state of the world as those whose actions appall us. We are adding to the state of world affairs without even realizing it, and this is not a good situation to be in. Yet how can we stop before we are aware of it? How can we break a habit that we do not even know exists? The answer is one step at a time. And it all begins within us.

Life is ours for the taking, but the way each of us conducts that life has a major effect on our corner of the world.

(I am I) I will help you understand what you do. I will help you see how you add to your own pain and heartache. Then I will help you stop. I will help you up and out of your rut until you can run again once more. I will hold your hand until you can go it alone. (I am I)

Only you can ever take the next step forward in your life, but first you must learn how you should do it. Once again the *I Ching* would be a great tool.

(I am I) I will help you recognize when to move forward and when to be still, when to be small and when to stand tall. Only you can learn these things for yourself with My help. (I am I)

Life will help you and work with you when you let it, but first you must remember how. You must learn to read the signals and signposts that surround you, whilst keeping your feet firmly on the ground. You alone can do this for yourself, by remaining utterly and completely in the moment you are in.

Whenever you feel your insides beginning to flutter or when you get over-excited, pull yourself back to your centre. Imagine roots under your feet that go deep into the ground, grounding, balancing and nourishing you. Imagine you can let yourself go. Imagine you are a flower in reverse. Bring in the petals of your head. Allow the flower to grow backwards back into the bud. Bring in your leaves and fold them back into bud formation too. Imagine the stem can grow backwards into the seed until you are once more as small as the seed, then open your eyes and continue as you should.

You have just closed yourself down and have drawn all your personal energy back into yourself. Energetically you are as safe and as small as a seed.

All of life must be in balance. Without hate we cannot know love. Without war we cannot know peace. Without pain and stress we cannot appreciate the peace and contentment of a quiet mind. All things have their opposites to highlight them. But any sign of over-emotion, either sadness or excitement, is an imbalance. All emotions have their place, but all things should be equally balanced within their time and place. As you reconnect to life, to yourself and the divine presence that surrounds you, you will naturally feel a quickening, an excitement, a buzz. Acknowledge this as it occurs, but remain firmly focused on the things that you should. You will feel as though you are being recharged, and indeed you are, but it is important that you do not let yourself float away in the process. Keep within the bounds of reality and at all times ask that your illusions be recycled and that only truth and light will ever prevail.

(I am I) Keep yourself grounded and focused on your day and I will be with you to help you. (I am I)

Only you can help yourself by remaining aware of your feelings. Only you know where your mind is, so only you can keep it in check. Only you can live your life and do what you are meant to do within it.

(I am I) This life is to be lived. This world is to be treasured, so it is up to man to look after it properly. (I am I)

This planet that we live upon is the body of God. It feeds us and provides for all our needs. Combined with the energies of the sky, it is our life force. Take care of it for all your life is worth. Respect it as you would respect your own home.

Only we can turn this planet around, literally. Only we can pull ourselves together and bring it back on track. Only we can take the chance we have been given to rectify the mistakes of the past, not by reliving them and feeding them to keep them prominent and alive, but by laying them to rest and moving on. This is a time for regrowth and for pastures new.

(I am I) I will lead you every step of the way if you will only give Me a spark of recognition, of faith and of love. This is our chance, combined, to place the 'now' on the map of time. It is here that I am and it is here that all things are possible. Life is asking for our help, so it is up to us to hear and acknowledge that call. It is up to us to conduct our life in a way that we can be proud of now. Don't wait until you get back home to spirit and then wish you had sorted things out. Re-establish all the things you should do and tidy your loose ends. Place order back into your bank balance and also into your affairs. Don't follow the pack and do what others do. Take your life back into your own control and walk beside Me. I will always lead you if you wish. (I am I)

It is probable that right now you are feeling a little sad, a little scared, but don't. You are where you are because that is where you are. The past is over, even yesterday, this morning… None of it can be used again. Instead, allow yourself to believe in the fresh start that awaits you. There may be repercussions that you must face up to, but do that with your chin held high and your shoulders back. Face up to your mistakes and move on. This life is far more precious than any amount of silver or gold will ever be.

(I am I) No amount of precious metal or stone can ever replace it. Treasure what you really are – your essence – and treasure all that you have achieved, despite the trials of your past. Lay down your defences and walk forward. Walk tall. Know that your life is just beginning. This is your time to shine. (I am I)

CHAPTER TWENTY-THREE

And So You Begin to Recover

(I am I) I am not a figment of your imagination. I am real. I am as real as the air that you breathe or the light that you see. I am in the words that attract your attention and the books that you read. I am in the thoughts that you think and the words that you say. I am you and you are Me. I am neither your jailer nor your judge. You are. You do all this and more to yourself. I do not hold the key to your heart and your chains. You do. You have it all. You are responsible for controlling your life. You first think the thoughts that put into play all that occurs around you. You program your own destiny with your thoughts and your words, your beliefs and your actions. You have total control of the being that is you. Recognize this and learn to accept your own power. Nobody anywhere can alter this truth. You are more, much more, than you can ever dream of, more than you can know in many lifetimes. You are a vital part in this living, breathing, thinking machine called Earth. The choices you make and the role you play are vital in the life of this planet. Together, you are strong. Alone, you believe you are small. But individually you play your part and it is a part that cannot be replaced. Without you there would be a gap, a hole, and holes have always been a nuisance. (I am I)

Only you can pick up the pieces and put yourself back together again. The years will have taken their toll. No one is able to travel through this material existence unscathed. Pain and turmoil are a necessary part of our life, of even our birth; without them, we would all live as zombies. How could we ever know and appreciate the joys that surround us and that await us if we did not have an opposite to measure against?

Life is like a ball of living energy. It contains all possible outcomes that could ever be, like a computer program. We push the buttons with our thoughts to release energies and all things that we need. We are in charge of the next step. We choose the category and level we will work within and respond to.

God made the world, in the ways that science has explained, but it is man who will now take it forward. He is the greatest invention that ever was made and it is he who now must shape and mend the world. He can make it a technological, mechanical world or he can take what he has learned and use it wisely. He can use his inventions to help him return to life, to freedom and to happiness.

(I am I) I can guide and help when My help is needed, but it is man who directs the future of his Earth. (I am I)

Only you can put your life back into balance and order. This is not a quest for outward advancement, but for reconnecting to the life that really is. It is about using the machines we have made to make our lives a little more comfortable, but then about loving and enjoying the time we have left. It is about connecting properly with each other in a heartfelt way. It is about understanding our parents, our children and our friends. It is about recognizing that we are all people. We are all on the same path of growth and understanding through life. It is about recognizing that we all have the same feelings, hopes, fears and dreams. It is about realizing that we are all connected on a spiritual level and it is about learning to see past the physical faults that mess us up.

Don't just point out other people's faults, as you too have your own. Help them to communicate, to move forward too – not with money or with a do-good attitude, but by your own example. Go within yourself first and foremost and understand exactly what has been holding you back and keeping you sad. Take this new day, this blank page, and use it a little differently from usual. Take your automatic pilot offline and make your own choices, as you used to when you were young, when you believed that the world really was your oyster, when you believed in yourself and in your life and when you believed in your ability to go forward and flow with that life, wherever it might take you.

Today is the first day of the rest of the life you have. Take it and live it. Yes, you have commitments, and yes, you have to work. Yes, the same old bills still drop onto your doormat, but you don't have to let them get you down. Instead work out how to get rid of them – how to get them down to a minimum. Look at the whole of your life from another perspective. Look at what you need to do to turn things around – to get out of debt, to remove the clutter and to enjoy your life. Are you doing a job you enjoy or are you simply working for your pay cheque? We all have to work in order to survive, but we should at least do it in a way that we enjoy. Life is too precious to let it dwindle away, to let it slip through our fingers day and night.

Change a few of the things that drain you. Learn where others are pulling your strings. Help yourself out of your rut by recognizing that you are probably in one. A book called *Emotional Clearing* by John Ruskan is a good starting point. It will help you recognize some of the behavioural habits that you stick with naturally. It will help you understand where you are, how you got there and, more importantly, how to get out. I, too, have read this book and it helped me recognize some truths that I did not really want to hear. I could not argue, though, with a book, and you cannot ignore the truth as it is. We all have our little quirky ways, but when we learn how these things do matter and hold us back, then we should take the adult approach and work them through.

Up until now we have lived only a half life. We believed that we were alone and that everything had to be done alone, under our own steam. Now we can learn a new truth – the actual truth. We can learn it for ourselves, by ourselves, one little bit at a time. We can learn real truths about ourselves instead of just dragging along other people's opinions of us. We are not bad through and through. Neither are we headed for hell. We live in a world that was made from love. We ourselves came from an act of love. We have love in our hearts and we want others to love us, but before they can, before we can let their love in, we must first learn to love and understand ourselves, to forgive ourselves our past mistakes and to recognize that we are worth more than we realized, not in a pretentious way but in a truthful, bottom-line sort of way. We must take a look at the essence of the person we really are and we must forgive the child within ourselves for all our wrongdoings. We can lay to rest all the indiscretions of the past and take each new day and live it in a better way – a non-impressive, truthful way. We have no one to impress, no one to prove a single thing to. We simply have to recognize the love and the joy that it is possible for us to have.

(I am I) I could not have put this better. I second these things with all that I am. (I am I)

The lump you feel inside now is your soul acknowledging the truth. This book has highlighted things that you can only admit deep within. It has accessed forgotten issues, things that you usually push away and cloud over. It has reached the essence of who you are.

This is not the end; it is the beginning. It is the start of a new life, of self-recognition and of a deeper understanding of those around you. People, everywhere, are just that – people. They don't always mean to hurt one another. They are just looking to be loved and understood, as you are. They want the best for themselves, as you do. They are the same as you are. When you find yourself in conflict or turmoil with another, at the point where you would normally lock horns, go inside instead and quietly ask for help. Ask for illusion to be gone and for truth and light and love to prevail. Ask that both of you may communicate on a correct level of understanding. Ask that you may hear each other's words. Just recycle all that stands in your way – always.

(I am I) Man is at the brink of a new age. What he thought would happen at the birth of the new millennium is upon him now. I am with him to help him live in the way he would like to, to take him back to love and happiness.

This is not a whim any more; it will be fact. Man is at a crossroads both physically and spiritually. He can stay as he is, but he will always struggle as he always has, or he can choose to change direction, to explore unseen realms within himself and to understand his mind and emotions on those deeper levels. He can make educated choices instead of haphazard, impulsive ones and he can set himself free. He can dance to the beat of his own tune, his own choices, instead of trudging through the rubbish and mire of his past.

Only you can look at the complete picture of your life so far. You can work out for yourself if it has been a good and happy one or if there are things that could have been better. The picture you will see has been built up over the years. Little by little you have slotted those pieces into place, some under your own steam and some through the intervention of others. When you look back, there is no judge, other than you. Only you can decide if you like all you see or not, if there were things you should have done or did not know. Only you can decide if you are happy as you are or if you want to go within to understand what keeps on going wrong, despite your best efforts.

Only you can help yourself, but first you must understand how. You are being given an opportunity to find the tools to do it. Until this moment in time you could only operate within the thoughts and beliefs that you already had in place, within the boundaries that had existed for you since your childhood. But now, through going within, you can refine, redraw and throw away some of the things you do unconsciously, some of the automatic things that do not serve you as they should. New growth will filter through and then take root. You can replant the garden of your mind and tidy up years of neglect and mistakes. You are going to learn a better way to live and in so doing you will cut the unconscious cords that others have played and tugged upon. They will no longer be able to pull your strings. They will understand the words you speak and the things you do in the way you mean. Your life will slowly reshuffle itself into a better working order and in the process you will clear the wooded arena of your mind. You will learn the power of your own thoughts and perhaps you will allow them to influence you in a positive way instead of a negative one. You will no longer feel bad for doing absolutely nothing, just because it was your pattern in life to do so. Life will take on a new and exciting look instead of being the automatic existence that has become the norm.

This book will open doors that until now have been tightly locked.

(I am I) I will help you from this moment on, if you let Me. I have never left your side yet, though you have not known it. I have had to watch and wait for you to realize that I was there. I have been powerless to interrupt. Now it can be different. Don't cry and don't be sad any more. Yes, life will still be life. It will always have its peaks and troughs, but then it is supposed to. Only now, you will turn to Me. You have a few tools that will help you along your way and you will pick up many more besides as you begin your studies. I will help you if you will learn how to help yourself. I will be there at all times. (I am I)

Life is good. It can be all that you want it to be, despite the problems that are yet to be overcome. All the problems that are occurring in your life are only versions of what is happening to everyone. The guise of these things may vary, but they are still the same for us all. No one is out of the woods yet, but we are all at different stages on our way. *(I am I) I must second this statement. (I am I)*

As we look back over time we can see the struggles that our ancestors lived through, like scars across the path of time. But we can also see how far man has come. He is not out of the woods yet, but he is well on his way. Life on the whole has never been so good and once we learn to get our own acts together it will be even better. The picture we will weave will be clearer than ever before. We can see the traps of the past and we will recognize the ones we are in. We all have a chance to clean ourselves up before we return back home to spirit. We are lucky. We are luckier than we can ever realize.

Those we have loved and lost will be with us, helping us as we continue on our way. They will be cheering us on. Just as the crowd is important at a sporting event, so they will play their part as we run the event of our life. All will play their part until you return home once more – until you cross your own finishing line. *(I am I) I must second this. (I am I)*

Only you can go forward now.

(I am I) I will be with you every step of the way. Don't be afraid or worried any more. Look at the moment you are in with truth and allow the illusions to fall away. Always look for the bottom line. If you are in doubt, then make yourself small and wait a short while until the picture is clear. I cannot do anything for you. You must do it yourself, but I can show you the way. I can smooth the edges and I can give you strength and support. This is your life, so only you can live it, but you will be helped till the end of your days. I will help you flow through your obstacles, especially when you feel that the world is against you. At these times you will be at your lowest ebb, but trust in Me and I will hold you up. Believe in Me. (I am I)

Man is always doing his best, but sometimes it seems that that best is just not enough. When the chips are down, don't ever give up.

(I am I) I will always lift your heavy mood so that you can carry on. I will always direct you to a glimmer of light and of hope. When you think you have tried all the avenues available to you, I will show you some more. (I am I)

Sometimes it is necessary to complete a cycle of events before the new can begin. Don't hold on to any illusions – let them go. Pain and sadness might be there from time to time, but they are sometimes a necessary conclusion to present events. You cannot let go of the old until you are ready to actually do so, so once more ask for help from above. Ask for the help that you need, even though you might not be sure what it is. Ask for the old to be recycled and love and light to remain. Never forget to recycle your pain and sadness. *(I am I) I will replace them with love. (I am I)*

Life is a gift to be treasured. It is fun and you can have as much of it as you wish. *(I am I) Provided that all things are kept in balance. (I am I)* I must also remember this as I go through my own life. Balance holds all things in their true and proper place. It is more important that we realize. Too much attention in any one direction will always throw another out of synch. All of nature must be always in balance and so must we. That is a fact of this life.

Only you can bring balance back into your life, but when you do, it will have a knock-on effect. As you pull yourself together, the little things around you will also readjust. *(I am I) I will help the whole process. (I am I)* Take your life back to the basics and release yourself from that which you no longer need. You will lighten your load in the process. I, too, have had to do this and in some ways I still must. Life should never stagnate, so allow it to go forward at its own pace. All you need do.is keep up. If you think it is going too fast, ask for it to be slowed down. Nothing can occur before the time it is destined to do so. Learn to be patient with yourself and with others around you. Take each day as it comes and learn to stay flexible within it.

We must all do these things for our own selves. No one person is ever more important or more in need than any other. All men are equal in the eyes of God, and the sooner we allow ourselves to recognize our gifts and our own worth, the sooner we can reconnect to and help the whole. Nothing you could ever do would alienate you from your birthright and that right is to live in love, in peace and in contentment. Reach out your hand for the help that you need and never turn your back on another. Help them not with money, but with the help you have received yourself, from the words of this book and others. Pass its details on where necessary and pass on your love as well. Send your thoughts up to highlight where healing and spirit intervention should come in. *(I am I) I will always be with you – no matter what. (I am I)*

Only you can give yourself another chance, another lease of life. Each new day that you live can be a good day, a day that is full of new experiences. Learn to embrace them. Don't tar them with the brushes of the past. Ask for your old fears, your old hang-ups, to be removed whenever you recognize their presence and try a few things that you usually would not do. I, too, must remember this. I, too, must let my hair down a little more than I do.

Only man can turn this world around once more. He can put the spring back into life or he can continue to wear it out. He does not even have to go overboard with his efforts. He just has to start from within. He must learn to live and to trust himself. He must give himself a reason to trust himself. He must realize that he has a new chance in every single day that he lives and he must learn to use it.

Man does not stand alone. He is an important part of the all that is and of the planet itself. The thoughts in his head have more effect than he can ever imagine, so he must realize that what he has in his mind is his offering to God – to the all that is. His thoughts direct his life and all that he finds himself doing. His thoughts are responsible for the way others treat and interact with him as well. Man must learn to respect and understand himself, and when he does, then other things will fall into place.

All we ever need is with us and it always has been. We are not alone, we never have been and never could be. We are an important working part of planet Earth and a spark of the divine energy that exists in all things. We are a part of a living, breathing, loving God.

(I am I) I am here. I am with you. I am in you. All that you will ever be you will be with Me. It can never be any other way. I am the spark of life, the consciousness that is in all living things and after your time is over and spent, you simply return home to Me. The life you are living is a gift, a joy to be experienced with love. You are love, even though you may have forgotten. You are a living part of Me. (I am I)

Learn to be happy. If you are not, then look at your life and figure out why. Not in an outward manner, by blaming others for this or that, or feeling sour with your lot. Look to understand how you have got to this point. Look for the reasons that are springing from inside you.

(I am I) Man is never too old to step out of behaviour patterns that no longer serve him. I am with him and I will help him to stay out of the fear. I will surround him with all that he needs if he asks Me. (I am I)

Your life will turn around, but be patient. Look for the little miracles that happen in your day. Ask for your troubles to be recycled, one at a time. In your thoughts, stay only in the day you are experiencing right now. Operate fully from this point. Now is the only time that really exists, for tomorrow is an illusion – until you get there. Be careful of placing energy and thoughts ahead of you in your own pathway. Recycle things 100 times if you need to, but learn to be positive and happy. This day is your day. Events may come and go, good as well as bad, but at the end of each day look at what you have achieved. Make each day count in one small way and slowly things will turn around for the better. You hold the key to your own life, to your heart, to your happiness and to your future. Learn to recognize the person you really are and let them out to live.

Only you can live the life that you have. You are unique. The mistakes of the past were just that, mistakes, and they are now behind you. Don't compound, repeat or drag them along with you any longer. Let them go. *(I am I)* *I second this. (I am I)*

Take each day and live it in a way you will be proud to own up to.

(I am I) I will be with you at all times. I am only one thought away. That is where I have always been and it's where you will always find Me. (I am I)

CHAPTER TWENTY-FOUR

Connections

(I am I) When we die, we return to our original energy form. When we are born, we come to Earth, to physical matter. We also form our part of the Earth's physical body.

The energy that is the sky consists of the life force the planet needs. Earth and sky are designed to integrate their energy through the catalyst that is man, through his spirit, but this is not occurring successfully at this time. Man is causing a blockage. He has forgotten that he is part of a thread. He has forgotten that he is part of a past, of a living heritage. He has forgotten that he comes from a long line of hundreds of ancestors. He has forgotten he is merely the latest link in a long chain that existed before he was born and will continue long after his own lifespan is through. In turn he, too, will become a link of the past. He, too, will have others attached in front of him, namely his children and their children in descent.

The Earth needs man to remember this. It needs him to re-establish links that have been forgotten. Blockages need to be removed.

The planet's surface depicts this picture. Its barren slopes and countries are a mirror image of the blockages that man is a contributory factor in. Barren lands represent the number of connections that need reconnecting in man himself. As he progresses into the light of the future, so he will return life and greenery, balance, peace and harmony to the Earth. But until he reawakes to who and what he is in terms of being an energy channel, he will simply add to the barren and dead lands that already exist.

Man is one of many energy conductors for physical Earth to exist and survive, and as such he will feed his energies to Earth for the whole of his life. He is capable of emitting both positive and negative vibrations. He alone has control of which, through his choices, his emotions and the life he leads. All through his life, and as a consequence of his life, he transmits all the forces that are his back into the Earth.

When energy is positive, it is able to assist the Earth in sustaining life. It is put to good use. Negative forces have the opposite effect. They can feed nothing. They have their effect on the planet in other ways, as they attract like to like in their own magnetic way and cause destruction.

All moving things on the surface of the Earth influence life as we know it. Man is the only variable that causes a disturbance to the planet's equilibrium and it is this that must be drawn back into balance once more.

There will always be dark areas, but over the course of the Earth's existence man has created and witnessed enough negative energy to last him through all eternity. From now until the end of time there is no need to create more. What the Earth must have now are light and a drawing together of positive energy. Only this can bring into focus the forces that it needs to repair the damage. It needs man to pull himself together.

As things now stand, Earth is slowly dying. It needs the help of man to assist it now, before it is too late. Man is its only hope of survival, because it is man who is the cause of most of the damage. Nothing is impossible at this point. I will help. I will help man overcome himself every step of the way, but first he must let Me in. He must wake up to the reality of himself and the part that he plays in the order of life, both his own and that of the planet that sustains his life. (I am I)

CHAPTER TWENTY-FIVE

Past, Present and Future

(I am I) The world of spirit is the past. It is the all that has been before this moment you are in, but it is also the future's potential.

Man is born into a physical now. His now is the only time-frame that is able to instigate anything at all. It is the only place that can turn possibility into material form and matter.

The future is yet to be, but it is created by the actions of the present.

Inside man there exists the potential of both good and bad, light and dark. These two possibilities exist side by side within him every day of his life. It is up to man alone to choose the path he will take. It is up to each individual in turn to make their own destiny.

The past can have little effect on the now, because those who live there have no influence in this time-frame, unless we allow their help to filter through.

Man holds in his hand the future outcome of Earth itself.

The present needs to reconnect with the past so that the future can be as it should. The present is not able to carry the world forward under its own steam. It does not have the necessary tools to do so.

The past has had the necessary tools, but has missed its opportunity to be effective in the now. Both past and present must combine to bring the now back into balance and peace.

The now is incapable of operating alone, because it is too deeply based in fear. It needs the love of the past to filter through to dilute the energies that presently overrule man.

Man needs the past to reconnect in his present to help him go forward truthfully and with confidence. Man is his own creator.

The world needs a balance of past and present to take it successfully into the future.

I need man to reconnect with Me, because I am all things. I am the past that was, the present that is and the future that will be.

I am all that there is and I need man to understand this. (I am I)

Further Reading

The following list is merely a sample of the literature available in the mind, body and spirit or self-help section of your local bookshop.

To connect with your inner self and your own personal guides or angels, simply still your mind for a few minutes and then browse through the following list, seeing which titles you connect with. Trust in your own inner guidance. You will be guided, one step at a time, along the path that is right for you.

When you browse through your bookshop or library, notice the titles that jump out and grab your attention. These are the books most likely to take you forward at this point in your journey.

Never read a book from back to front, but always from front to back. Many can be read from beginning to end fairly quickly, but it will be better if you read others more slowly, chapter by chapter, to give the information time to sink in. Because you are on a journey, you will likely experience the things you have read – in your life. This is good. It is part of the experience and the path of learning.

Some books will feel flat in the middle, but don't worry and don't be tempted to skip over these sections.

They are flat because at this particular time the information might not relate to your needs. But if you read it, your mind will place it in store until it does. Other books will be hard going because they are not right for you at this time. Put them down and go back to them at a later date if you wish.

This mode of reading will help you outgrow outdated boundaries and beliefs that may have lingered since your childhood. It is a process that will take you forward to a place where you can operate more efficiently. It will open you up to the flow of life that is waiting to help you. It will connect you once more to your guides.

Good luck!

- Juan Arias, *Paulo Coelho: Confessions of a Pilgrim*, HarperCollins, 2001
- Richard Bach, *Jonathan Livingston Seagull*, Macmillan, 1970
- —, *Illusions*, Bantam Doubleday Dell, 1977
- —, *The Bridge across Forever*, William Morrow & Co., 1984
- —, *One*, Bantam Books, 1992
- DeSersa Esther Black Elk, Pourier Olivia Black Elk, Lori Utecht and Charles Trimble, *Black Elk Lives: Conversations with the Black Elk Family*, University of Nebraska Press, 2000
- Wallace Black Elk, *Black Elk: The Sacred Ways of a Lakota*, HarperOne, 1991
- Wallace Black Elk and William S. Lyon, *Black Elk Speaks Again*, HarperCollins, 1990
- Brian Browne Walker, *The I Ching or Book of Changes*, St Martin's Press, 1992
- C. Maxwell Cade and Nona Coxhead, *The Awakened Mind*, Delacorte Press, 1978

- Jack Canfield and Mark Victor Hansen, *Chicken Soup for the Soul*, Health Communications, 1993
- Patricia Carrington, PhD, *Learning to Meditate*, Pace Educational Systems, 1979
- Susan Chernak McElroy, *Animals as Teachers and Healers*, Thorndike, 1997
- Deepak Chopra, *The Path to Love*, Harmony Books, 1997
- Anthea Church, *Inner Beauty*, Brahma Kumaris Information Services Publications, 1995
- John Cleese and Robin Skynner, *Families and How to Survive Them*, Methuen, 1983
- Paulo Coelho, *The Alchemist*, HarperSanFrancisco, 1993
- —, *The Valkyries*, HarperSanFrancisco, 1995
- —, *The Fifth Mountain*, Thorsons, 1998
- —, *The Pilgrimage*, Thorsons, 1999
- Diana Cooper, *A Little Light on Angels*, Findhorn Press, 1996
- —, *Angel Inspiration*, Hodder Mobius, 2001
- *A Course in Miracles*, The Foundation for Inner Peace, 1977
- Janki Dadi, *Wings of Soul*, Brahma Kumaris Information Services Publications, 1998
- Lama Surya Das, *Awakening the Buddha Within*, Bantam Doubleday Dell Publishing Group, 1997
- Michael Drosnin, *The Bible Code*, Weidenfeld and Nicolson, 1997
- Susan Forward, *Toxic Parents*, Bantam Doubleday Dell Publishing Group, 1989
- Shakti Gawain, *Living in the Light*, Harcourt Brace Co., 1986
- John Gray, *Men Are from Mars, Women Are from Venus*, HarperBusiness, 1992

- —, *Men Are from Mars, Women Are from Venus – Children Are from Heaven*, Vermilion, 1999
- J. Arthur Findlay, *The Rock of Truth*, Psychic Press, 1948
- Suzie Hayman, *The Relate Guide to Second Families*, Vermilion, 1997
- Susan Hayward, *A Guide for the Advanced Soul*, Little, Brown & Co., 1989
- James Hillman, *The Soul's Code*, Random House, 1996
- Stephanie J. King, *Just for Today*, Inner Sanctum Publications, 2005; reissued as *Life is Calling*, Hay House, 2009. This book was written to go hand-in-hand with *And So It Begins...* Life stops for no-one, no matter how hard you work at it... The way you approach it can be the difference between make or break – always. You control everything, even when it would appear otherwise. Nothing is by chance. Everything has the force of positive or negative as its outcome, again the choice of which depends on us. Co-written with spirit, designed to be opened seemingly at random, this book connects completely with where you and your life are right now. You will be guided to lessons and information most appropriate for you at the moment. Communicating and connecting directly with your own guardian/angel/guide, it will enable you to cultivate balance, inner peace, purpose, perspective, direction and strong personal growth – amongst many other things. No matter where you are – just like *And So It begins... Life is calling...* is completely for you...
- Naomi Levy, *To Begin Again*, Random House, 1998
- Denise Linn, *Signposts*, Rider, 1996
- Sarah Litvinoff, *The Relate Guide to Starting Again*, Vermilion, 1993
- Lynne McTaggart, *The Field*, HarperCollins, 2001

- Gustavus Hindman Miller, *A Dictionary of Dreams*, Gallery Books, 1991
- Dr H. C. Moolenburgh, *Meetings with Angels*, C. W. Daniel, 1992
- John G. Neihardt, *Black Elk Speaks*, University of Nebraska Press, 1932
- M. Scott Peck, *The Road Less Travelled*, Hutchinson, 1983
- —, *The Road Less Travelled and Beyond*, Rider, 1997
- Edwin Raphael, *The Complete Book of Dreams*, Foulsham, 1992
- James Redfield, *The Celestine Prophecy: An Adventure*, Warner Books, 1994
- —, *The Tenth Insight*, Warner Books, 1996
- James Redfield and Carol Adrienne, *The Celestine Prophecy: An Experiential Guide*, Bantam Books, 1995
- —, *The Tenth Insight: An Experiential Guide*, Time Warner, 1996
- John Ruskan, *Emotional Clearing*, R. Wyler & Co., 1993
- Betty Shine, *A Mind of Your Own*, HarperCollins, 1998
- Stephen Turoff, *Seven Steps to Eternity*, Elmore-Chard, 1989
- Iyanla Vanzant, *One Day My Soul Just Opened Up*, Pocket Books, 1998
- —, *In the Meantime*, Simon & Schuster, 1998
- —, *Yesterday I Cried*, Simon & Schuster, 1999
- Neale Donald Walsch, *Conversations with God*, Book 1, G. P. Putnam's Sons, 1996; Book 2, Hampton Roads, 1997; Book 3, Hampton Roads, 1998
- Ambika Wauters, *Ambika's Guide to Healing and Wholeness*, Piatkus Books, 1995
- Richard Webster, *Spirit Guides and Angel Guardians*, Llewellyn, 1998

- Dr Brian Weiss, *Messages from the Masters*, Warner Books, 2000
- Linda Williamson, *Finding the Spirit Within*, Rider, 2000
- www.channelledbyspirit.com

FOOTPRINTS

One night a man had a dream. He dreamed he was walking along the beach with the Lord. Across the sky flashed scenes from his life. For each scene, he noticed two sets of footprints in the sand, one belonging to him and the other to the Lord.

When the last scene of his life flashed before him, he looked back at the footprints in the sand. He noticed that many times along the path of his life there was only one set of footprints. He also noticed that it happened at the very lowest and saddest times in his life.

This really bothered him and he questioned the Lord about it. 'Lord, you said that once I decided to follow you, you'd walk with me all the way, but I have noticed that during the most troublesome times in my life, there is only one set of footprints. I don't understand why you would leave me when I needed you most.'

The Lord replied, 'My precious, precious child, I love you and I would never leave you. During your times of trial and suffering, when you see only one set of footprints, it was then that I carried you.'

THE LAST WIND

We must pull in one direction – together. This is the only way that we can survive. This is the only way that we can go forward. We create our reality with our own thoughts and wishes. To believe in the power of thought is to re-establish our link with the universal consciousness – the all that is.

A Closing Note...

(I am I) Thank you for taking the time and the trouble to wake up to Me and to life. Not everyone will do so in this lifetime. Not everyone needs to and not everyone will bother. Not everyone will know that they should... But you did...

The life experiences you have gained thus far have been largely by personal choice. But the place you are in now is the place you should be in – to open up, to remember and move on. How can you know what you definitely are until you definitely know what you're not? Without any one of your experiences you would be somewhere else, someone else. You would not be in the position you are in – ready to trust and to learn.

Man thinks the world he lives in is getting worse, falling apart, breaking down. This is true at the moment, but each person has within them the capacity to change something, no matter how small or seemingly insignificant or unimportant. Each one is part of Earth life, rooted and active in the present, right now. Each one can try to change something, even if only to wake up to the truths and real life that surround them, if only to wake up to themselves... (I am I)

Because the guidance in this book is unique, do not keep it on a shelf with all your other books, but in a place where you will see it and use it often. It is a life tool that will interact with you daily. The more frequently you use it, the more you will benefit, and the more your life will visibly change. No one on Earth will charge to your rescue – you must do everything yourself. And so it begins...